...LEGE OF FOOD, TOURISM & CREATIVE ... DIES

...ARY SUMMER ...

22

2005.

The Economics of Tourism
Destinations

The Economics of Tourism Destinations

Norbert Vanhove

ELSEVIER
BUTTERWORTH
HEINEMANN

AMSTERDAM BOSTON HEIDELBERG LONDON NEW YORK OXFORD
PARIS SAN DIEGO SAN FRANCISCO SINGAPORE SYDNEY TOKYO

Elsevier Butterworth-Heinemann
Linacre House, Jordan Hill, Oxford OX2 8DP
30 Corporate Drive, Burlington, MA 01803

First published 2005
Reprinted 2005

British Library Cataloguing in Publication Data
A catalogue record for this book is available from the British Library

Library of Congress Cataloguing in Publication Data
A catalogue record for this book is available from the Library of Congress

ISBN 0 7506 6637 4

For information on all Elsevier Butterworth-Heinemann
publications visit our website at www.bh.com

Working together to grow
libraries in developing countries

www.elsevier.com | www.bookaid.org | www.sabre.org

ELSEVIER   BOOK AID
International   Sabre Foundation

Typeset by Charon Tec Pvt. Ltd, Chennai, India
www.charontec.com
Printed and bound in Great Britain by Biddles Ltd, Kings Lynn, Norfolk

Contents

List of figures

List of tables

Foreword

In his new book *The Economics of Tourism Destinations*, Professor Norbert Vanhove sums up current economic thinking in the area of tourism. His approach is quite different from the usual way knowledge is produced in this field, which is to a great extent devoted to business administration aspects and in particular to marketing.

This book is an ideal introduction to the economics of tourism. Its systematic development of the theme is highly persuasive. It includes everything that an expert in the field of tourism needs to know about the basic economics involved. Furthermore, it brings the reader up to date with the latest thinking in the ongoing scientific debate in this sector.

The author also makes a convincing presentation of the methodology and instruments most commonly employed in current tourism analysis. The reader will find the latest thinking on forecasting and the compilation of statistical data in tourism. It even includes an analysis of the tourism satellite accounts in the national economy, as well as various case studies of forecasting models.

Professor Vanhove is an economist specializing in tourism and regional development who is equally at home with theory and practice. His book thus makes a particular effort to explain the factors that make for the success and competitiveness of a destination. He is indeed one of the leading specialists in this field.

It is worth noting too that the author evaluates the impact of tourism projects at the macro-economic as well as the micro level, on the basis of many years' experience. One of the undoubted strengths of this book is his ability to go to the heart of the subject and illuminate the reader regarding all the essentials.

Professor Peter Keller
President of the International Association of Scientific Tourism Experts

Preface

This book has two sources. The first is related to my research in tourism. In 1962, O. Vanneste, Director of the WES (West Flemish Study Office), asked me to start a new department in WES called 'Tourism economic research'. For many years I was involved in tourism research, and this brought me into contact with the AIEST (International Association of Scientific Experts in Tourism), of which I have been Vice-President for the last ten years, and the TRC (Tourist Research Centre), an association of tourism experts and institutes specializing in tourism and strongly linked to the AIEST. The annual TRC meetings focusing on the exchange of research, and particularly on research methods, were a source of permanent inspiration and enrichment. This research background was extremely valuable in the preparation of this book.

The second relates to a teaching task. In 1990, J. Van den Broeck, Professor at the RUCA (Rijks Universitair Centrum Antwerpen, now incorporated into the University Antwerpen), insisted on teaching 'Economics of Tourism' in the newly created 'Minor of Tourism'. The preparation of a course guideline is the first task for a professor of a new course, and although I had had a long research career in tourism, I was surprised by the shortage of handbooks on the subject. Most handbooks at that time focused on the management aspects of tourism and, more particularly, marketing. My friend Professor R. Medlik referred me to a publication by Mathieson and Wall (1982); however, he suggested that I should myself write a handbook on the economics of tourism. It was many years before I responded. Meanwhile, a number of books on this subject (for example, Bull, 1995; Sinclair and Stabler, 1998; Tribe, 1999 and Tisdell, 2000) had been published. The present publication is the result of continuous improvement and revision of course guidelines.

This publication is in four respects different from previous publications on the subject. First, this book emphasizes new aspects such as the measurement of tourism (e.g. Tourism Satellite Account), supply trends, competition models, the macro-evaluation of tourism projects and events, and the role of tourism in a development strategy. Secondly, an effort is made to deal with many different economic aspects of tourism in a single publication. Thirdly, each chapter seeks to combine theory and practice. Fourthly, the economics of 'tourism destinations' is a central theme of this publication.

The first chapter provides the up-to-date definition of tourism and provides a review of its economic characteristics.

Measurement of tourism is not an easy task, and this is discussed in Chapter 2. In the last decade there has been a growing interest in the tourism world in new methods for measuring the demand for and supply of tourism. Tourism information systems, Tourism Satellite Account, tourism surveys, production indexes and tourism barometers are exponents of these research efforts, and are presented here.

The economics of tourism implies particular attention to demand and supply, which are covered in Chapters 3 and 4. Tourism demand focuses on four main subjects: determinants of tourism demand, trends in tourism demand, the evolution of holiday participation in a number of European tourism-generating countries, and the phenomenon of seasonality. Chapter 4 pays particular attention to the market structures in tourism, the pricing mechanisms and new supply trends.

Chapter 5 can be considered an extension of the supply side. The key point of this chapter is not the individual enterprise, but the 'tourism destination'. The economic literature on tourism during the last decade is characterized by many publications dealing with the competitiveness of destinations. This chapter tries to give an insight into the complexity of competition in tourism, and to provide a synthesis of the different developed models – Porter, Poon, WES, Bordas, and Ritchie and Crouch.

Chapter 6 builds on the third chapter. It is surprising how many publications are related to forecasting tourism demand. Forecasting tourism demand is not an easy task; there is not only a lack of reliable data, but also many other determinants apart from economic factors influence the demand. Therefore it is necessary to make a distinction between qualitative and quantitative methods of forecasting. A number of case studies illustrate the complexity of the quantitative approaches.

The economic impact of tourism is discussed in Chapter 7. Several facets are considered: tourism as a strategic dimension of economic development, economic advantages and disadvantages, balance of payments aspects, employment characteristics, and the magic tourism multiplier. The main focus, however, is on the methods of measuring the income and employment generation of tourism expenditure.

Evaluation of tourism projects is a central point of tourism policy, and Chapter 8 is dedicated to micro- and macro-evaluation. Micro-evaluation deals with the scientific discounting methods, while macro-evaluation is of great importance in tourism and is directly related to cost–benefit analysis. Here, a systematic approach to measure the economic return of projects and events is developed.

The last chapter is an epilogue on two themes. The first raises the question, to what extent can the slogan 'tourism is a growth sector' be applied to all tourism destinations? The answer is related to productivity levels, price evolution, sustainable development and the management of tourism growth. The second theme concerns tourism as an economic development strategy, where a distinction is made between developed and developing countries.

The philosophy of this publication is to serve as a handbook for students studying the economic aspects of tourism at graduate level. However, the book is also addressed to researchers in tourism and people involved in tourism policy.

Professor Norbert Vanhove

Acknowledgements

I am indebted to the WES, World Trade Organization and many AIEST and TRC colleagues for the documentation and data provided. I would like to thank especially Mrs B. Declercq, librarian at the WES. I wish to express my warm gratitude to Mr M. Cumberledge for polishing the English. I also thank Mrs F. Pille for logistical support in unlocking the secrets of the computer, and J. Bisschop, who assisted me by drawing the figures. Last but not least, I thank my wife Elisabeth for the support and encouragement.

1

Economic characteristics of the tourism sector

The purpose of this first chapter is to focus on a number of economic characteristics of the tourism sector. They are the fundamentals of many aspects of the economics of tourism to which we shall refer in further chapters of this book. However, before starting with an overview of the economic characteristics, let us define what we understand by 'tourism' and what do we not consider to be tourism.

What is tourism?

What is tourism? This is not such a simple question as it seems. Colloquially, free time, leisure, recreation, travel and tourism are used synonymously and are almost interchangeable. This is not quite correct. From a scientific and practical point of view, the reality is quite different. The case of Austria is a simple illustration. In 1999, based on the Tourism Satellite Account, tourism represented, in terms of value added (direct and indirect effect), 8.7 per cent of GDP. However, tourism and recreation together make up a total of 15.5 per cent of GDP (Franz *et al.*, 2001). The difference is clear.

In the tourism literature, a distinction is made between conceptual and statistical (technical or operational) definitions of tourism.

Conceptual definitions

One of the oldest conceptual definitions of tourism was given by two pioneers of tourism research, Hunziker and Krapf (1942), who defined tourism as 'being a sum of relations and phenomena resulting from travel and stay of non residents, in so far a stay does not lead to permanent residence and is not connected with any permanent or temporary earning activity'. For a considerable time this definition was generally accepted – including by the AIEST (Association International d'Experts Scientifiques du Tourisme) – although it had more than one shortcoming. For example, a stay in a hospital could be considered to be tourism, and a business trip would be excluded as being related to an earning activity. Moreover, under this definition non-residents were identified with foreigners – in other words, domestic tourism was totally excluded.

The AIEST discussed the definition once again on the occasion of the annual congress in Cardiff in 1981. This congress accepted the following definition:

> The entirety of interrelations and phenomena which result from people travelling to and stopping at places which are neither their main continuous domiciles nor place of work either for leisure or in the context of business activities or study.

A clearer definition can be found at the British Tourism Society, which in 1979 adopted a definition based upon the work of Burkart and Medlik (1974):

> Tourism is deemed to include any activity concerned with the temporary short-term movement of people to destinations outside the places where they normally live and work, and their activities during the stay at these destinations.

Within this definition we can identify the inclusion of those activities that are involved in the stay or visit to the destination. There is no insistence on overnight stays or foreign visits, and it allows for domestic as well as day visits (Gilbert, 1990).

According to Burkart and Medlik (1974) – and this still applies today – conceptually, tourism has five characteristics:

1. Tourism is an amalgam of phenomena and relationships rather than a single one
2. These phenomena and relationships arise from a movement of people to, and a stay in, various destinations; there is a dynamic element (the journey) and a static element (the stay)
3. The journey and stay are to and in destinations outside the normal place of residence and work, so that tourism gives rise to activities which are distinct from those of the resident and working populations of the places through which tourists travel and of their destinations
4. The movement to the destinations is of a temporary, short-term character
5. Destinations are visited for purposes not connected to paid work – that is, not to take up employment.

A conceptual definition that deserves special attention is the one given by Gilbert (1990) and proposed for a social understanding of tourism:

> Tourism is one part of recreation which involves travel to a less familiar destination or community, for a short-term period, in order to satisfy a consumer need for one or a combination of activities.

The merits of this definition are several. It places tourism in the overall context of recreation; retains the need for travel outside the normal place of work habitation, and focuses on the reasons for travel.

Operational or technical definitions

The main practical need for exact definitions of tourism and the tourist has arisen from the necessity to establish adequate statistical standards (Mieczkowski, 1990). Furthermore, many people, including tourism experts, have difficulty in considering business trips and vocational travel as tourism activities. They are often included with tourism because they respond to the characteristics described in the preceding section, and their economic significance is also the same (see Burkart and Medlik, 1974). Business travellers are pure consumers, and it is difficult or impossible in practice to separate them from those travelling for pleasure. The main difference is purpose, but most hotelkeepers or accommodation providers are unable to make a distinction between holidaymakers and business travellers.

In the opinion of Burkart and Medlik (1974), a technical definition of tourism must:

- Identify the categories of travel and visits that are and are not included
- Define the time element in terms of length of stay away from home (i.e. the minimum and maximum period)
- Recognize particular situations (e.g. transit traffic).

A well-known definition is the one recommended on the occasion of the United Nations Conference on Travel and Tourism held in Rome in 1963, although it should be recognized that the UN definition was not the first (see Committee of Statistical Experts of the League of Nations, ETC, IUOTO, OECD and IMF, in Gilbert, 1990). The UN Conference recommended the following definition of 'visitor' in international statistics:

> For statistical purposes, the term 'visitor' describes any person visiting a country other than that in which he has usual place of residence, for any reason other than following an occupation remunerated from within the country visited.

This definition covers:

- *Tourists*, i.e. temporary visitors staying at least 24 hours in the country visited and the purpose of whose journey can be classified under the headings of

3

either (a) leisure (recreation, holiday, health, study, religion, and sport) or (b) business, family, mission, meeting.
- *Excursionists*, i.e. temporary visitors staying less than 24 hours in the country visited (including travellers on cruises).

The statistics should not include travellers who, in the legal sense, do not enter the country (for example, air travellers who do not leave an airport's transit area, and similar cases).

Later the phrase '24 hours' became a point of discussion, and was replaced by 'overnight' (United Nations Statistical Commission of 1967 and the IUOTO meeting of 1968, in Gilbert, 1990). This precision does correspond better to the reality (a trip with an overnight stay may last less than 24 hours), but is after all of minor importance.

The UN definition refers to international tourism (visiting a country other than that in which a traveller usually resides), but there is no reason to neglect domestic tourism. A person travelling from New York to California (domestic tourism) to visit the city of San Francisco is no less a tourist than is a Belgian visiting Paris (international tourism). The 1980 Manilla Declaration of the WTO extends the definition implicitly to all tourism, both domestic and international. Excluded from the definition are returning residents, immigrants, migrants (temporary workers staying less than one year), commuters, soldiers, diplomats and transit passengers.

This was the standard definition for a long time, although it was not applied in all countries. In that respect, the USA is a typical example. Even within the USA the definition of tourism and tourists varies from state to state (De Brabander, 1992).

There was, however, still not a common language of tourism statistics. Many scientists and organizations were aware of the problem, and the early 1990s saw a long period of preparation, in which several international organizations participated (Eurostat, OECD, WTO and UN Statistic Division), to solve the problem. This ended, in 2000, with the adoption by the United Nations Statistical Commission of the *Tourism Satellite Account: Recommended Methodological Framework* (Eurostat *et al.*, 2001). The Vancouver Conference of 2001 was a celebration of 10 years of scientific and intellectual international cooperation leading to a consensus on the development of the tourism satellite account. This remarkable achievement by the tourism industry was the culmination of the life's work of the late Enzo Paci – the WTO's former chief of statistics (see Enzo Paci World Conference on the Measurement of the Economic Impact of Tourism, Nice, 1999, in Eurostat *et al.*, 2001). At the same time it was a reformulation of a technical definition of tourism which was (or should have been) accepted worldwide:

> Tourism comprises the activities of persons travelling to and staying in places outside their usual environment for not more than one consecutive year for leisure, business and other purposes not related to the exercise of an activity remunerated from within the place visited.

where the persons referred to in the definition of tourism are termed 'visitors', a visitor being defined as:

> Any person travelling to a place other than that of his/her usual environment for less than twelve months and whose main purpose of trip

is other than the exercise of an activity remunerated from within the place visited.

This definition differs in two respects from the former UN description: first, the maximum duration of stay (one consecutive year) outside the usual place of residence is determined; and secondly, 'usual place of residence' is replaced by the term 'usual environment'.

In the new definition, 'usual environment' is a key element. In the *Tourism Satellite Account: Recommended Methodological Framework* (Eurostat, 2001), this corresponds to the geographical boundaries within which an individual moves during his or her regular routine of life. The usual environment of a person therefore consists of the direct vicinity of his or her home place of work or study and other places frequently visited, and has several dimensions:

- Frequency – places that are frequently visited by a person (on a routine basis) are considered as part of the usual environment even though these places may be located at a considerable distance from the place of residence
- Distance – places located close to the place of residence of a person are part of the usual environment even if the actual spots are rarely visited
- Time – how much time does the visitor spend between leaving the place of residence and returning home?
- Definition – the definition of places where people perform routine activities (homework, shopping, study, etc.).

To determine the usual environment, there are two different approaches in survey research: endogenous and exogenous. In the endogenous approach, the researcher has to define distance and time thresholds and must indicate what is 'frequent'. The available international applications show how different the interpretations of the abovementioned dimensions are. Many factors are influential, including the size of the country, population density, spreading of regional city centres etc. In rural areas the usual environment can be quite large, whereas in an urban centre the people living in one part of the city might never (or seldom) visit another part although the distance between them is relatively small.

In the exogenous approach, visitors are supposed to indicate themselves if the place visited is within their usual environment. The latter method is preferred by the WTTC (World Travel and Tourism Council), but it is a very dangerous path because the interpretation of individuals is very subjective.

All the discussion seminars attended on the subject of 'usual environment' have led to the conclusion that there is no general rule. The researcher has to be very pragmatic. There is always a grey line between tourism and recreational activities, and between tourism and routine activities. In practice, this will not greatly influence research results.

Dimensions of travel and tourism

Notwithstanding the many international and/or scientific definitions of tourism, there seems not to be a universally accepted definition. There is, however, more agreement on the dimensions of tourism. De Brabander (1992) makes a distinction between the 'travel' and 'stay' dimensions. As far as the travel component is concerned, he refers to three sub-dimensions:

1. Distance – short-, medium- and long-haul
2. Origin – domestic and international
3. Mode of transport – car, coach, train, plane, boat and other.

For the 'stay' dimension, there are another three classifications:

1. Duration – less than 24 hours (excursions) and more than 24 hours; for the latter group a further distinction is very often made between short holidays (one to three nights) and holidays (four nights or more)
2. Purpose – leisure, business, congress and personal (family, religion, health, education)
3. Accommodation – hotel, boarding house, camping, holiday village, rented apartment or – villa, cruise, farm and other.

It is evident that excursions do not involve an overnight stay.

Types of tourism

It is important to locate the tourist (and related consumption) geographically in order to analyse the impacts on a country of reference. This applies not only when statistics are established at the national level, but even more when they are compiled at the regional level. In the tourism satellite account, tourism is divided into the following categories (taking France as an example):

■ Domestic tourism – the tourism of residents of a country visiting destinations in their own country. The tourism satellite account makes a distinction between resident visitors travelling only within their country and resident visitors with a final destination outside the country (e.g. a French visitor from Paris travelling to Madrid and spending one night in Montpellier).
■ Inbound tourism – the tourism of non-resident visitors within the country.
■ Outbound tourism – tourism of nationals (e.g. French) visiting destinations in other countries.
■ Internal tourism – the combination of domestic and inbound tourism.
■ National tourism – the tourism of resident visitors (e.g. French) within and outside the economic territory of the country of reference (France).
■ International tourism – the combination of inbound and outbound tourism.

Based on the types and categories of tourism, and taking into account that consumption is an activity of visitors, the following aggregates for visitor consumption can be derived:

■ Domestic tourism consumption – the consumption of resident visitors within the territory of, for example, France.

- Inbound tourism consumption – the consumption of non-resident visitors within the country of reference and/or of goods and services provided by residents.
- Outbound tourism consumption – the consumption of resident visitors outside the country of reference and/or of goods and services provided by non-residents.
- Internal tourism consumption – the consumption of both resident and non-resident visitors within the country of reference and/or or goods and services provided by residents.
- National tourism consumption – the consumption of resident visitors within and outside the country of residence.

Although tourism consumption will be dealt with in greater detail in Chapter 2, a number of remarks should be made with respect to some of the abovementioned categories of consumption. First, with regard to domestic consumption, the final destination of the visitor might be within or outside the country of reference (e.g. France), but the consumption activity that is referred to must take place within France. In other words, the domestic portion of outbound tourism consumption is part of domestic tourism consumption (see the example above regarding the French tourist travelling from Paris to Madrid with a visit to Montpellier).

Secondly, inbound consumption does not include purchases that took place in other countries (such as an air transport provided by a foreign company, or a bottle of whisky bought in the tax-free airport shop). However, goods and services purchased in the destination country may have been imported.

Thirdly, outbound tourism consumption does not include the goods and services acquired before and after the trip and within the country of residence, which is traditionally identified as the domestic portion of outbound tourism consumption.

Fourthly, inbound tourism consumption is an 'export' for the country concerned, whereas outbound tourism consumption is an 'import'.

Tourism and related concepts

Tourism should be seen in relationship with and distinguished from a number of related concepts. The first of those concepts is 'free time' – i.e. the time available to the individual, after completing necessary work and other survival activities and duties, to be spent at his or her own discretion (Miller and Robinson, 1963; Mieczkowski, 1990). In other words, free time can be defined as 'empty time'.

The second concept is 'leisure'. Leisure time is 'part of free time devoted to activities undertaken in pursuit of leisure, which may, through recreative processes and playful activities, or may not, be attained'. Leisure is time filled with specific kinds of activities. There is, however, another wider and more pragmatic understanding of the term, identifying it with free (uncommitted, discretionary) time as contrasted to work, work-related and subsistence time, called by some authors 'existence time' (Clawson and Knetsch, 1964; Mieczkowski, 1990). The relationship between the two notions remains hazy, and there is a grey transition zone between them. Fully committed time is, for example, essential sleep, eating, travelling to work and essential shopping; highly committed time concerns activities such as child-raising, religion, house repairs and overtime work. Therefore there is nowadays a general agreement that leisure should be described as the time available to an individual when work, sleep and other basic needs have been met (Cooper et al., 1993).

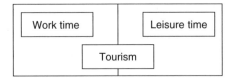

Figure 1.1 Tourism, work and leisure time

'Recreation' is the third concept. According to Cooper *et al.* (1993), 'Recreation can be thought of as the pursuits engaged in during leisure time, and an activity spectrum can be identified from recreation around the home, at one end of the scale, through to tourism where an overnight stay is involved, at the other'. As we have seen in the preceding section, day trips outside the usual environment are also a tourism activity.

Essential and /or possible characteristics of leisure are:

- The revitalizing function for work (may be old fashioned)
- That it is a non-working activity engaged in for pleasure
- Its voluntary character without external compulsion.

Mieczkowski makes it very clear when he states that 'In leisure the emphasis is on the time element where recreation refers to the content, to the way leisure time is spent'. Most authors express the opinion that recreation consists of 'activities' (Clawson and Knetsch, 1964; Mieczkowski, 1990, Cooper *et al.*, 1993) The latter make a distinction between home-based recreation (gardening, watching TV, reading, etc.), daily leisure (visiting sports, visiting restaurants, etc.), day trips (visiting attractions, theme parks or beaches, etc.), and tourism.

However, not all tourism is carried out during leisure time; business tourism takes place during work time. Indeed, part of tourism is associated particularly with working time, including business meetings and conventions (see Figure 1.1).

The last related concept is 'travel'. On the one hand, travel is more than tourism – it may also be undertaken for such reasons as commuting, migration and other movements of people which are beyond the scope of tourism. However, it is also possible to defend the thesis that tourism is more than travel, for travel constitutes only one component of tourism.

Colloquially, travel is often used as a substitute for tourism – indeed, Mieczkowski (1990) makes the humorous remark that a WTO publication is called 'World Travel' in English, and 'Tourisme Mondiale' in French. The term 'tourism' is more frequently used in Europe, whereas in the United States the more common term is 'travel'. Two of the oldest tourism scientific journals are *Tourism Review* (AIEST, and more European-based) and the *Travel Research Journal* (American-based).

The economic characteristics of tourism

Tourism has a number of typical economic characteristics which influence to a large extent the economics of tourism or lead to special methods of measurement and economic impact analysis. This section deals with the most relevant points.

Is there a tourism industry?

In reports, speeches, articles and publications in general, 'the tourism industry' is common language. Nevertheless, there is an ongoing debate in the literature regarding whether tourism constitutes an industry or a sector in its own right (Wahab, 1971; Burkart and Medlik, 1974; Chadwick, 1981; Jefferson and Lickorish, 1988; Medlik, 1988).

What is an industry? An industry or an economic sector in general comprises firms that produce the same products or services, or the same group of products and services, and/or are based on the same raw materials (leather, rubber, etc.). The System of National Accounts defines 'industry' as groups of establishments engaged in the same kind of productive activities.

A tourist travelling abroad buys services provided by the travel trade, transportation services, accommodation, foods and drinks, souvenirs of all kinds, entertainment services, etc. Clearly all these commodities and services belong to the same category of products or services, and this explains why there is not a sector in the national accounts called tourism. The hotel and catering industry (*horéca* in French) can hardly be considered as a substitute, as it is only a part of the total tourism sector. On the other hand, many firms in the catering industry have no or few links with tourists.

Nevertheless, Burkart and Medlik (1974) defend the thesis of the existence of a tourism industry based on the idea that all the components mentioned above have the one common function of supplying tourist needs:

> Although it is difficult to apply to these services the normal concept of an industry – in view of the special nature and complexity of their respective contributions to the tourist product – they may be described as the *tourist industry*: they include that part of the economy which has a common function of supplying tourist needs. This enables us to link demand and supply in tourism and to analyse the impact of tourism on the economy.

This is any case a strong argument.

Smith (1988) also agrees with the notion of tourism industry and, like Medlik (1988), has formulated an operational measurement for tourism industry activity. In his supply-side view he makes a distinction between firms that serve tourists exclusively (e.g. hotels) and a second group that serves a mix of tourists and local residents (e.g. a restaurants or pubs).

The fact that in reality the components of a tourist product belong to different sectors of national accounts, and that some firms serve exclusively tourists and other serve tourists as well as non-tourists, makes it difficult to measure the real significance of tourism. All this created the need for a Tourism Satellite Account (TSA).

The International Conference on Travel and Tourism Statistics held by the WTO in Ottawa in 1991 was the culmination of the great efforts made in the late 1970s and in the 1980s by international organizations (United Nations, WTO, OECD), tourism experts and countries (Canada and France) in the measurement of the economic impact of tourism. The United Nations (through its statistical commission), Eurostat, the OECD and the WTO are the international organizations that have established a set of definitions and classifications for tourism, the well-known Tourism Satellite Account (Eurostat *et al.*, 2001). There were two main purposes for this; first, the achievement of international comparability, and secondly, to serve as a guide to countries for the introduction of a statistical system for tourism.

How can the tourism satellite account be defined? We find a very good description of the philosophy in Franz *et al.* (2001):

> Countries measure economic activities – GDP, employment or demand – on the basis of internationally agreed standards for national accounts (NA). As part of the overall economy tourism is already represented in NA; the respective commodities produced by suppliers and purchased by visitors are also included in the core accounts. However, they are not visible as such because tourism is not identified as a separate activity, and the commodities produced and consumed by tourism demand are buried in other elements of the core accounts. In the overall national accounts framework there is little room for analysis by function. In order to overcome this problem, Satellite Accounts are proposed which are conceptually based on the same core accounts, able to highlight a particular aspect of the economy at the same time. The basic NA concepts are applied to tourism as well, taking into account those industries supplying tourism output and which are identified in the production account; at the same time these industries determine demand characteristics of tourism (e.g. visitors), which are identified by function.

More generally speaking, 'satellite account' is a term developed by the United Nations to measure the size of economic sectors that are not included in their own right in national accounts. The basic content of the TSA is dealt with in Chapter 2 of this book.

The five main sectors of the tourism industry are:

1. The attraction sector
   - natural attractions
   - cultural attractions
   - theme parks
   - museums
   - national parks
   - wildlife parks
   - gardens
   - heritage sites
   - entertainment
   - events
2. The accommodation sector
   - hotels
   - motels
   - bed and breakfast
   - guest houses
   - apartments, villas and flats
   - condominium timeshares

- ■ campsites
- ■ touring caravans
- ■ holiday villages
- ■ marinas
3. The transport sector
   - ■ airlines
   - ■ railways
   - ■ bus and coach operators
   - ■ car rental operators
   - ■ shipping lines
4. The travel organizer sector
   - ■ tour operators
   - ■ travel agents
   - ■ incentive travel organizers, etc.
5. The destination organization sector
   - ■ national tourist offices
   - ■ regional tourist offices
   - ■ local tourist offices
   - ■ tourism associations.

The tourist product is an amalgam

A tourist product can have a very different meaning, depending on whether the viewpoint is that of the supplier or that of the visitor. For the hotelkeeper the hotel room is the product; the air carrier supplies seats, and the restaurateur sells meals. These are the products that are supplied to the holidaymaker. In the narrow sense, the tourist product consists of what the tourist buys.

In fact, the tourist buys much more. The holidaymaker purchases a holiday experience – or everything from the moment he leaves home until he returns (the experience chain). That is the meaning in the wider sense – 'The tourist product is an amalgam of what he does at the destination and the services he uses to make it possible' (Burkart and Medlik, 1974). Attractions, accessibility, amenities at the destination (accommodation, catering, entertainment, internal transport and communication, incoming tour operators, etc.) and many intangible elements (such as atmosphere, ambience and friendliness of the local population) are the components of the amalgam, and these components complement each other. For Gilbert (1990), a tourism product is 'an amalgam of different goods and services offered as an activity experience to the tourist'. The composer of the product can be the tour operator, a travel agency, the accommodation sector, the destination management organization, other organizers or, last but not least, the individual tourist.

Tourism is a service activity

Earlier in this chapter tourism was considered as a sector in its own right, but it is not an industry in the strict sense of the word. Tourism has all the characteristics of services. Middleton, in the excellent book *Marketing in Travel and Tourism* (Middleton and Clarke, 2001), mentions a number of characteristics that distinguish services

Table 1.1 Generic characteristics distinguishing services from goods

Goods	Services
■ are manufactured	■ are performed
■ are made on premises not normally open to customers (separable)	■ are performed on the producer's premises, often with full customer participation (inseparable)
■ are delivered to places where customers live	■ customers travel to places where the services are delivered
■ purchase conveys ownership and right to use at own convenience	■ purchase confers temporary right to access at a prearranged place and/or time
■ possess tangible form at the point of sale and can be inspected prior to sale	■ are intangible at the point of sale, and often cannot be inspected
■ stocks of product can be created and held for future sale	■ are perishable; services can be inventoried but stocks of product cannot be held

Source: Middleton with Clarke (2001), *Marketing in Travel and Tourism*, published by Butterworth-Heinemann and reproduced with kind permission.

from goods. For the sake of this book, three characteristics of services are of great significance.

First, all tourism services are *intangible*. In terms of international trade and balance of payments, inbound and outbound tourism are invisible exports and imports respectively (see Chapter 7).

The *inseparability* of tourism services is a second important characteristic. Production and consumption take place on the premises or in the equipment of the producer (e.g. aircraft), and not in the residence of the tourist. As a consequence, the staff of the tourism suppliers have some consumer contact and are seen by the tourists to be an inseparable aspect of the service product. Whereas commodities can be tested and guaranteed, and product performance can be enforced by consumer protection laws, this is much more difficult with tourism services (see Table 1.1). The performance in an aircraft or a hotel is determined by the attitude of the staff, and normal guarantees or legal enforcement cannot be expected. The inseparability has direct consequences not only for tourism marketing but also in managing the competitive position of a tourism provider or destination (see Chapter 5).

Indeed, the attitude of the staff (e.g. friendliness, helpfulness) is often a vital element in delivering tourism products. Human beings are not machines, and one group of hotel tourists may be very satisfied with the staff's behaviour whereas another group arriving a week later may have a lot of complaints – perhaps owing to the staff's pressure of work. Together with climate, attitude is to a large extent responsible for the heterogeneity of performance. Heterogeneity is directly related to the characteristic of inseparability.

For our purpose, *perishability* is the most important character of services with respect to tourism. For this reason, the following paragraph is dedicated to this characteristic.

Tourism products are perishable

The perishability of tourism products can best be illustrated by a practical example. A hotel with 100 rooms has a production capacity of 100 rooms for rent every day, and the hotelkeeper will try to sell this full capacity every day. On most days of the year he will not be successful. Unlike goods, the hotelkeeper cannot save the unsold rooms in stock for the next day or week, and nor can he reduce the capacity. Supply in tourism is relatively inflexible, and rooms that are not rented on the day of the performance are totally lost – or 'perishable'. All hotels with a fixed number of rooms (which is the normal case) and transport operators with a fixed number of seats (railway, air carrier, bus/coach companies, etc.) face identical situations of matching perishable supply to the available demand. The production capacity that is not sold on a particular day is lost and can never be recovered.

As a direct consequence of perishability, it is not possible to create a stock of hotel rooms or train seats. However, this is not a phenomenon specific to the tourism sector. Many service industries with fixed capacity are confronted with the same problem. To cope with the perishable character of tourism products, many hotelkeepers, air carriers and railway companies apply more and more price differentiation and yield management. Yield management is a method for managing capacity profitably, and has gained widespread acceptance, particularly in the airline and hotel industries, over the last two decades. Yield management is a method that can help a firm to sell the right inventory unit to the right customer, at the right time, and for the right price (Kimes, 1999). In Chapter 4 we will see that a number of necessary conditions should be fulfilled for yield management – a firm should have a fixed capacity, high fixed costs, low variable costs, a segmented market, time-varied demand and similarity of inventory units.

The seasonality of tourism demand

Demand for tourism products is characterized by an unequal temporal distribution. Annually, there are weeks and months with a great demand and others with a low demand. This temporal peaking pattern is called seasonality. This uneven distribution is different from receiving country to receiving country, and from destination to destination. Some regions have a high season of a maximum of six weeks, whereas for other destinations high season lasts several months. There are also regions that attract tourists all year round, although with some months of lower occupancy rate. The peaking pattern is not necessarily restricted to one peak – for example, many Alpine regions have two peaks (see Figure 1.2). The tourism sector refers to two seasons; however, there are not only seasonal but also weekend peaks. The relationship between 'seasonality' and 'perishability' is quite evident.

The main factor responsible for the seasonal peaks is climate – for example, residents of northern Europe tend to take their main holidays in the summer period of June to mid-September. However, in the Pacific, Mediterranean or Caribbean tourist destinations, where the climatic variations are less important, there is also a seasonal pattern of demand. Two factors are responsible for this. The first is the organization of the school holidays in the main generating markets. Many people are involved in education-related activities – children, students, the parents of those children and students, teachers and school-related persons – and in developed countries this group constitutes a high percentage of the population.

The second factor also has an institutional origin. The organization of annual paid leave in business is well defined in several generating markets. Many firms

13

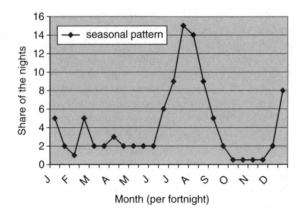

Figure 1.2 A possible seasonal pattern of tourism demand in a tourist region

in Europe are closed during the annual period of paid leave, while others work at a reduced capacity. The choice of the period of paid leave is also influenced by the annual school summer holidays.

This appears to be a self-reinforcing system, because many people without links to school or business prefer to take holidays in the peak season – perhaps because of a psychological 'vacation pressure', or in some cases because people may prefer to take holidays when their neighbours are away from home (Vanhove, 1974).

Seasonality has a number of unpleasant economic and ecological consequences for tourist destinations:

1. The seasonal pattern of demand affects the occupancy rate of accommodation providers, and it is impossible to run a hotel in a profitable way with only 100 days of operation. This is a typical example of under-utilization of resources.
2. The general tourism infrastructure (manmade attractions, beach equipment, parking, roads, marinas, etc.) is under-occupied at certain times. This is a typical example of wrong (or partly wrong) use of capital.
3. To cope with the peaks, the public sector is confronted with high operational costs (police force, fire brigade, hospital capacity, etc.). These cost are not restricted to the high season, but have repercussions all year round.
4. In many tourism regions, seasonality leads to seasonal employment, and the correlative seasonal unemployment can cause welfare problems. Clearly the reality is a little bit more complex. During the season working hours are sometimes very long, and during the off-season unemployment benefit for tourist workers is in some tourism regions more or less 'institutionalized', or a blind eye is turned.
5. The tourist as a consumer is confronted with high prices, over-concentration, traffic congestion and very often low service performance during the high season. This causes dissatisfaction on the part of the tourists.
6. The concentration of demand in a few weeks in many cases provokes ecological dangers or leads to exceeding the carrying capacity of natural or cultural attractions.

It is therefore not surprising that several countries are making efforts to achieve better management of tourism demand by staggering holidays (see Stäblein,

1994, and Chapter 3). The general trend in most generating countries is to take more than one holiday a year, with a reduction in the duration of the main holiday and a growing demand for short breaks (one to three nights), and this has flattened the seasonal pattern in many destinations.

Interdependence of tourism products

Interdependence of tourism products is a direct consequence of the characteristics mentioned earlier – a tourist product is an amalgam. Even an individual tourist buys a whole set of products supplied by different firms – the attractions have no economic value without the necessary accommodation, but the latter cannot function properly without the supporting factors and resources – infrastructure, accessibility, facilitating resources and hospitality (Ritchie and Crouch, 2003). A destination is a cluster of activities, and a bad performance by one sub-sector influences the profitability of the other sectors of the cluster. Different suppliers always benefit from combining their respective efforts.

In a wider sense, there can be an interdependence of destinations and/or resorts. The benefits offered by two neighbouring destinations are more than the sum of the two individual destinations. Bruges as a cultural destination is a real support for the seaside resorts at the Belgian coast and for the other cities of culture in Belgium, and *vice versa*. This has encouraged the Flemish cultural cities to organize their promotion partly together.

Relatively low investment costs but high fixed cost of operation

It may be hard to prove that the tourism sector has low investment costs, as low investment cost is a relative notion. Comparisons must be made with other sectors, and the tourism sector itself does not exist in the strict sense of the word as it is composed of many sub-sectors. However, there are several indicators that support the thesis of low investment costs. The investment per person employed in the accommodation sector (e.g. a hotel) and other facilities is relatively low. Many natural attractions are free goods, or only need marginal investments to make them operational. Most cultural attractions, such as churches, castles, abbeys and museums, were built for non-tourism purposes, and only later became tourism attractions too.

Not all tourism investments have relatively low investment costs. Airports, aircraft, highways, railways, cruise ships, cruise terminals, waterworks and cable railways all require high investment costs. However, some of them not only serve the tourism sector but also other activities in the national economy.

More important are the high fixed costs of operation. The cost for a firm can be divided into fixed and variable costs. Fixed costs are costs that are independent of the number of customers and must be paid anyhow, whereas variable costs are costs that are incurred as a function of the number of customers received at any given time.

A hotel, an air charter or a tourism attraction has in any case to finance the following costs in order to be open and to receive customers (Middleton, 2001):

- Depreciation of premises and equipment
- Maintenance

- Energy and utilities
- Insurance
- Property taxes
- Wages and indirect salary costs for full-time employees
- Overheads
- Marketing costs.

The point is that these costs are mostly committed in advance for the whole year, and have to be met whether the hotel or air charter draws few or many visitors. It is a general rule that a hotel cannot be profitable with an occupancy rate of less than 60 per cent, and air charters should have a load factor of more than 90 per cent. Owing to the relatively high fixed costs of operations, many holiday villages offer off-season or mid-week arrangements at very low prices, which cover the variable costs and provide a little surplus to contribute to the payment of the annual fixed costs.

As a consequence of the typical cost structure, many tourist firms make substantial and fast-growing profits once they exceed the breakeven point but make great and increasing losses when they stay below that breakeven.

Tourism is a growth sector

During the second half of the last century, tourism became one of the most important and rapidly growing sectors in the world economy. Figure 1.3 shows the evolution of international tourist arrivals worldwide during the period 1960–2000, and a forecast up to the year 2020.

The forecast data for the period 2000–2020 are based on the WTO publication *Tourism: 2020 Vision* (WTO, 1998). During the 1980s the average world annual growth rate of tourism in terms of arrivals amounted to about 5 per cent, but this decreased to 4.3 per cent in the 1990s. However, for the subsequent two decades the WTO foresees an annual growth rate of about 4.4 per cent. In terms of international tourism receipts – a comparison in real terms is much more difficult – an even higher growth rate can be noted. Here, however, we stick to the international tourist arrivals. The predicted annual growth rate (as a percentage) is the average of unequal rates per receiving region, and is shown in Table 1.2.

However, all regions register a very positive growth rate. Even more important is the fact that there are not many economic sectors that can stand comparison with tourism in terms of growth.

High income-elasticity
The relatively high growth rate of tourism demand is partly the result of the high income-elasticity of international arrivals and receipts. Demand for tourism reveals a high degree of sensitivity to changes in incomes – i.e. it is generally considered to be income-elastic. What does this mean? Income-elasticity is the reaction of demand to rising or falling incomes, and is measured as a ratio between changes in demand and corresponding changes in income. For example, if a 1 per cent increase in income causes a 1.5 per cent growth in tourism demand, then the

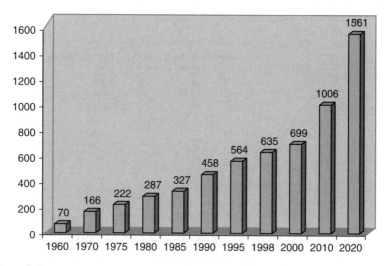

Figure 1.3 International tourist arrivals (millions) (Source: WTO).

Table 1.2 Predicted percentage annual growth rate in international tourist arrivals

	2000–2010	*2010–2020*
Europe	3.2	3.1
East Asia/Pacific	8.2	6.8
Americas	4.0	3.8
Africa	5.7	5.1
Middle East	7.1	6.5
South Asia	6.8	5.8
World	4.5	4.4

income-elasticity of tourism demand is equal to 1.5. The coefficient of elasticity can be expressed as the following formula:

$$E_Y = \frac{\Delta D/D}{\Delta Y/Y} \tag{1.1}$$

where

E_Y = coefficient of income-elasticity;
ΔD = change of tourism demand;
D = tourism demand;
ΔY = change of income;
Y = income.

A tourism demand is considered to be income-elastic when E_Y is bigger than 1; an E_Y value of between 0 and 1 is an indication of an inelastic demand.

Tourism income-elasticity varies from country to country and from period to period. Smeral (1994) calculated the income- and price elasticity for the

Table 1.3 Income- and price-elasticity for inbound tourism, by country

	Income-elasticity	Price-elasticity
Australia	1.24	−1.32
Austria	1.21	−0.87
Germany	0.61	−0.43
Switzerland	1.60	−1.15
Denmark	1.36	−0.99
France	1.11	−0.91
Italy	2.12	−1.41
Japan	2.10	−1.69
Spain	2.45	−1.39
Sweden	2.47	−1.76
USA	2.06	−0.44
UK	0.52	−0.72

inbound tourism (export) of a number of countries over the period 1975 to 1992 (see Table 1.3).

For all but two countries of the countries in Table 1.3, income-elasticity is greater than 1. However, the coefficients differ from country to country, and 5 of the 12 countries show an income-elasticity greater than 2. This means that in the case of Italy, with an E_Y equal to 2.12 and a real welfare increase in Italy's generating countries of 2.5 per cent, the inbound consumption increases by $2.12 \times 2.5 = 5.3$ per cent.

As well as income-elasticity, price-elasticity is very important in the tourism sector. This is the reaction of demand to changes in price, and is calculated in a similar way to income-elasticity. Smeral's exercise shows that tourism demand is sensitive to price variations, and the price-elasticity is higher than commonly stated. The tourism business is highly competitive. It is clear that coefficients of price-elasticity have a negative sign. When the independent variable of 'price' increases, a decrease in tourism demand (dependent variable) can be expected, and *vice versa* – when prices decrease, demand will increase.

For the measurement of coefficients of elasticity, refer to Chapter 7.

Predominance of SMEs

Another economic feature of tourism is the predominance of small and medium-sized enterprises (SMEs) in the tourism industry. Middleton (1998) has estimated the number of SMEs in the UK alone to be 170 000 (he uses the term 'micro-businesses'), and these comprise some 95 per cent of all the enterprises providing tourism services. In many well-known tourism countries, the hotel sector is no exception. Cooper *et al.* (1993) made a comparison between the USA and Europe with respect to rooms owned by publicly quoted companies. Although the 1991 data are no longer very current, they are illustrative. The share of rooms in so-called quoted companies varied from 30 per cent in the USA, 23.5 per cent in the UK and 20.4 per cent in The Netherlands to 3.2 per cent in Spain, 1.7 per cent in Italy and 1.0 per cent in Greece. Although not fully comparable, Marvel (2004) has recently published data regarding the chain penetration (chains are hotel groups with at least 10 properties) as a percentage of total hotel stock. These data confirm the abovementioned differences. In 2004, branded rooms represent 65 per cent of the total hotel stock in North America and only 25 per cent of that in Europe (11 EU countries plus Switzerland); the penetration (in 2003) varied from 37 per cent in France and 32 per cent in the UK to 8 per cent in Switzerland and 6 per cent each in Italy and Austria. It should be emphasized that the chain penetrations is much lower in terms of hotel units. In Europe, the 87 brands with at least 10 properties represent no more than 6 per cent of the total stock.

Middleton (2001) lists a number of economic advantages and disadvantages of these micro-businesses:

- The money earned by micro-businesses tends to stay in the local community – they typically purchase locally and are part of the fabric of the local money circulation cycle
- They are a vital element in job creation in rural areas and less developed regions in general
- They do not have the commercial rationale that dominates big enterprises
- Typically, 'Numbered in their hundreds of thousands, micro-businesses are unique as individual enterprises and they cannot be standardized – to attempt to do so would destroy their contribution. Unfortunately this makes them amorphous and difficult to measure and "badge" as a coherent sector'.

It should be recognized that in many developing countries tourism is a gateway to 'entrepreneurship', and this is considered to be one of the positive points of tourism in the development process of many countries and regions (Mathieson and Wall, 1982; Vanhove, 1986).

The characteristics dealt with in this first chapter should be seen as an introduction to the more 'economic' chapters of this book.

References and further reading

Boniface, B. and Cooper, C. (1987). *The Geography of Travel and Tourism.* London: Heinemann.

Burkart, A.J. and Medlik, S. (1974). *Tourism. Past, Present and Future.* London: Heinemann.

Chadwick, R.A. (1981). Some notes on the geography of tourism: a comment. *Canadian Geographer,* 25.

Chadwick, R.A. (1994). Concepts, definitions and measures used in travel and tourism research. In J.R. Brent Ritchie and Ch. R. Goeldner (eds), *Travel, Tourism, and Hospitality Research.* New York: John Wiley & Sons.

Clawson, M. and Knetsch, J.L. (1964). *Economics of Outdoor Recreation.* Baltimore: Johns Hopkins Press.

Cooper, C., Fletcher, J., Gilbert, D. and Wanhill, S. (1993). *Tourism. Principles & Practice.* London: Pitman Publishing.

De Brabander, G. (1992). *Toerisme en economie.* Leuven: Garant.

Eurostat, OECD, WTO and UN Statistics Division (2001). *Tourism Satellite Account: Recommended Methodological Framework*. Luxembourg: UN.

Franz, A., Laimer, A. and Smeral, E. (2001). *A Tourism Satellite Account for Austria*. Vienna, Statistik Austria and WIFO.

Gilbert, D.C. (1990). Conceptual issues in the meaning of tourism. In C.P. Cooper (ed.), *Progress in Tourism, Recreation and Hospitality Management, Vol. 2*. London: Pitman Publishing.

Jefferson, A. and Lickorish, L. (1988). *Marketing Tourism – A Practical Guide*. Harlow: Longman.

Kimes, S. (1999). Yield management: an overview. In I. Yeoman and A. Ingold (eds), *Yield Management. Strategies for the Service Industries*. Cassell: London.

Marvel, M. (2004). European hotel chain expansion. *Travel & Tourism Analyst*, Mintel, May.

Mathieson, A. and Wall, G. (1982). *Tourism: Economic, Physical and Social Impacts*. London: Longman.

Medlik, R. (1988). *What is Tourism? Teaching Tourism into the 1990s*. Guildford: University of Surrey.

Middleton, V.T.C. (1998). SMEs in European tourism: the context and a proposed framework for European action. *Revue de Tourisme*, 4.

Middleton, V.T.C. with Clarke, J. (2001). *Marketing in Travel and Tourism*, 3rd edn. Oxford: Butterworth-Heinemann.

Mieczkowski, Z. (1990). *World Trends in Tourism and Recreation*. New York: Peter Lang.

Miller, N. and Robinson, D. (1963). *The Leisure Age. Its Challenge in Recreation*. Belmont: Worldworth Publishing Company.

Ritchie, J.R.B. and Crouch, G. (2003). *The Competitive Destination*. Wallingford: CABI Publishing.

Rogers, J. (2002a). Crossing an administrative boundary: a new approach to leaving the usual domestic environment. *Enzo Paci Papers on Measuring the Economic Significance of Tourism, Vol. 2*. Madrid: WTO.

Rogers, J. (2002b). Have you crossed the line? A discussion of measurement challenges in leaving the usual domestic environment. *Proceedings of the 33rd Annual TTRA Conference*. Boise: Travel and Tourism Research Association.

Smeral, E. (1994). *Tourismus 2005*. Vienna: Ueberreuter.

Smith, S. (1988). Defining tourism: a supply side view. *Annals of Tourism Research*, 15(2).

Smith, S. (1997). *Tourism Analysis. A Handbook*, 2nd edn. Edinburgh: Longman.

Stäblein, F. (1994). School holidays. Presentation of an experience: rolling system of school holidays. *Conference on Staggering of Holidays*, Düsseldorf. Hannover: Niedersächsisches Kultusministerium.

Vanhove, N. (1974). *Vakantiespreiding. Een nieuw voorstel voor België, No. 6*. Brugge: Facetten van West-Vlaanderen.

Vanhove, N. (1986). Tourism and regional economic development. In J.H.P. Paelinck (ed.), *Human Behaviour in Geographical Space. Essays in Honour of Leo H. Klaassen*. Aldershot: Gower.

Wahab, S. (1971). An introduction to tourism theory. *Travel Research Journal*, 1.

WTO (1998). *Tourism: 2020 Vision*. Madrid: WTO.

2

The measurement of tourism

Introduction

Measurement of tourism activity is important for both public and private sectors. Without reliable data it is impossible to demonstrate the economic importance of the sector in terms of value added, employment, exports and imports. In many countries the amount of tourism activity is still underestimated due to a lack of correct statistical information. An efficient policy also requires data on the supply and demand structure and the development of the sector. Furthermore, a good information system is the basis for a good planning process at the local and regional levels. Strategic planning (both marketing and physical) begins with a situation analysis – which are the priority markets, what is the necessary capacity of hospitals, parking, waste treatment installations, police force, etc.?

The characteristics dealt with in Chapter 1 already provide an indication that it is not easy to measure tourism activities of a country or region. What is the tourism demand and supply of a country? This is a very important question, as the answer provides the basis for the economic impact analysis.

At the risk of oversimplification, until recently tourism supply was defined only in terms of the numbers of beds, rooms, camping places, etc., and tourism demand was expressed only in the numbers of arrivals and nights. From Chapter 1 it is evident that the numbers of rooms and arrivals provide a poor indicator of the tourism activity of a country. These statistics are useful, but far from complete. This explains the numerous efforts, mainly over the last decade, by scientists and regional, national and international organizations to improve the tourism data system.

This chapter focuses on a number of measurement systems applied in practice. They can be classified in five groups:

1. A general tourism information system
2. The Tourism Satellite Account
3. Tourism and holiday surveys
4. The tourism production index
5. The tourism barometer.

All these systems have different objectives and are as such not comparable, sometimes being complementary. Besides these instruments, each country has its own (sometimes updated) registration system.

A general tourism information system

A general tourism information system (TIS) can be described as a system used to collect, in a permanent and systematic way, the tourism supply and demand data at the destination level (national, regional or local) necessary for an efficient tourism policy (e.g. general policy, tourism marketing, physical planning). The elements of the TIS depend largely on the content of the tourism policy.

Table 2.1 shows the possible content of such a system. A clear distinction is made between the demand items and the supply elements. The demand and supply categories are further divided into 'basic' and 'secondary' items. In the context of a TIS, 'basic' means that each destination should dispose of these items; it does not exclude that for marketing purposes some secondary items are also important. Table 2.1 is only a possible example, and its contents are not exhaustive. It can be adapted in function of the policy purposes. A destination marketing information system will have a different outlook (Ritchie and Ritchie, 2002).

The preparation and the upkeep of a TIS is demanding and expensive, but the cost can be reduced if the following suggestions are taken into consideration. First, for several elements it is not necessary to repeat the measurement annually – for example, the expenditure pattern of visitors to a destination is unlikely to change fundamentally from one year to the next. Secondly, for several items costs can be saved by working with a representative sample – a good sample gives better results than a poor exhaustive inquiry. In sampling, particular attention should be paid to three topics:

1. The sample method (random sampling, systematic sampling, stratified sampling, cluster sampling, quota sampling or random walk)
2. The method of delivering the survey (personal interviews, telephone surveys, postal surveys or the Internet)
3. Questionnaire design (phrasing and content of questions) (Cooper et al., 1993; Smith, 1997).

Table 2.1 Primary and secondary items of a TIS at destination level

Type	Items	Frequency	Method of data collection
Actual demand	Basic items ■ number of arrivals ■ number of nights ■ period ■ origin of arrivals ■ purpose of trip ■ accommodation ■ final destination ■ combination of duration – purpose/origin/accommodation	yearly	exhaustive survey or representative sample
	■ expenditure per person and per family ■ breakdown of expenditure per major category ■ combination of expenditure and other attributes	each three years	sample
Actual demand	Secondary items ■ family size ■ age ■ profession ■ travel organisation ■ transport ■ first or repeat visitor ■ information gathering ■ activities on the destination (visits to …) ■ evaluation	each three to four years	representative sample
Potential demand	■ socio-economic trends in generating markets ■ tourism trends in generating markets ■ awareness of the destination in generating and potential markets ■ potential demand in a number of countries or regions ■ image of the destination ■ strengths with respect to main competitors	each three years	survey desk research and information from the trade

(Continued)

Table 2.1 (*Continued*)

Type	Items	Frequency	Method of data collection
Other marketing information	■ choice distribution channel (independent, trade) ■ use of the internet; consultation of the web-site ■ ecological indicators ■ target groups and communication instruments ■ efficiency of the communication instruments of the destination ■ price level in competitive destinations	each three years yearly	sample desk research sample
Day tourism	■ number ■ expenditure (type of expenditure) ■ origin ■ profile (transport, age etc.)	yearly or every two years	sample
Supply	Basic items ■ number of units per accommodation type ■ commercial and non-commercial accommodation ■ location ■ price level ■ operational periods ■ capacity per accommodation type (beds, rooms, sites, etc.) ■ characteristics of the accommodation (hotel classification; classification of camping sites, apartments and other) ■ employment and type of employees ■ cultural attractions	yearly	permanent inventory
Supply	Secondary items ■ restaurants and cafes ■ recreational facilities ■ capacity recreation facilities ■ sports facilities ■ shopping facilities ■ health care ■ meeting facilities (capacity)	each three years	desk research

A number of macro-indicators can be derived directly from the TIS. This is the case with tourism turnover and occupancy rates at the destination level.

The Tourism Satellite Account

Background, definition and objectives

It must be clear that this section is restricted to a conceptual framework of TSA. For the extensive methodology and purely technical aspects, we refer to the specialized reports and manuals on the subject listed under References and Further Reading.

A tourism satellite account (TSA) is quite different from a general information system. The concept is on the one hand much wider, on the other far narrower. This will become clear in the following paragraphs.

Statistics regarding tourism have often been restricted to data on the volumes of arrivals, number of nights, length of stay, purpose of visit, type of accommodation, origin of visitors and their socio-economic profile, accommodation capacity and corresponding occupancy rate, and a few other elements. It should not be difficult to make the link to the basic items of the TIS of the preceding section. These are still elements of the TSA, but the latter offers much more. However, elements that important for an environmental or marketing policy are not retained in the TSAs.

How can we define a TSA? According to the WTO (2000), 'A TSA is no more than a set of definitions, classifications integrated into tables, organized in a logical, consistent way, which allows one to view the whole economic magnitude of tourism in both its aspects of demand and supply'. As we noted in Chapter 1, the 'satellite account' was developed by the United Nations to measure the size of economic sectors that are not included in their own right in national accounts. In other words, it is a system of tourism information integrated with the system of national accounts.

Many organizations and tourism scientists felt, in the 1990s, the need for a comprehensive tourism measurement system. Many were frustrated because of a real underestimation of the sector. This is well expressed in a WTO brochure (WTO, 2001): 'Tourism is an activity that many in the world participate in but which few appreciate beyond its abilities to delight the traveller and facilitate business'.

Why is the TSA needed? Governments often underestimate the economic benefits that tourism provides because it is not visible in the same way as industries such as machine construction and textiles. Business enterprises often fail to realize the role tourism plays in their success, and they do not take full advantage of opportunities in this growing activity because it is not measured in the same way as other industries. Citizens, too, may not seriously consider the job opportunities that tourism provides. Tourism activity generates substantial amounts in personal spending, business receipts, employment, value-added creation and government revenue. Only a small part of tourism spending takes place in what are normally considered to be tourism industries (hotels and trade), and in fact a very large part takes place outside the classical tourism industries such as self-catering, museums, retail shops, public transport, etc. However, until now there has been insufficient attention to measuring these economic benefits on an equal footing with other sectors such as machine construction, textiles or insurance.

The objectives of tourism satellite accounting are very diverse, and include the following (Eurostat *et al.*, 2001):

- To describe the structure of a country's or region's tourism activity
- To provide macro-economic aggregates to describe the size and the economic importance of tourism, such as tourism value-added and tourism GDP
- To provide detailed data on tourism consumption and how this is met by domestic supply and imports
- To provide detailed production accounts of the tourism industries, data on employment, linkages with other productive activities and capital formation
- To provide a link between economic data and the basic items of TIS.

Designed with a view to its subject as well as its purposes, according to Franz *et al.* (2001), the TSA is not just a set of statistical tables but a self-contained, comprehensive system of specific definitions, and inter-relating numbers, compilations and analyses. However, this perception of the TSA is still only half the story; the other half is its being embedded in the greater context of the overall national accounts system of a country. Franz *et al.* (2001) call it the 'holistic' view.

The fundamental structure of the TSA is based on the general balance existing within an economy between the demand of goods and services generated by tourism and their supply. The idea behind the TSA is to analyse in detail all the aspects of demand for goods and services which might be associated with tourism within the economy, to observe the operational interface with the supply of such goods and services within that economy, and to describe how this supply interacts with other activities (Eurostat *et al.*, 2001).

The demand and supply perspectives are the subject of the next two sections.

The demand perspective

Two key elements of the demand perspective are the 'visitor' and 'tourism consumption'. The term 'visitor' (tourist and excursionist) was defined in Chapter 1. Tourism consumption is the central element of the system and the basis for the economic impact analysis of tourism. The WTO and OECD use the following definition: 'expenditure made by, or on behalf of, the visitor before, during and after the trip and which expenditure is related to that trip and which trip is undertaken outside the usual environment of the user'. It is important to notice that some expenditure before the trip (e.g. passports, inoculation, small items to be brought along as gifts) and afterwards (developing of photos) is included, as long as its usage is clearly directed to the trip.

The different aggregates or categories of tourism consumption (domestic, inbound, outbound, internal and national) are linked to visitors, and were dealt with in Chapter 1. These aggregates of tourism consumption go far beyond visitors' purchases on the trip. They also encompass all expenditures on goods and services by other institutional units on behalf of visitors. If cash or financial assets are transferred to the visitor to finance the trip, the purchases funded by these are included in visitor consumption. Along with this are all forms of transfers in kind

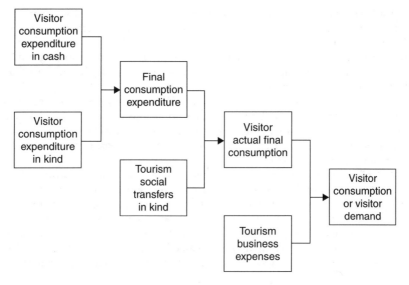

Figure 2.1 Components of visitor consumption

and other transactions benefiting visitors where it is not cash or financial assets that are provided to the visitor but goods and services themselves.

The components of visitor consumption are shown in Figure 2.1.

There are four main categories:

1. Visitor final consumption expenditure in cash
2. Visitor final consumption expenditure in kind
3. Tourism social transfers in kind
4. Tourism business expenses.

These categories and Figure 2.1 need explanation.

Visitor final consumption expenditure in cash covers what is usually meant by 'visitor expenditure', and is part of the final demand in input–output terms. It always represents the most important component of total consumption. Here, special attention should be paid to consumer durable goods. With respect to tourism, a distinction should be made between 'tourism single-purpose goods', which are goods used exclusively on trips (e.g. skiing equipment, camping equipment, luggage, etc.) and 'multipurpose consumer durable goods', which are used on holidays but also within the usual environment (such as cameras and cars). In the framework of the TSA convention, a different treatment of both categories of durables is seen. Tourism single-purpose durable goods are always included, whether purchased before, during or after a trip, or even outside the context of a specific trip. Multipurpose consumer durables are only included if purchased during a holiday.

Visitor consumption expenditure in kind consists of non-monetary transactions, and includes barter transactions (exchange of a residence for holiday purposes), production for own final use (e.g. second homes on own account or free of charge), and income in kind (holidays offered by the employer).

Tourism social transfers in kind relate to non-market services provided by governmental organizations or non-profit institutions serving households (NPISH). Examples of these non-market services are health services provided to visitors (e.g. spas), and activities such as museum visits, where the total costs may not be fully attributed to the tourist. The charges for museums paid for by the tourist are included in visitor consumption in cash.

Tourism business expenditure includes tourism expenses that are classified as intermediate consumption of businesses, government organizations and NPISH. They mainly concern expenditure on transport and accommodation of employees on business trips, and are considered as intermediate consumption of the corresponding production units.

As well as visitor consumption, attention should be paid to tourism collective consumption. In the case of tourism, collective services refer (among other things) to the provision of legislation and regulations regarding tourism, the promotion of tourism by public agencies, the maintenance of order and security, and the maintenance of the public domain. So far, tourism collective consumption is not a part of the TSA and remains as the actual final consumption of general government. However, in TSA system, a table of tourism collective consumption is predicted.

A special category is tourism gross fixed capital formation. This is important for tourism because the existence of a basic infrastructure in terms of attractions, transport, accommodation, airports, public utilities and many others determines the nature and intensity of tourist flows. Furthermore, it requires a large amount of investment from the public as well as from the private sector. For the moment, the identification of capital goods whose acquisition or production is driven by the needs of visitors presents both conceptual and practical difficulties. However, Table 8 of the UN/WTO TSA concerns 'tourism gross fixed capital formation' (Eurostat *et al.*, 2001).

Final remarks at the end of this section concern the estimation of expenditure. This is a very important and delicate point, especially when a breakdown per category of tourist expenditure is necessary. The guidelines for developing the TSA give an overview of applied expenditure estimation methods (WTO, 2000), which are of a very varied nature and include:

1. Existing data (Country's National Statistical Office)
2. Household surveys
3. Visitor surveys
   - diary surveys
   - surveys at accommodation establishments
   - surveys at border entry/exit points
   - surveys on board transport vehicles
   - surveys at popular visitor places
4. Tourism establishment surveys – interviews with selected guests, or giving questionnaire to selected guests
5. Central bank data
6. Expenditure models
   - expenditure ratio model
   - cost factor expenditure model (a hybrid of household surveys and establishment surveys).

The supply perspective

Tourism-specific products

The economic analysis of tourism requires the identification of tourism-specific products – i.e. the resources used by tourists on their holiday, their consumption of goods and services, and therefore the identification of the economic units that provide those goods and services. General economic classifications of activities are established from the point of view of supply by producers and from the characteristics of the production process, but for tourism some adaptation of these classifications is required. Indeed, tourism is a phenomenon that was originally defined from the point of view of demand.

The starting point is the classification of goods and services. Not all goods have the same relevance for the estimation of tourism consumption. The level and structure of an individual's consumption at home is not the same as when that individual is away from the usual environment. This has the consequence that classifications that are meaningful for the description of household consumption in general may not be so meaningful when the focus is specifically on tourism (Eurostat *et al.*, 2001).

The 1993 System of National Accounts (SNA) suggests a number of steps in the identification of different groups of products (see Figure 2.2).

In the TSA concept, production can be split into three categories. The first is tourism-characteristic goods and services – those products which, in most countries, would cease to exist in meaningful quantity (or the consumption of which would be significantly reduced) in the absence of tourism, and for which it should be possible to obtain statistical information (e.g. accommodation, travel services, cable cars, etc.). To make an international comparison on a worldwide basis possible, a list of tourism characteristic products is available. TSA tables make a distinction between seven groups – each subdivided – of tourism characteristic products:

1. Accommodation services
2. Food- and beverage-serving services
3. Passenger transport services
4. Travel agency, tour operator and tourism guide services

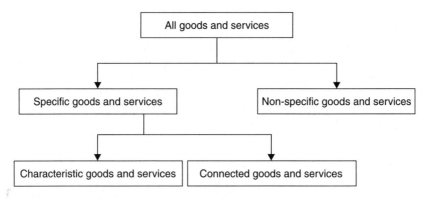

Figure 2.2 TSA and classification of goods and services

5. Cultural services
6. Recreation and other entertainment services
7. Miscellaneous tourism services.

The second category consists of tourism-related or connected goods and services – those products which are consumed by tourists in volumes significant to the visitor and/or the provider but are not included in the list of tourism characteristic products (e.g. taxicab transportation, currency exchange). Tourism characteristic and tourism-related goods and services together are called 'tourism-specific products'.

The third category consists of non-specific or non-tourism characteristic production (e.g. toothpaste and, in general, most retail trade).

In practice, the borderline between the different groups is not always clear. In the Austrian TSA, tourism-connected and non-characteristic products are combined into one group.

Tourism-specific activities

The activities in which the above mentioned tourism characteristic products originate are called characteristic activities. The 1993 System of National Accounts (SNA) emphasizes the analysis of characteristic *producers*: 'In a satellite account the main emphasis when looking at production is on the analysis of characteristic activities and producers'.

To assure international comparability, a list of tourism characteristic activities has been defined. The production accounts of the TSA retain 12 tourism characteristic activities:

1. Hotels and similar
2. Second-home ownership
3. Restaurants and similar
4. Railway passenger transport services
5. Road passenger transport services
6. Water passenger transport services
7. Air passenger transport services
8. Transport supporting services
9. Transport equipment rental
10. Travel agencies and similar
11. Cultural services
12. Sporting and other recreational services.

One important feature of tourism characteristic activities is the direct contact between the consumer and the provider of the products. Some activities may be considered to be characteristic of tourism because of the importance of their products and services for the tourist, although the major part of their typical output is not sold to tourists. This is the case for transport services and restaurants – restaurant meals are consumed by visitors and non-visitors alike.

TSA tables

The next step is the integration of the demand and the supply side into tables. This allows examination of the magnitude of tourism in both demand and supply aspects. The 10 tables of the TSA are derived from or related to the tables of the 1993 SNA that concern supply and the use of goods and services.

The TSA consists of a set of 10 tables:

- Tables 1–4: tourism consumption by products and type of tourism (domestic, inbound, outbound and internal tourism consumption)
- Table 5: production accounts of tourism industries (see Appendix 2.1)
- Table 6: domestic supply and internal tourism consumption of services by products (see Appendix 2.2)
- Table 7: employment
- Table 8: tourism gross fixed capital formation
- Table 9: tourism collective consumption
- Table 10: quantitative indicators without monetary expression (e.g. number of arrivals, nights, or establishments).

To illustrate the content of Tables 1–6, the Austrian TSA tables, in a condensed form, are shown as an example. Table 2.2 is a condensed form of the Austrian TSA Tables 1, 2 and 4. Table 2.3 relates to TSA Tables 5 and 6 (also in a condensed form).

Note that in the TSA Table 5 (see Table 2.3), every tourism industry is listed vertically in rows and every product is recorded horizontally in columns. Each cell of the spreadsheet provides the value of a specific product produced in a given year by a given tourism industry (called the make matrix). TSA

Table 2.2 TSA Tables 1, 2 and 4: results for Austria (1999) in a condensed form (in millions of Austrian schillings)*

Products	Inbound tourism consumption (TSA Table 1)	Domestic tourism consumption (TSA Table 2)	Internal tourism consumption (TSA Table 4)	
			In kind	In cash and kind
Characteristic products:	142 814	108 478	10 249	261 541
1. Accommodation services	37 135	23 170	10 249	70 554
2. Food- and beverage-serving services	62 384	48 585		110 889
3. Passenger transport services	19 601	19 880		39 481
4. Travel agency, tour operator and tourist guide services	2 179	470		2 657
5. Cultural activities				
6. Recreation and other entertainment services	21 595	16 365		37 910
7. Miscellaneous tourism services				
Total connected and non-specific products	17 378	20 532		37 910
Value of domestically produced goods (net of distribution margin)	160 192	129 010	10 249	299 451
Distribution margins	1 583	1 127		2 710
Total	161 775	130 137	10 249	302 161

* €1 = 13.76 Austrian Schillings
Source: Franz *et al.* (2001).

Table 2.3 TSA Tables 5 and 6: results for Austria (1999) in a condensed form (in millions of Austrian schillings)*

Products	TSA Table 5: Production account of tourism industries and other industries				TSA Table 6: Domestic supply and internal tourism consumption by products (d)					
	Hotel & restaurant[a]	Total tourism industries[a]	Tourism connected & non-specific industries	Total output of domestic producers (at basic prices) domestic supply (gross)	Total output of domestic producers (at basic prices) domestic supply (net)[b]	Imports	Taxes less subsidies on products of domestic output and imports	Domestic supply (at purchaser price)	Internal tourism consumption	Tourism supply ratio
Characteristic products	173 776	401 385	31 775	433 140	433 004	5 629	−5 078	433 554	261 540	0.60
1. Accommodation services	171 832	188 368		189 489	201 846		4 524	206 370	181 443	0.88
2. Food and beverage serving services										
3. Passenger transport services	215	122 274	28 266	150 540	172 540	2 142	−16 327	158 355	39 480	0.25
4. Travel agency, tour operator and tourist guide services	27	40 477	136	40 613	2 049[b]	609	−1	2 657	2 657	1.00[b]
5. Cultural activities	585	27 060	267	27 317	27 433	395	557	283 853	37 960	0.57
6. Recreation and other entertainment services	1 107	23 161	1 126	24 288	28 243	2 482	6 169	36 894		
7. Miscellaneous tourism services		35	858	893	893			893		
Total connected and non-specific products	1 630	8 716	4 314 079	4 322 796	4 322 931	1 230 432	302 948	5 856 311	40 621	0.02
Value of domestic output	175 396	410 081	4 345 854	4 755 935	4 755 935	1 236 060	297 870	6 289 865	302 161	0.05
Distribution margin	806	12 225	108 806	110 031	110 031	63 982	−	174 013	2 710	0.02

Value of domestic output (net of distribution margin)	174 590	408 856	4 237 048	4 645 904	4 645 904	1 172 078	297 870	6 116 852	299 461	0.05
Value of imported goods[c]	x	x	x	x	x	x	x	x	x	x
Total output (net of distribution margins)	174 590	408 856	4 237 048	4 645 904	4 645 904	1 172 078	297 870	6 116 852	299 461	0.05
Intermediate consumption (at purchases prices)	69 675	182 123	1 881 436							
Total gross value added (at basic prices)	105 721	227 958	2 484 072	2 702 030						
Tourism ratio on supply	0.88		0.02							
Tourism value added (TVA) (Holiday and business trips)	93 034		51 961	194 421						
Share on GVA (in %)	0.88		2.09	7.17						

* €1 = 13.76 Austrian Schillings

[a]The other tourism industries are included in total tourism industries; in the Austrian case hotels and restaurants are combined.

[b]According to SNA 93, the output of travel Agency services represents the value of service charges of agencies (commission charges) and not the full expenditure incurred by travellers to the travel agency. As stated in UN TSA, 'TSA requires all components of a package tour, including the value of the service of the tour operator himself, to be considered as directly purchased by the visitors. This entails a so-called "net" valuation of package tours'. This means that the output of tour operators consists of a margin whereas the elements of the package are directly distributed to the respective products (e.g. accommodation).

[c]Does not apply.

[d]The rows of TSA Table 6 are similar to those of TSA Table 5. In the condensed form they are shown only once. The first block of rows details output by tourism characteristic product. Total output of an activity is obtained as the sum of its outputs by product. The remaining block of rows shows intermediate consumption by product. The difference between total output (at basic prices) and the total input (at purchasers' prices) provides value added at basic prices. The last block of rows presents the components of value added.

Source: Franz *et al.* (2001).

Table 5 (production account or supply) provides the data basis for TSA Table 6 (demand and supply). This table presents an overall illustration of internal tourism consumption with domestic supply, from which tourism value added and the GDP generated by internal tourism consumption can be derived. This table is the core element of the TSA system.

The internal tourism consumption (see the final column of Table 2.2) is integrated into Table 2.3 (TSA Table 6), and allows us to calculate the 'tourism ratio' of supply (also called 'tourism share'). To calculate the tourism ratio of any given supply of commodities, the amount purchased by tourists is related to the total supply of the respective commodity. For Austria, the tourism ratio of the combination 'hotels, restaurants and similar' equals 0.88 – in other words, 88 per cent of the domestic supply is consumed by domestic and inbound tourists. These tourism ratios vary from product to product. For hotel services this ratio is very high, but for air transportation it only amounts to 22 per cent. This an indication that a relatively high proportion of supply is used by non-tourists.

These tourism ratios, applied to the gross value added (GVA) of the symmetrically corresponding industry in TSA Table 5, result in the direct tourism value added (TVA) of each industry. The total TVA of the 12 tourism industries is related to the overall GDP, which leads to the share of tourism in the total GDP.

The valuation principles applied in TSA Tables 5 and 6 need clarification. In the TSA, the valuation principles are essentially the same as those advocated by SNA 93. 'Use' (TSA Table 6) is valued at purchasers' prices, while 'production' (TSA Table 5) is valued at basic prices.

The SNA defines basic value as:

> The amount receivable by the producer from the purchaser for a unit of good or service produced as output minus any tax payable, and plus subsidy receivable, on that unit as a consequence of its production or sale. It excludes any transport charges invoiced separately by the producer.

Purchasers' prices are defined as (OECD, 2000):

> The amount paid by the producer, excluding deductible VAT or similar deductible tax, in order to take delivery of a unit of a good or service at the time and place required by the purchaser. The purchasers' price of a good includes any transport charges paid separately by the producer to take delivery at the required time and place.

So far, this provides the conceptual framework of the TSA. The TSA is an ideal instrument to measure a number of macro-economic aggregates, and this is discussed in Chapter 7.

WTO tourism statistics

The WTO is not only active in the field of TSA, but is also primarily known for a very comprehensive database of tourism statistics worldwide. It offers a selection of statistics and correspondent analysis on inbound tourism (tourist arrivals, tourism receipts, travel by purpose and means of transport) and outbound tourism (outbound tourism by region of origin and tourism expenditure), as well as on the WTO's long-term prospects – *Tourism 2020 Vision* (WTO, 1998).

In the publication *World and Country Trends*, produced annually by the WTO, we find comprehensive, comparable and up-to-date sources for an assessment of world tourism statistics by country, region and sub-region. It provides an analysis of international tourist arrivals, international tourism receipts, region of origin of arrivals, purpose of visit, means of transport, international tourism expenditure, etc. (see *Yearbook of Tourism Statistics*, published annually by the WTO). Country data are also available on the WTO website 'Tourism Factbook'. This gives the latest and most up-to-date statistics for all the countries around the world, easily accessed by either alphabetical or geographical selection.

For the quality of the data, the WTO depends on the national data providers. A critical attitude towards some country data is recommended. The WTO is more a coordinator of tourism data than a data collector. As coordinator, it helps national and regional authorities to collect the data (see *The Technical Manuals Set*, published by the WTO). This package provides all the knowledge needed for the collection, interpretation and presentation of tourism statistics. It contains general concepts and definitions as well as technical guidelines and methods for different users and various segments of tourism research. The package includes volumes 1–4, respectively titled *Concepts, Definitions and Classifications for Tourism Statistics*; *Collection of Tourism Expenditure Statistics*; *Collection of Domestic Tourism Statistics*; and *Collection and Compilation of Tourism Statistics*.

In 2003, the WTO started using the WTO world tourism barometer, with the aim of monitoring the short-term evolution of tourism in order to provide the tourism sector with adequate and timely information. The WTO world tourism barometer is scheduled to be published several times a year. At the outset it contained three permanent elements: an overview of short-term tourism data from destination countries and air transport; the WTO Panel of Tourism Experts with a retrospective and prospective evaluation of tourism performance; and selected economic data relevant for tourism. The objective for future editions is to extend the content and improve coverage gradually over time.

Tourism and/or holiday surveys

Tourism and holiday surveys are of a completely different nature, and have different objectives to TSAs. They are mainly used to provide a view of the holiday pattern of a country's population. However, there are also surveys that focus on incoming tourism, and these surveys can be useful sources in the preparation of a TSA – especially for the demand side.

Typical surveys in the UK

The UK uses a number of typical tourism surveys and has a long tradition in the matter. The main sources in the UK are:

- The International Passenger Survey (IPS)
- The United Kingdom Tourism Survey (UKTS), or the former British Home Tourism Survey
- The United Kingdom Day Visits Survey (UKDVS).

All three can be seen in relationship to the TSA, although the origin of each of these surveys has nothing to do with the TSA. Here, the main characteristics as reported by Allin (Allin, 1998) and information provided by 'VisitBritain' are presented.

The IPS is carried out by the Office for National Statistics, and collects information from passengers as they enter or leave the UK. The survey is based on face-to-face interviews with a sample of passengers travelling via the principal air and sea routes or the Channel Tunnel. The sample is stratified to ensure that it is representative by mode of travel, port or route, and time of day. The sampling scheme used is multi-stage, and is carried out separately for air, sea and tunnel routes, with interviews carried out throughout the year. Information from overseas visitors is only collected from those on the return leg of their journey, amounting to around 50 000. The same practice in reverse is applied to UK residents travelling abroad.

Information collected in the survey covers the traditional variables, such as country visited, up to five towns stayed in overnight in the UK (overseas visitors only), number of nights spent in each town, length of stay, accommodation, package or independent, purpose, fares, expenditure excluding fares, money spent by UK residents on alcohol and tobacco, mileage travelled, etc.

A breakdown of spending by overseas visitors is collected from a sub-sample from time to time. The last sub-sample was carried out in 1997, and included about 3000 interviews. Information was collected in respect of 14 categories:

1. Accommodation
2. Meals out
3. Alcohol included with meals
4. Taxi or car hire;
5. Public transport/petrol
6. Clothing/fabrics
7. Food from retail shops
8. Souvenir/gifts, books/newspapers
9. Entertainment and admissions
10. Medical services
11. Hair and beauty treatments
12. Telephone/fax/postage services
13. Other services
14. Other items.

The knowledge of these data is very useful in the preparation of the TSA table inbound tourism consumption.

The United Kingdom Tourism Survey is the second source. The UKTS is jointly commissioned by the national tourist boards, and collects information on tourism activity by UK residents involving trips within the UK that include a stay of at least one night away from home. The survey has been running since 1989, and is conducted each month on a continuous basis. In 2000 the methodology changed from face-to-face interviewing to telephone interviews, using random digit dialling with a representative sample of UK adults aged 16 years or more (in total, about 50 000 interviews). In each interview information is sought on all trips taken in the previous two months, thereby minimizing the risk of poor reporting due to failing memory. The results are weighted to a constant profile of adults in the UK each month.

A wide range of data is collected in the survey (e.g. purpose, accommodation, organization of trip, type of location stayed in, activities pursued as main purpose of holiday, activities pursued on holiday, etc.). Information on expenditure is collected in nine categories:

1. Package trip
2. Accommodation (non-package trip)
3. Travel
4. Service or advice
5. Buying clothes
6. Eating and drinking
7. Other shopping
8. Entertainment
9. Other expenditure.

The third important tourism survey in the UK is the United Kingdom Day Visitor Survey(UKDVS). This survey was conducted for the first time on a full yearly basis in 1994, and has been repeated in 1996, 1998 and 2002. The scope for the survey comprised all adults aged 16 years and over, resident in private households within England, Scotland and Wales. The sample was designed to ensure that an adequate number of interviews was completed in each of these three countries to support separate analysis rather than ensuring an even distribution of the sample across Great Britain.

Within each of the countries, a three-stage clustered design was used, namely:

1. The selection of census enumeration districts
2. The selection of delivery points (addresses) within these areas
3. The selection of adults within addresses.

The initial targets for achieved sample sizes in each of the three countries were 3500 for England, and 2000 each for Scotland and Wales. However, in the 2002 survey this sampling approach was developed a stage further to ensure that an agreed minimum number of interviews was completed in each of the government regions within England. A target of a minimum of 400 interviews per region was agreed upon, and consequently the target sample for England was increased to almost 4000. The procedure is to select persons to interview. In the UKDVS, a tourism day trip is defined as a leisure trip taken away from a person's usual environment, and therefore should exclude local trips. The preferred definition of non-local trips is those trips that last longer than three hours and are taken irregularly.

The survey seeks information on day trips over the last two weeks, and then asks for recall over the last year. Besides the classical data, the survey collects information on 11 expenditure categories:

1. Purchase of petrol/diesel on the trip
2. Fares on buses/coaches/trains
3. Parking charges

4. Admission tickets, including ticket bought in advance
5. Tolls
6. Alcoholic drinks
7. Meal/snacks and non-alcoholic drinks
8. Gifts/souvenirs
9. Hire of equipment/facilities;
10. Clothes
11. Anything else.

These surveys give a substantial amount of information regarding the volume and value of tourism expenditure by UK residents and overseas visitors to the UK, and UK residents travelling abroad. However, there are a number of discrepancies for TSA applications (Allin, 1998):

■ Variation in the questions used to solicit information on the breakdown of expenditure between the different surveys
■ The depth of information on expenditure breakdown available
■ The limited data on day business trips.

In addition, in the UK there are a several other regular and *ad hoc* surveys that focus on particular types of tourism – for example, surveys of visits to visitor attractions, surveys of Conference and Exhibition activity, and the NOP Holiday Survey, which focuses on holiday-taking by British residents at home and abroad and more specifically those lasting more than four nights. In 1998 the former BTA stopped sponsoring the British National Travel Survey, but the research agency conducting the survey (NOP) has continued with it since that time as the NOP Holiday Survey. This is a random survey, conducting about 4000 face-to-face interviews with a representative sample of the British population. It takes place in November of each year, and asks details of holidays of four or more nights taken during the previous 12 months. This brings us to holiday surveys.

Holiday surveys

Most European countries perform a holiday survey. A few examples of reliable holiday surveys are:

■ In Austria, the Urlaubsreisen der Österreicher – Statistik Austria
■ In Belgium, the Belgisch vakantieonderzoek – WES
■ In France, the Déplacements touristiques des Français – INSEE
■. In Italy, the Viaggi e vacanze – ISTAT
■ In Germany, the Reiseanalyse – Forschungsgemeinschaft Urlaub und Reisen e.V.
■ In The Netherlands, the ContinuVakantieOnderzoek – CVO, NIPO, NRIT and TRN
■ In Norway, the Holiday Survey – Statistics Norway
■ In Spain, the Familitur (Movimientos Turisticos de los Españoles) – IET
■ In Switzerland, the Travel Market Switzerland – University of St Gallen
■ In the United Kingdom, the NOP Holiday Survey – NOP.

Among these holiday surveys, the Belgian holiday survey (WES) is well known and can be considered as an example. It covers the period 1967–2003, and relates to holidays (four nights or more) and short holidays (one to three nights). For more than 20 years the Belgian Holiday Survey has been conducted in a similar way, based on two samples of 6000 persons each. The persons selected are the same in both samples. A first sample covers the summer holidays (April–September) and the second covers the winter holidays (October–March).

The survey is based on a two-stage stratified sample. In the first stage there is double stratification, first by province. The number of sampling points (600 in total) and interviews per province is proportional to the population of each region. Within each stratum, further selection is based on a self-weighting stratification per size class of villages and towns. In the second stage the selection of the interviewees is based on a quota sample, with 10 people per sampling point. The interviewees are selected per street, sex, age and profession.

Holiday surveys provide a lot of information about the holiday behaviour of a country's population. Holiday participation is one of these behaviours. A distinction is made between net and gross holiday participation, where net participation expresses the number of holiday-takers in one year per 100 inhabitants and gross participation gives the number of holidays taken in one year per 100 inhabitants. Chapter 3 shows the results for a number of countries.

It is worth making one statistical note here. All these surveys are based on samples. Very often questions are raised such as: 'How reliable are the results based on a sample?' and 'How big should the sample size be?'. The following test provides a reliable guideline. The best sampling method is undoubtedly a random sample, where each person has the same chance of being selected. In tourism surveys at a national level, a 100 per cent pure random sample is seldom or never applied because of the high costs. In cases of random sampling, the following formula is applicable (with a 95 per cent confidence level):

$$P_s - 1.96\sqrt{\frac{P_s(1 - P_s)}{n - 1}} \sqrt{\frac{N - n}{N - 1}} \le P_p \le P_s + 1.96\sqrt{\frac{P_s(1 - P_s)}{n - 1}} \sqrt{\frac{N - n}{N - 1}} \quad (2.1)$$

where

P_p = population proportion (the real value in the universe)
P_s = sample proportion
N = population size
N = sample size.

Applied to the net participation rate of the Belgian population in the holiday survey for the year 2000, using the hypothesis of a random sample (which is not the case), and where $P_s = 0.63$, $N = 10\,000\,000$ inhabitants and $N = 6000$, the P_p value varies (with a 95 per cent confidence level) between 61.8 and 64.2 per cent – indeed, the corresponding error term or confidence interval amounts to 1.2 (see Table 2.4). A confidence level of 95 per cent (i.e. it is accurate 19 times out of 20) is standard in most tourism research, and gives a very reliable result. The problem is that most surveys are not based on a random sample but, as in the UK surveys, on a stratified random sample or a quota sample (or a combination of both). In that case a more complex statistical formula should be applied. However, the formula applicable for a random sample can be used as a proxy, although it is important to be aware that in such a case the error term will be slightly higher.

Table 2.4 Error terms (with a 95 per cent confidence level) in function of sample proportion P_s and sample size N

Sample size N	Sample proportion P in %						
	5	10	20	25	30	40	50
	95	90	80	75	70	60	50
100	4.3	5.9	7.9	8.5	9.0	9.7	9.8
200	3.0	4.2	5.6	6.0	6.4	6.8	6.9
500	1.9	2.6	3.5	3.7	4.0	4.3	4.4
1000	1.4	1.9	2.5	2.7	2.8	3.0	3.1
2000	1.0	1.3	1.8	1.9	2.0	2.1	2.2
5000	0.6	0.8	1.1	1.2	1.3	1.4	1.4
6000	0.6	0.8	1.0	1.1	1.2	1.2	1.3
10000	0.4	0.6	0.8	0.8	0.9	1.0	1.0

Table 2.4 provides details of error terms with varying sample proportions and sample size, and with a 95 per cent confidence level. If in the Belgian case P_s takes a value of 0.50 and the sample size is reduced to 1000, the P_p will take a value of (50 ± 3.1) – i.e. 46.9 per cent and 53.1 per cent (see Table 2.4).

Regarding the above formula, another point should be noted. For most samples from big populations, the factor $\sqrt{(N-n)/(N-1)}$ equals 1. This implies that the error term is independent of the population size – i.e. a sample size of 6000 from a population of 10 million has the same value as a sample of 6000 from 100 million people. This is a very important conclusion. The sample size should consider carefully the possible breakdowns (e.g. result per region). The more breakdowns, the larger the sample required.

The tourism production index – WES

Tourism arrivals or nights are, for many regions, not a good indicator for the tourism performance, as such destination data are very often unreliable or only relate to hotel nights. Camping, rented apartments, second homes and other accommodation forms are very often not considered. It is also well known that official tourism data totally neglect day visitors. Furthermore, the official data are only available long after the tourism activity took place.

These are the reasons why the WES started in 1962 to design a tourism production index for the West-Flanders region in Belgium (coastal region, Bruges and hinterland area). It had a dual aim: to collect data covering all aspects of the tourism business in the region, and provide information rapidly about the performance of the tourism sector. Table 2.5 gives the components of the WES tourism index, which can be compared with an index of manufacturing production.

Each category of the index was given a certain weight factor, and within each category a weight was attributed to the components of the category. The number and variety of the components was such as to guarantee coverage of all measurable aspects of the tourism activity of the region. The results were published no later than four weeks after each month of tourism production, and this was possible due to a successful data collection system, high participation of the sector and the use of a representative sample in the major components.

Table 2.5 Components of the WES tourism index (TI)

Tourism categories (j)	Components (i)	Weight	
		Component i	Category j
Accommodation	■ hotel ■ rented apartment/villas ■ camping ■ social tourism		
Traffic	■ rail transport ■ road traffic ■ road accidents ■ road assistance		
Trade	■ turnover retail trade ■ fuel consumption cars		
Attractions	■ theme parks ■ museums ■ ticketing swimming pools ■ visits to casinos		
Consumption public utilities	■ water consumption ■ waste collection ■ telephone communications ■ post traffic ■ patients in coastal hospitals ■ information provided by local tourism offices		
Tourism activity Bruges	■ information tourism office ■ boat trips on the canals ■ nights		
Tourism activity hinterland	■ nights ■ recreation		

The WES index was produced monthly for the months April–September of each year from 1962 to 2001. Although the index was considered to be the only reliable method of measurement of the performance of the sector in the region, production stopped in 2001 for financial reasons. The concept provides an example for many other tourism regions.

The 'tourism index' (TI) is an application of the following formula:

$$TI = \sum_{j=1}^{j=n} \left[\sum_{i=1}^{i=n} \left[w_i \, \Delta \, comp.i \right] \right] w_j \qquad (2.2)$$

where

Δ comp.i = change component i with respect to the reference period
w_i = weight component i within the corresponding category
w_j = weight of each category j.

Taking into account that data are collected monthly and the high season months are more important than off-peak periods, weight should be given to the individual months.

The Swiss tourism barometer

The Swiss tourism barometer, designed by Müller and Schmid (Müller and Schmid, 2003; Schmid, 2003) is, like the WES tourism index, a reaction to the problem of lack of reliable data in the tourism sector. It was inspired by the remarks of tourism professionals and scientists who criticized various aspects of tourism statistics for the following reasons:

■ The focus is too narrow because it pays too much attention to accommodation
■ The production period is excessively long
■ Data on self-catering accommodation are poor or inexistent
■ The method of data collection does not use modern technology
■ Present statistics focus on physical data and neglect largely monetary aspects.

A tourism barometer in its generic form was not new. The term 'tourism barometer' had already been used in Voralberg, Austria (the Voralberger Tourismus-barometer) since 1981; the Côte d'Azur, France since 1987; and former Eastern Germany since 1998. Later the DWIF extended the field of application to other German regions (Schleswig-Holstein, Niedersachsen) and the German tourism barometers were brought under a common denominator, Das Sparkassen-Tourismusbarometer (the barometer is financed by the Sparkassen-und Giroverbandes). Recently the WTO started to produce a periodical publication *WTO Barometer on Travel and Tourism*.

The concept of the Swiss tourism barometer is in several respects original, and it deserves a special attention as a tourism monitoring system. The Swiss started trials in 2001 in two regions (Berner Oberland and Grisons). However, due to financial constraints the barometer is not yet operational at a national level. The barometer is based on voluntary cooperation of the following sectors:

■ Hotels
■ Youth hostels
■ Weekend homes
■ Camping firms
■ Restaurants
■ Cableways
■ Sports, (ski and sport schools), culture and entertainment enterprises
■ Tourism organizations.

The participating firms of each branch report physical and monetary data on a monthly basis. Only one important sector (rented apartments and holiday homes in general) is not included. Tourism organizations are asked to report on information provided to tourists, and provide estimates of excursionists and bed-nights in private weekend houses.

The Swiss tourism barometer is composed of three parts. The first is systematic monitoring of relevant factors influencing tourism demand. Income and price are very important indicators, but national instruments on income and prices are not published on a monthly basis and are not adapted to the tourism sector. Therefore, more specific indicators are used as a substitute:

■ The consumer climate index, published every three months, represents income
■ The price for overnight visitors is based on the Swiss Consumer Price Index (only items relevant to tourists are included)

- Price movements in competing destinations are based on the price of package tours
- The rate of exchange of a basket of the currencies of the main countries of origin
- The number of hours of sunshine per month (for day visitors).

For each of these items the changes are registered with regard to the same month of the previous year.

The second part concerns the abovementioned branches of the industry. For each branch, a frequency indicator (e.g. number of overnight stays), a turnover indicator and one to three specific indicators (hotels: average turnover per night; restaurants: average turnover per seat; cableways: first entrances, etc.) are calculated.

To calculate frequency changes per branch, the following formula is applied:

$$\Delta \text{Freq}_t = \frac{\sum_{i=1}^{n} \text{Freq}_{i,t,cj} - \sum_{i=1}^{n} \text{Freq}_{i,t,py}}{\sum_{i=1}^{n} \text{Freq}_{i,t,py}} \qquad (2.3)$$

where

ΔFreq_t = change frequency (e.g. overnights) in the month t compared with the same month of the previous year

$\sum_{i=1}^{n} \text{Freq}_{i,t,cj}$ = sum of the frequency of the individual enterprises i for the month t during the current year

$\sum_{i=1}^{n} \text{Freq}_{i,t,py}$ = sum of frequency of the individual enterprises i for the month t during the previous year.

The changes in turnover are not based an absolute figure but on relative data (turnover month t compared with the same month of previous year). For the result of any branch, the individual results ΔTo_t are weighted with the turnover of each participating enterprise.

$$\Delta \text{To}_t = \sum_{i=1}^{n} w_i \, \Delta \text{To}_{i,t} \qquad (2.4)$$

where

$$\sum_{i=1}^{n} w_i = 1$$

To = turnover
$\Delta \text{To}_{i,t}$ = turnover change of enterprise i in month t over previous year.

The third part is an aggregation of the results of the branches to give a tourism performance index (TPI). This aggregation is based on turnover data, as not all branches can provide frequency data. The TPI is obtained using the formula:

$$\text{TPI}_t = \sum_{i=1}^{n} w_i \, \Delta \text{To}_{i,t} \qquad (2.5)$$

The weighting of each branch corresponds to its contribution to tourism value added.

Such a tourism barometer not only allows monitoring of the tourism perform-ance of the individual branches and the region as a whole, but also provides an explanation for the positive or negative results. Participating firms can compare their performance with the enterprises of their sector.

References and further reading

Allin, P. (1998). *A Feasibility Study for Compiling a Tourism Satellite Account for the UK*. London: The Department for Culture, Media and Sport.

Cooper, C., Fletcher, J., Gilbert, D. and Wanhill, S. (1993). *Tourism. Principles & Practice*. London: Pitman Publishing.

Cooper, A. and Wilson, A. (2002). Extending the relevance of TSA research for the UK: general equilibrium and spillover analysis. *Tourism Economics*, 1.

Delisle, J. (1999). The Canadian national tourism indicators: a dynamic picture of the satellite account. *Tourism Economics*, 5.

Eurostat (1998). *Community Methodology on Tourism Statistics*. Luxembourg: Eurostat.

Eurostat, OECD, WTO and UN Statistics Division (2001). *Tourism Satellite Account: Recommended Methodological Framework*. Luxembourg: Eurostat.

Franz, A., Laimer, A. and Smeral, E. (2001). *A Tourism Satellite Account for Austria*. Vienna: Statistik Austria and WIFO.

Franz, A., Laimer, P. and Manente, M. (2002). *European Implementation Manual on Tourism Satellite Accounts*. Luxembourg: Eurostat.

Heerschap, N.M. (1999). The employment module for the Tourism Satellite Account of the OECD. *Tourism Economics*, 5.

Lickorish, L.J. (1997). Travel statistics – the slow move forward. *Tourism Management*, 18.

Maschke, J. (2000). *Das Sparkassen-Tourismus-Barometer 2000*. Yearly Report. Ostdeutscher Sparkassen- und Giroverband.

Meis, S. (1999). The Canadian experience in developing and using the Tourism Satellite Account. *Tourism Economics*, 5.

Müller, H. and Schmid, F. (2003). Tourism barometer – developing and testing an instrument for monitoring the tourism market in Switzerland. *Tourism Review*, 3.

OECD (2000). *Measuring the Role of Tourism in OECD Economies. The OECD Manual on Tourism Satellite Accounts and Employment*. Paris: OECD.

Ritchie, J.B. and Ritchie J.R.B. (2002). A framework for an inquiry supported des-tination marketing information system. *Tourism Management*, 23.

Rubben, M. and Verhaeghe, A. (2002). *Ontwikkeling van een toeristisch infor-matiesysteem op Vlaams niveau*. Antwerp: University Antwerpen and Katholieke Hogeschool, Mechelen.

Schmid, F. (2003). *Tourismusbarometer*. Bern, FIF.

Smith, S. (1997). *Tourism Analysis. A Handbook*, 2nd edn. Edinburgh: Longman.

WES (2002). *Toeristische Index WES-Kust, Brugge en Achterland*. Brugge: WES.

WTO (1998). *Tourism: 2020 Vision*. Madrid: WTO.

WTO (2000). *General Guidelines for Developing the Tourism Satellite Account, Measuring Total Tourism Demand*. Madrid: WTO.

WTO (2001). *The Economic Impact of Tourism*. Madrid: WTO.

Appendices to Chapter 2

Appendix 2.1: Production accounts of tourism industries and other industries (*Net valuation*)

Products	TOURISM INDUSTRIES					
	1 – Hotels and similar	2 – Second home ownership (imputed)	3 – Restaurants and similar	4 – Railway passenger transport	5 – Road passenger transport	6 – Water passenger transport
A. Specific products						
A.1 Characteristic products						
1 Accommadation services						
1.1 Hotels and other lodging services (3)		X				
1.2 Second homes services on own account of for free	X		X	X	X	X
2 Food and beverage serving services (3)		X				
3 Passenger transport services (3)		X				
3.1 Interurban railway (3)		X				
3.2 Road (3)						
3.3 Water (3)		X				
3.4 Air (3)		X				
3.5 Supporting services		X				
3.6 Transport equipment rental		X				
3.7 Maintenance and repair services+		X				
4 Travel agency, tour operator and tourist guide services		X				
4.1 Travel agency (1)		X				
4.2 Tour operator (2)		X				
4.3 Tourist information and tourist guide		X				
5 Cultural services (3)		X				
5.1 Performing arts		X				
5.2 Museum and other cultural services		X				
6 Recreation and other entertainment services (3)		X				
6.1 Sports and recreational sport services		X				
6.2 Other amusement and recreational services		X				
7 Miscellaneous tourism services		X				
7.1 Financial and insurance services		X				
7.2 Other good rental services		X				
7.3 Other tourism services		X				
A.2 Connected products		X				
distribution margins		X				
services		X				
B. Non specific products		X				
distribution margins		X				
services		X				
Value of domestic produced goods net of distribution margins		X				
Value of imported goods net of distribution margins	X	X	X	X	X	X
TOTAL output (at basic prices)						
1. Agriculture, forestry and fishery products						
2. Ores and minerals						
3. Electricity, gas and water						
4. Manufacturing						
5. Construction work and construction						
6. Trades services, restaurants and hotel services						
7. Transport, storage and communication services						
8. Business services						
9. Community, social and personal services						
Total intermediate consumption (at purchase price)						
Total gross value added of activities (at basic prices)						
Compensation of employees / Other taxes less subsidies of production / Gross mixed income / Gross operating surplus						

X does not apply; (1) Corresponds to the margins of the travel agencies; (2) Corresponds to the margins of the tour opeartors; (3) The value is net of the amounts paid to travel agencies and tour operators.

7 – Air passenger transport	8 – passenger transport supporting services	9 – Passenger transport equipment rental	10 – Travel agencies and similar	11 – Cutural services	12 – Sporting and other recreational services	TOTAL tourism industries	Tourism connected industries	Non specific industries	TOTAL output of domestic producers (at basic prices)
X	X	X	X	X	X		X		
X	X	X	X	X	X	X	X	X	X
							X	X	X
							X	X	X
							X	X	X
							X	X	X
							X	X	X
							X	X	X
							X	X	X
							X	X	X

Appendix 2.2: Domestic supply and internal tourism consumption, by products (*Net valution*)

	TOURISM INDUSTRIES							
	1–Hotels and similar		2–Second home ownership (imputed)		***		12–Sporting and other recreational services	
Products	output	tourism share	output	tourism share	output	tourism share	output	tourism share
A. Specific products								
A.1 Characteristic products								
1 Accomodation services								
1.1 Hotels and other lodging services (3)			X	X				
1.2 Second homes services on own account of for free	X	X			X	X	X	X
2 Food and beverage serving services (3)			X	X				
3 Passenger transport services (3)			X	X				
3.1 Interurban railway (3)			X	X				
3.2 Road (3)			X	X				
3.3 Water (3)								
3.4 Air (3)			X	X				
3.5 Supporting services			X	X				
3.6 Transport equipment rental			X	X				
3.7 Maintenance and repair services			X	X				
4 Travel agency, tour operator and tourist guide services			X	X				
4.1 Travel agency (1)			X	X				
4.2 Tour operator (2)			X	X				
4.3 Tourist information and tourist guide			X	X				
5 Cultural services (3)			X	X				
5.1 Performing arts			X	X				
5.2 Museum and other cultural services			X	X				
6 Recreation and other entertainment services (3)			X	X				
6.1 Sports and recreational sport services			X	X				
6.2 Other amusement and recreational services			X	X				
7 Miscellaneous tourism services			X	X				
7.1 Financial and insurance services			X	X				
7.2 Other good rental services			X	X				
7.3 Other tourism services			X	X				
A.2 Connected products			X	X				
distribution margins			X	X				
services			X	X				
B. Non specific products			X	X				
distribution margins			X	X				
services			X	X				
Value of domestic produced goods net of distribution margins			X	X				
Value of imported goods net of distribution margins	X	X	X	X	X	X	X	X
TOTAL output (at basic prices)								
1. Agriculture, forestry and fishery products								
2. Ores and minerals								
3. Electricity, gas and water								
4. Manufacturing								
5. Construction work and construction								
6. Trades services, restaurants and hotel services								
7. Transport, storage and communication services								
8. Business services								
9. Community, social and personal services								
Total intermediate consumption (at purchasers price)								
Total gross value added of activities (at basic prices)								
Compensation of employees Other taxes less subsidies of production Gross mixed income Gross operating surplus								

X does not apply; *** Means that all tourism industries of the proposed list have to be considered one by one in the enumeration; *The imports referred here are exclusively those which are purchased within the country of reference; (1) Corresponds to the margins of the travel agencies; (2) Corresponds to the margins of the tour operators; (3) The values is net of the amounts paid to travel agencies and tour operators

TOTAL tourism industries		Tourism connected industries		Non specific industries		Total output of domestic producers (at basic prices)	Imports*	Taxes less subsidies on products of domestic output and imports	Domestic supply (at purchasers price)	Internal Tourism consumption	Tourism ratio on supply
output	tourism share	output	tourism share	output	tourism share						
X	X	X	X	X	X			X	X		
										X	X
X	X	X	X	X	X	X		X	X		
		X	X	X	X	X					
		X	X	X	X	X					
		X	X	X	X	X					
		X	X	X	X	X					
		X	X	X	X	X					
		X	X	X	X	X					
		X	X	X	X	X					
		X	X	X	X	X					
		X	X	X	X	X					

3

Tourism demand

Determinants of tourism demand

The determinants of tourism demand are those factors at work in any society that drive and set limits to the volume of a population's demand for holiday and travel (Burkart and Medlik, 1981). The determinants of tourism demand explain why the population of some countries has a high propensity to participate in tourism whereas that of other countries shows a low one.

These determinants should be distinguished from motivations and buyer behaviour. Burkart and Medlik describe motivations as 'the internal factors at work within individuals, expressed as the needs, wants and desires that influence tourism choices'. Marketing managers should know why and how consumers make their holiday choices, but it is also necessary to understand how internal psychological processes influence individuals in choosing between different holiday destinations and particular types of product. These processes are known within marketing as aspects of buyer behaviour (Middleton and Clarke, 2001). Here, only determinants are discussed.

Middleton summarizes the determinants under nine headings:

1. Economic factors
2. Comparative prices
3. Demographic factors
4. Geographic factors
5. Socio-cultural attitudes to tourism

6. Mobility
7. Government/regulatory
8. Media communications
9. Information and communication technology.

However, tourism demand is also sensitive to changes in the supply of products and the capacity of supply. As an example, owing to the excellent fast train connections the city of Lyon has become a short-break destination for Belgians.

Economic factors: income, time and price

Probably the most important group is the economic factors, and more particularly the income (or specifically the disposable income) of the population of the generating markets. According to Middleton, in the late 1990s there were 30 countries of origin that accounted for over 90 per cent of world international travel spending. The concentration of the demand is even more remarkable when it is noted that the top 10 countries alone account for some two-thirds of international tourism spending. Under these circumstances, it is quite logical that most destinations are fishing in the same ponds.

In the relationship between tourism and income, the latter can be measured in different ways – for example, by GDP, personal income or disposable income. Disposable income is the most adequate independent variable. Discretionary income (or the income that is left after all necessary expenditure) would be an even better variable. In periods of rising oil prices, discretionary income is under high pressure and so is tourism demand, but unfortunately there are no data available regarding this possible variable. A notion directly derived from the relationship between tourism demand and income is income-elasticity, or the relative change in tourism demand to a relative change in income. In Chapter 1 we saw that outbound tourism shows a high income-elasticity – in other words, when income increases by 1 per cent, tourism demand increases by more than 1 per cent.

With respect to the income factor, there are two significant points that should be noted. First, disposable income per capita is an average, and as such this indicator neglects the personal income distribution within the country. It is well known that, particularly in some Middle Eastern countries, the higher incomes are concentrated in the hands of just a few people.

Secondly, there can be a time lag between tourism expenditure and income creation. More evident, however, is the possible 'time lead'. Consumers very often anticipate income expectations; they can be optimistic or pessimistic, and sometimes a positive or negative over-reaction is the result (WTO, 1990).

There are no holidays without time available for travel. For many years, the free time available was a major determinant. This is no longer the case in many developed economies, where employees have four to six weeks of paid leave each year and the number of working hours per annum is not higher than 1700–2100. For a long time increased paid leave has enhanced holiday participation, especially the second holiday and the shorter breaks; however, at present additional free time no longer has such a great impact. Marginal utility is decreasing, and many people don't have the money to take more (short) holidays a year. However

Table 3.1 Amount of paid leave and public holidays per year, per country (1999)

Country	Paid leave (days)	Public holidays
Austria	30	13
Italy	20–30	12
France	25	11
Germany	24	11
Japan	10–20	14
UK	23	8
Australia	20	8
South Africa	14	12
Canada	10–15	11
Malaysia	12	13
USA	10	9
China	10	7

more flexible working time has an impact on off-peak holidays and stimulates the staggering of holidays.

Free time is, however, still a determinant factor in developing countries, and even in many developed countries such as Japan and the USA. Not all populations have 30 days of paid leave each year. Table 3.1 compares the situation in the late 1990s in a number of countries at very different stages of development (WTO, 1999).

The introduction of a second week of paid leave in the Republic of China in the late 1990s, linked to the National Holiday, created a travel boom in the first week of October. The Great Wall of China became very overcrowded during that week, and a visit there was not without danger. A third and fourth week off in China would open a very important market for many destinations in the world. In reality there is a dichotomy between the money rich/time poor and the time rich/money poor.

A factor that is often overlooked is the age of retirement and early retirement. The lowering of retirement age is another factor that has increased free time available, and as such has stimulated tourism demand. However, owing to the ageing population and the costs of retirement, in some countries the value of pensions is being reduced and the retirement age raised over a transitional period (WTO, 1999).

Price is a third important economic determinant. The relationship between tourism demand and price leads to price-elasticity. In Chapter 1 we noted that price-elasticity is very often close to -1 – in other words, when the price of a tourist product in a destination increases by 1 per cent, the demand in the generating country decreases by about 1 per cent. This is classic price-elasticity.

Due to economies of scale, technological improvements in transport and communication, deregulation in air transport and stronger competition, prices of tourism products have not followed the general inflation rate. This movement has stimulated the tourism purchasing power of potential travellers and made travel more accessible.

Price is a complicated issue. It is not only the absolute amount that should be considered but also the relative price of a tourist product against other similar products, as this will be a key factor in tourism demand. Indeed, tourism demand can also be influenced by the price of a competitive or complementary product. In such a case we are confronted with cross-elasticity, or the responsiveness of the demand for one commodity (e.g. a holiday in Italy) to changes in the price of another commodity (e.g. a holiday in Spain). In mathematical form, this can be considered as:

$$E_{cr} = \frac{\frac{\Delta D}{D}}{\frac{\Delta P_c}{P_c}} \tag{3.1}$$

where

E_{cr} = cross-elasticity;
ΔD = change of demand;
ΔP_c = change of price of a competitive (complementary) product.

Returning to the Spanish–Italian example, a price increase of 10 per cent in Spain can lead to an increase in demand for a similar Italian tourism product of 7 per cent. In this case, the cross-elasticity equals 0.7. Competitive or substitute products always show a positive sign. Complementary products show a negative cross-elasticity – for example, an increase in the price of charter flights to Spain will lead to a decrease of demand for hotel rooms in Spain.

The price of tourism relative to other products must also be considered (Holloway, 1992). For an individual consumer, tourism competes with other products or services (such as a personal computer, home improvements or fitness services) for a share of the budget. A widespread reaction to special offers on the occasion of a national car fair can lead to a shift in demand in that country.

A comparison between prices should be based on similar products. Seaside destinations can be compared, but the sun and a beach in Rimini cannot be compared with a cultural tourism product in Tuscany. If the products are very similar, there are two other important price components in international tourism: the inflation rate in the generating and receiving countries, and the relative exchange rates between the generating country's currency and that of the receiving destination. In Europe, before the introduction of the euro Spain suffered much more from inflation than its competitors in the Mediterranean area. A switch in demand to the competitors of the region was the logical consequence, followed by devaluation of the Spanish peseta. As a member of the European Monetary Union, Spain now has to respect the famous Maastricht norms and can no longer devaluate the national currency. In the 1980s and 1990s, devaluation of the peseta was the weapon used to keep the Spanish tourism sector competitive.

This brings us to the second important price component in international tourism: the relative exchange rate between generating and receiving countries. Prices should be adjusted for the exchange rate (see Chapter 5, and Dwyer *et al.*, 2000). The variability of exchange rates is very great. Let us illustrate this with the evolution of the relationship of the US dollar to the British pound during the period 1980–2003 (see Figure 3.1).

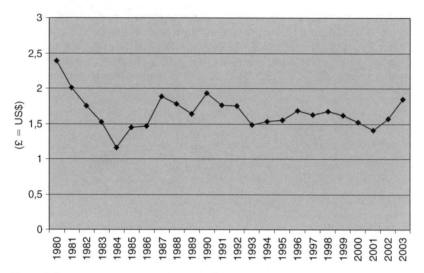

Figure 3.1 Relationship of the US dollar to the British pound, 1980–2003

With such variability in exchange rates, it is not surprising that tourism flows between the USA and the UK are fluctuating. The number of Britons travelling to the USA fell drastically in the early 1980s and recovered during second half of the decade. In 2003, US tourism products were again cheap for the British and European in general. An unfavourable change in the exchange rate means less travel abroad, travel to different locations, a reduction in expenditure and/or length of stay, and possibly changes in the mode of transport.

The combination of exchange rates and price evolution leads to the important notion of 'real exchange rates'. Real exchange rates are based on market rates of exchange between each origin country's currency and each destination country's currency, adjusted by the relative price levels between the origin country and each destination. In other words, to calculate the trend in real exchange rates, the index of market rates is adjusted by an index of relative inflation rates between the origin country and each of the various destinations (Economist Intelligence Unit, 1995).

A special feature of price is the 'perceived costs'. Special attention will be paid to this aspect in Chapter 5.

Economic determinants alone, however, cannot explain tourism demand in its entirety (see Crouch, 1992). Many other factors influence the volume of holidays and limits to travel.

Other determinants

First among other determinants are demographic factors. The size or volume and the growth of the population of the generating markets are very important. In many cases it is not the total population but the size of the relevant market segments that counts. This brings us to the age structure of the population of several generating markets. In Europe and the USA the ageing population has become a real challenge (Müller, 2001), and for the tourism sector this is providing threats but also opportunities. The senior market is growing very fast. This segment has the purchasing power and time to travel, and travel experience. Other age segments are declining. The question arises as to how long some Western economies can go on with retirement at the age of 55–58, or even earlier. Owing to the disequilibria in the age structure, in the near future the active population will be obliged to work for longer. Countries with developed economies are confronted with other demographic trends: one-person and two-person households have emerged, smaller households are the rule, and divorce and remarriage have become common.

With respect to geographical factors (e.g. climate, urbanization, etc.), Middleton's (2001) statement is quite important: 'In the twenty-first century cities and towns are the magnets for modern stay and day visit tourism'. Large cities are generators for attractions (seaside resorts, theme parks and other) within accessible distance, but at the same time several of them attract tourists for their heritage. Prague, St Petersburg, Paris, Barcelona and many others attract millions of visitors each year.

There are also several socio-cultural attitudes that affect tourism. People from northern climates believe that lying on beaches has a therapeutic value, but more and more people are concerned about depletion of the global ozone layer and the toxic effects of too much exposure to unfiltered sunlight. This might change the holiday pattern of many people, or at least the holiday behaviour of tourists at sun-belt destinations.

In many western countries there is a common belief that holidays are 'rights' and 'necessities for relieving stress', and paid holidays have become an institution. Government regulations may have a much greater impact on tourism than generally believed. We see government interventions with respect to tourism in several fields:

- Guaranteeing fair competition between suppliers
- Consumer protection
- The timing of school holidays
- Frontier formalities for international travellers (e.g. the Schengen agreement)
- Environment and sustainable development
- Regulations in the field of transport, tour operating, time-sharing, and compulsory environmental impact assessments.

The role of mass media communications is considerable. As Middleton puts it, 'the cumulative effect of television over the years in shaping travel and tourism expectations in the major demand-generating countries cannot be overestimated'. Television has a major influence on tourism demand; it is not only a medium for advertising but also, and above all, it brings destinations, attractions, people and events into millions of households worldwide on a daily basis. The impact of regular television holiday programmes is widespread in all social classes. The ability of television to draw attention to things that go wrong for tourists also has an effect on demand. Besides television we should pay particular attention to the Internet, especially as a new information medium, distribution channel and booking instrument, and even as providing virtual enterprises. Finally, it is important not to forget the exposure of prospective holidaymakers to newspapers, magazines, radio, DVDs etc., which also contribute to creating awareness and attitudes.

Tourism is confronted with a number of constraints, too. The carrying capacity of most places is not unlimited. More and more destinations are limiting further quantitative growth (e.g. Bermuda, The Seychelles) and/or introducing a visitor management system (Amsterdam, Bruges, Salzburg, Venice, etc.).

Terrorism is a recent constraint of the last decade. More and more, tourists have become target groups for terrorist movements to exert political pressure. Unfortunately, the list of examples is long – Egypt, Indonesia, Kenya, Peru, Colombia, Spain, Italy, Sri Lanka, etc. The terrorist attacks in the USA on 11 September 2001, although not directed towards tourism, discouraged (and continue to do so) many international tourists from visiting the USA.

The growth of crime in tourism destinations – or at least the perception of escalating crime – is a further handicap for international tourism.

The ageing population has made the over-60s an increasingly important group, and has had an impact on holiday choice. Countries without a developed health-care service have become less and less attractive for older travellers.

Trends in tourism demand

In this section we deal with a number of trends within tourism demand. There is no doubt that these trends are partly related to the socio-economic determinants discussed above.

Globalization of tourism demand

Globalization is a generic term comprising three basic elements. The first is the geographic element, which covers intra-regional and inter-regional travel. In French, we speak of the '*mondialisation*' of tourism, or its expansion to global scale. Others see globalization in terms of convergence in world tastes, product preferences and lifestyles, which leads to the second element, the growing standardization and market homogenization. There is a trend towards similar customer preferences worldwide. The third element is the existence of inter-nationally similar practices, such as distribution systems, marketing, product development, etc. All three features are present in modern tourism development. The first and second characteristics are more demand-oriented; the third is supply-oriented.

On a world scale, long-haul travel and inter-regional flows are already important and are predicted to increase their market share from 18 per cent in 1995 to 24 per cent in 2020 (WTO, 1998). The expected evolution of the intra-regional/long-haul split of international tourist arrivals is very unequal per receiving region. Table 3.2 gives the share of long-haul arrivals per receiving region in 1995 and 2020.

By and large, it is expected that more originating and receiving countries will become involved in the process of globalization.

Globalization of tourism over the last two or three decades cannot be explained in terms of demand factors only. However, these are important when

Table 3.2 Share of long-haul arrivals per receiving region in 1995 and 2002

	1995	*2020*
Africa	42	36
Americas	23	38
East Asia and Pacific	21	17
Europe	12	15
Middle East	58	63
South Asia	76	86

considering Baum's (1995) key factors in explaining the growth of international tourism. It would be unwise to overlook the great influence of technology. Technology has affected two different aspects of travel – transportation and communication. Without changes in aviation (air fares included), the globalization of tourism would have been impossible. The same probably applies to the changes in information technology.

Nonetheless, demand and technology together still provide an insufficient explanation. Supply factors, such as international hotel chains and the increasing number of cruise carriers, are important, and the role of the destination countries is very often underestimated. Many developing countries consider tourism to be a main source of wealth, and the benefits can be great (Vanhove, 1997). The incentive to encourage tourism is often related to demand as well; the broadening of tourist interest not only leads to a greater diversification of tourism development in established destinations but also to more destinations entering the tourism market.

Fragmentation of annual holidays

For several years there has been an increase in the number holidaymakers taking more than one holiday per year. More free time, higher personal income and double-income families have led to the phenomenon of fragmentation. The main holiday has become shorter, but people are taking two or more additional (short) holidays a year. However, we are also confronted with time-efficient development. In a period of greater leisure time, an increasing proportion of the population finds less time to travel and is in a 'time poor–money rich' situation. The outcome of this trend is an increasing number of products that offer the tourist the maximum excitement in a minimum of time (WTO, 1998).

More attention to the environment and the growing importance of eco-tourism

The environment is becoming one of the main concerns of our society, and everyone is aware of this. Tourist resorts are sometimes much less worried about it, but the holidaymaker wants to escape from negative aspects of the environment.

The landscape in all its diversity is the basic element, the main ingredient, the raw material of tourism. It is the very essence of tourism, and constitutes its driving force. From the tourist's point of view, the attraction of the landscape owes much to its diversity and the contrast it offers with his or her daily environment. It is the degree of this contrast that will determine the attraction for tourists. There is therefore a search for the real and authentic, and European travellers increasingly want nature to be more prominent in their vacations (Poon, 1993).

A direct consequence of this movement is the boost in eco-tourism in Europe and the US. Eco-tourism (a new buzzword) can mean a number of things, and is often old wine in a new barrel, but it is generally used to describe tourism activities which are conducted in harmony with nature, as opposed to more traditional mass tourism activities. According to Hawkins (1994), eco-tourism offers opportunities for many developing countries.

Certain resorts or regions are running the risk of or have already fallen victim to over-development and subsequent rejection by tourists. This is a consequence of this movement.

Changed values

In today's society there are several indications of changed values, such as a growing consciousness of nature and a search for the real and authentic. However, there is much more. Individualization is gaining in importance in our society, and for the tourism sector this implies that 'a' consumer no longer exists, but rather 'this' consumer. The consequence is evident – the tourist product has to be adapted to 'this' consumer. We can refer to a set of building blocks where the parts are assembled differently according to the personality of the consumer.

Poon (1993) indicates two other changed values. She is convinced that there are growing signs today that the fashion for sun is beginning to fade, and sunshine is no longer sufficient to build a viable and sustainable tourism industry. Destinations have to begin to offer 'sun-plus' holidays, such as sun plus spas, plus nature, plus fishing. The second changed value is the search for the different: 'The new traveller wants to experience the inexperienced, see the unexpected, gain impressions of new cultures and a new horizon'.

Changing lifestyles

Krippendorf (1987) argues that society has moved through three phases since the industrial era. In the industrial era, tourists were drawn from a population that 'lived to work', but over the past two decades people have begun to 'work to live'. Travel motivations have changed from 'to recover, to rest, to have no problems' to 'to experience something different, to have fun, to have a change, to be active'. Today there is a third phase, which has been described as the desire to experience 'the new unity of everyday life'. In this phase, the polarity of work and leisure has been reduced.

The vacation motivations of this group include:

- To broaden their horizon
- To learn something new

- To encourage introspection and communication with other people
- To discover the simpler things in life and nature
- To foster creativity and open-mindedness
- To experiment and take personal risks.

Some speak of a 'global lifestyle', which is a consequence of improved educational levels and the revolution in communication technology. The world is becoming increasingly cosmopolitan, with all its people influencing each other. This globalization process has many impacts on and implications for tourism. The most fundamental of these is the fact that increased travel is both a reason for, and the result of, the global lifestyle (WTO, 1999).

Tourism demand modifies quickly, and is no longer always coherent. The rapid modifications are revealed in the Mediterranean region, where the market share of the Mediterranean countries in the European market varies from year to year. Demand is not always coherent either. We may expect that a chairman of a large company will take his or her holiday in a five-star hotel, in an exotic destination – but is that really so? Not any more. That same chairman may also ask for a cycling holiday, which will allow travel from one place to another. This proves that we are no longer dealing with 'the' consumer but 'this' consumer, and provides a clear illustration of the so-called hybrid consumer.

A 'healthy lifestyle' is another trend: 'The practice of healthy living reflects itself in holiday and tourism lifestyles and is responsible for the proliferation of health spas, saunas, fitness centres, "fat farms", gyms, massage … and other such additions to many hotels and resorts' (Poon, 1993). Müller (2001) speaks of 'wellness tourism'.

More independent tourists as opposed to mass tourism

Fordian tourism was for a long time the prevailing paradigm, with mass tourism based on economies of scale and standardization (see, for example, hotel trademarks, franchise systems and tour operator vacations). In the 1980s we witnessed a great change in the operational paradigm of the tourism industry (Fayos-Solá, 1996; Cuvelier, 2000), which responded to the profound changes that Poon grouped under the headings: (a) new consumers; (b) new technologies; (c) new forms of production; (d) new management styles and (e) new prevailing circumstances. Fayos-Solá calls this phenomenon the 'New Age of Tourism' (NAT). He compares the Fordian paradigm and the NAT paradigm with respect to demand, inputs, management and environment. With respect to demand, the differences are very clear (see Table 3.3).

The new age of tourism is characterized primarily by a much greater segmentation of demand, the need for flexibility of supply and distribution, and achieving profitability through diagonal integration (economies of scope, system gains and synergies) instead of economies of scale (see Chapter 5). Segmentation of demand requires a good knowledge of the market in order to identify groups of customer traits and needs (see Cockerell, 1997; Smith, 1997). For Fayos-Solá, flexibility is important in several areas: in the organization, production and the distribution of tourism products, in reservation, purchasing and payment systems, and in ways in which the tourism product is consumed (Fayos-Solá, 1996).

Table 3.3 Comparison of the Fordian and NAT paradigms with respect to demand

Fordian age	NAT
Sun	Complex motivations
'Massification'	Individualism
Lack of tourist's own criteria	High expectations
Non-differentiated markets	Complex motivation

There is evidence of this change of paradigm in the British tour operating market in the late 1980s. Indeed, Middleton (1991) posed the question, 'Whither the package tour?', demonstrating that the UK outbound market for traditional forms of air-inclusive package holidays reached maturity in the mid-1980s and declined in the latter half of the decade. The evidence also shows that profitable future growth for both tour operators and resorts lies in developing new forms of IT products. Mature tourists look for the core advantages of packages (price, reliability etc.) without the traditional requirement and stigma of travelling and staying together in highly visible groups on chartered flights and in hotels. The following statement by Middleton is very important: 'So far as possible, customers should not be aware of being labelled and identified as tour groups. They will, of course, continue to be bound by the specific times and product options which are the basis on which bulk purchase prices can be obtained from suppliers'.

Poon (1993) holds similar ideas. For her, new tourism exists if and where the following six conditions hold:

1. The holiday is flexible and can be purchased at prices that are competitive with mass-produced holidays (cruises v. land-based holidays)
2. Production of travel and tourism-related services is not dominated by scale economies alone; tailor-made services will be produced while still taking advantages of scale economies where they apply (yield management)
3. Production is increasingly driven by the requirements of consumers
4. The holiday is marketed to *individuals* with different needs, incomes, time constraints and travel interests; mass marketing is no longer the dominant paradigm
5. The holiday is consumed on a large scale by tourists who are more experienced travellers, more educated, more destination-oriented, more independent, more flexible and more environmentally conscious
6. Consumers consider the environment and culture of the destinations they visit to be a key part of the holiday experience.

New types of holidays and special interest

It is not surprising to learn that, in the light of changing values and lifestyles, new types of holidays and recreation have arisen under the slogan: 'to experience something during the holiday'. Holidaymakers want to enjoy their holidays thoroughly, and this has resulted in an increasing interest in holidays devoted to sports or other hobbies; urban tourism; natural, health, wellness, culture, adventure and language holidays; second homes, etc. We speak of 'targeted product market development' (especially theme-based) oriented towards one or more of the three Es: entertainment, excitement and education.

There is a net polarization of tourist tastes: the comfort-based and the adventure-oriented. With respect to the latter, there is a trend to travel to high places (mountains), under water (tourist submarines) and the ends of the earth (e.g. the Antarctic Peninsula).

As well as the desire to experience something, there is also an increasing demand for animation and activity. Many tourists need to be encouraged to discover their own capacities and to develop them within the framework of holidays with a real content. That is why tourist 'animation' is very important. This can take different forms – movement, social life, creative activities, education and discovery, self-discovery, quietness and adventure.

Increased quality-consciousness

Another trend can be summarized as the search for 'greater quality'. This is in agreement with the trend towards new forms of holidays. Increased quality does not mean more luxury, but what the Germans call *Erlebnistiefe* – holidays with meaning.

Martin and Mason (1987) clearly emphasize this:

Different types of people will make new and varied demands on the tourism products. For example: older people will look for better quality, and more secure surroundings while single people seek more social contact through tourism. In addition, there will be accompanying shifts in what people want out of their lives, which will affect their choices as tourists. Likely changes in attitude are:

■ the development of greater awareness of the range of tourism choices available and demands for a higher standard of service and value for money from tourism operators and,
■ growing concern about the quality of the tourism experience in all senses, including the nature of the facilities used, the state of the environment visited, and the health-enhancing (or detrimental) features of the activities undertaken.

The attraction of the countryside, quiet holidays with a content, holidays with attention to the environment and health, and visits to cultural cities are predominant trends. In the United Kingdom, the term 'green tourism' is a perfectly integrated concept that goes beyond 'rural tourism' (Green, 1990).

More experienced and educated holidaymakers

The holiday participation rates speak for themselves. One holiday per year has for a long time been a must for most people from developed countries. 'More experienced' does not only mean 'more quality conscious', but also:

■ An increased requirement for variety
■ A greater desire for communication and personal attention on holiday

- The need for greater variety and choice
- More activity and adventure.

As well as having more experience, tourists are very often better educated than they were in the past.

More flexible tourists

New consumers are more flexible. What does this mean? Poon (1993) emphasizes two characteristics:

1. New consumers are hybrid in nature and consume along unpredictable lines
2. New consumers are more spontaneous (e.g. there are shorter lead times before booking a holiday).

Tourism demand worldwide

In 2002, according to WTO estimates, international tourist arrivals increased to 703 million whilst international tourism receipts reached $US 474 billion. International tourist arrivals have witnessed an uninterrupted growth during the second half of the twentieth century, although the growth rate is declining (see Table 3.4).

The year 2001 was the first to show real stagnation (i.e. little decline) in international arrivals and receipts (expressed in $). The growth rate of 4.3 per cent over the last decade is still a good performance in comparison to most other sectors.

Over several decades, growth rates have proved to be resilient – at least on a global scale – to factors such as economic recession, variable exchange rates, terrorist activities and political unrest in many parts of the world (see Table 3.5, Figure 3.2). Of course there has been a levelling off of movements due to specific circumstances, and the steady growth has slowed down or even declined on several occasions (1967–1968, 1973–1974, early 1980s, early 1990s and 2000s).

Looking now at tourism receipts, during the 1990s these grew in current US dollar terms at an average annual rate of 6.4 per cent (Todd, 2001). It is also important to emphasize that international tourism receipts at a global level have increased faster than other important export sectors. According to WTO–GATT–UNCTAD sources, the average annual percentage growth in

Table 3.4 Growth rate of international tourist arrivals, 1950–2000

Date	Percentage
1950–1960	10.6
1960–1970	9.1
1970–1980	5.5
1980–1990	4.8
1990–2000	4.3

Table 3.5 Tourist arrivals and receipts from international tourism, 1975–2002

Year	Arrivals (millions)	Receipts (billions of US$)
1975	222	41
1980	286	105
1985	327	118
1990	458	269
1995	565	405
2000	687	473
2001	684	460
2002	703	474

Source: WTO.

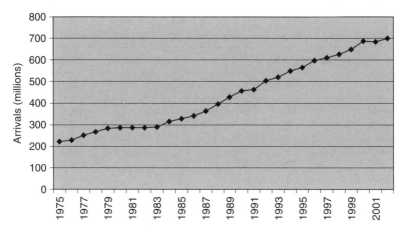

Figure 3.2 International tourist arrivals, 1975–2002

current terms of tourism during the 1980s and 1990s was 9.6 per cent for tourism, 7.5 per cent for commercial services and 5.5 per cent for merchandise exports.

The growth rates are very unequal per region. For the period 1980–2001, the East Asia/Pacific region shows an annual growth rate of 8.5 per cent as opposed to 3.4 per cent for the Americas and 3.8 per cent for Europe. A logical consequence is a changed market share of the regions mentioned in Table 3.6; Europe and the Americas have been the losers and the East Asia/Pacific region is the great winner.

However we must not wrongly interpret the evolution of the market share. International tourism on a large scale started in the less developed world much later than in Northern America and Europe. All this is related to the later economic take-off in many developing countries. The result is a decrease in the market share of the Americas and Europe.

The very high market share of Europe can to a certain extend be attributed to the welfare level in Europe and the richness of tourist attractions. However, it is also important to take into account the fact that Europe is composed of a large number of small countries, which makes it favourable to international tourism. A trip of 300 km in several European countries is quite often a trans-border trip.

Table 3.6 International arrivals by region (millions), 1980–2001

Region	1980	2002	Annual growth rate 1980–2001* (%)	Market share 1980	2001
World	286.0	702.6	4.3	100.0	100.0
Africa	7.3	29.1	6.8	2.6	4.1
Americas	61.3	114.9	3.4	21.5	16.3
East Asia/Pacific	21.5	125.4	8.5	7.5	17.9
Europe	186.1	399.8	3.8	65.1	56.9
Middle East	7.5	27.6	5.5	2.6	3.9
South Asia	2.2	5.9	4.8	0.8	0.8

*Based on $(1 + (r)/100)^n$ or compound annual growth rate.
Source: WTO.

Table 3.7 Forecast inbound tourism by region, 1995–2020 (million arrivals)

Receiving region	Forecasts 1995	2010	2020	Growth rate 1995–2020	Market share 1995	2020
World	565	1006	1561	4.1	100.0	100.0
Africa	20	47	77	5.5	3.6	5.0
Americas	109	190	282	3.9	19.3	18.1
East Asia/Pacific	81	195	397	6.5	14.4	25.4
Europe	338	527	717	3.0	59.8	45.9
Middle East	12	36	69	7.1	2.2	4.4
South Asia	4	11	19	6.2	0.7	1.2
Intra-regional	464	791	1183	3.8	82.1	75.8
Long-haul	101	216	378	5.4	17.9	24.2

Source: WTO database, July 2000.

Two major sources are available for forecasting the future of international tourism: the Economist Intelligence Unit (EIU) and the World Tourism Organization (WTO). The EIU produces forecasts on international tourism at irregular intervals. The results in Table 3.7 are WTO data based on adapted *Tourism: 2020 Vision* (WTO, 1998). A distinction has been made between inter-regional (long-haul) and intra-regional travel. Although there are problems with forecasts for such a long period, four points should be noted:

1. The expected growth rate for the next two decades is very similar to the annual increase over the preceding two decades
2. Europe registers a falling growth rate from about 4 to 3 per cent; the regions with a strong growth rate are all situated in Asia
3. The market share of Europe in total inbound tourism is predicted to fall from 60 per cent to about 46 per cent
4. Long-haul trips will represent about one-quarter of all international tourism in 2020; long-haul travel worldwide will also grow faster, at 5.4 per cent per year over the period 1995–2020, and inter-regional travel at 3.8 per cent.

Consequently, the ratio between intra-regional and long-haul travel will shift from around 82:18 in 1995 to 76:24 in 2020.

Holiday propensity and holiday frequency

The net and gross holiday propensity, also called net and gross travel participation, are important indicators for tourism demand.

Net holiday participation

In Europe, several countries make a distinction between net holiday participation (four nights or more) and net short holiday participation (one to three nights – see Table 3.8). The net holiday propensity refers to the percentage of the population who take at least one holiday (tourism trip of four nights and more) in a period of one year, and is a measure of the penetration of holiday-taking among individuals in a population. In richer countries, the net holiday propensity varies between 40 and 80 per cent (see Table 3.8). The many travel constraints ensure that the net travel propensity never approaches 100 per cent; 80 per cent seems to be a ceiling.

A comparison between national holiday surveys is not always possible. The applied definitions are very often unequal – are we talking of the total population, or only adults? In Norway, only the population in the age group 16–79 years is considered. What is the treatment of non-commercial holidays, such as visits to friends and relatives (VFR) and a (short) holiday in a second residence? How are business trips dealt with?

Table 3.8 Net and gross (short) holiday propensity in a number of European countries, 2002 (per cent)

Country	Net holiday participation	Gross holiday participation	Net short holiday participation	Gross short holiday participation[a]
Austria	48.0	76.0	30.1	106.6
Belgium	58.6	95.4	29.4[b]	45.5[b]
France[c]	66.1	158.6	44.7	131.5
Germany (2003)	76.8	102.9	36.8	83.6
Italy	n.a.	81.7	n.a.	62.5
Netherlands (2003)[d]	74.7	144.2	41.1	81.9
Norway (2003)[e]	76.6	164.4	n.a.	n.a.
Switzerland (2001)	69.0	152.6	n.a.	65.4
UK (2003)	57.0	123.0	n.a.	n.a.

[a] Should be handled with care
[b] Non-commercial short holidays excluded
[c] Population 15+
[d] Domestic VFR excluded
[e] Population aged 16–79.

With respect to the data in Table 3.9, there are two features that are notable. First, the net holiday propensity of the population of the countries listed has not increased over the past decade (see Figure 3.3). In many European countries, net holiday participation seems to have reached a ceiling. Secondly, since the year 2000 there has even been a slight decrease in the net participation. This decline is not of a structural nature; it is probably caused by the economic situation in the early years of the twenty-first century.

Gross holiday participation

Gross holiday propensity (gross trip propensity) expresses the total number of holidays taken during a period of a year as a percentage of the total population. This is a measure of penetration of holidays, and not individual holidaymakers.

In several developed countries the gross propensity exceeds 100 per cent, and often approaches 120 and even 160–170. In other words, several people are taking two, three or more holidays a year.

Table 3.10 shows the gross holiday propensity for a number of European countries (see also Figure 3.4). Once again, the variability between European countries is very great. It is surprising that the UK, with a relatively low net travel participation, shows a high gross holiday propensity.

The evolution, over the last decade, of gross travel propensity in Europe is very similar to that of the net propensity: stagnation for a number of years and a slow decrease in the recent past.

Table 3.9 Net holiday propensity per country, 1990–2002 (per cent)

	Austria	Belgium	France[a]	Germany[b]	Netherlands	Norway[c]	UK[d]	Switzerland
1990	45			69	70			76 (83)[e]
1991		61		67	71		60	
1992				71	70		59	(83)
1993	45			75	71		61	
1994		63		78	73		60	
1995			68	78	72		61	
1996	48	61	68	72	72		58	(75)
1997			66	74	72		57	
1998		63	66	76	74		59	(79)
1999	50		66	75	74	76	55	
2000	56	63	64	76	74	75	59	
2001	54		64	76	74	76	60	69 (72)
2002	48	59	66	75	74[f]	75	59	
2003				77[g]	75	78	57	

[a] Personal trips; population 15+
[b] 14 years and more
[c] 16–79 year-olds
[d] 16 years and older
[e] Figures for Switzerland in brackets refer to three or more overnights
[f] Not fully comparable with former years
[g] Increase due to methodological improvements.

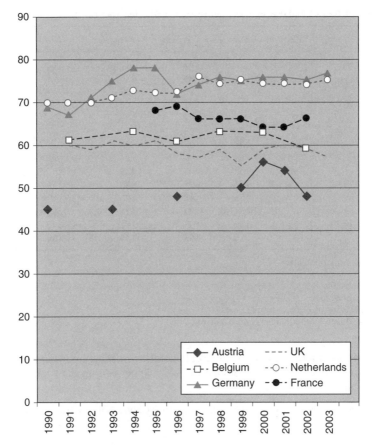

Figure 3.3 Net holiday participation, 1990–2002/2003

It might be questioned whether this stagnation or decline of holiday participation is compensated for by short holiday participation. Using available data, the answer to this question is affirmative:

■ In Austria, the gross short holiday participation increased from 79 per cent in the year 1990 to 145 per cent in the year 2000, but in 2002 the rate dropped to 107 per cent.
■ In Belgium, the gross short holiday participation (non-commercial holidays excluded) increased from 26 per cent in 1988 to 50 per cent in the year 2000, but fell to 46 per cent in 2002.
■ In the Netherlands, the number of short holidays was about 9.1 million in 1990; this had grown to 13.1 million by 2002. The corresponding gross short holiday participation increased from 65 per cent to 77 per cent in 2000, and 86 per cent in 2002.
■ In Switzerland, although not 100 per cent comparable, the data indicate the same trend.

Table 3.10 Gross holiday propensity per country, 1990–2002 (per cent)

Year	Austria	Belgium	France[a]	Germany[b]	Netherlands	Norway[c]	UK[d]
1990	67			87	117		
1991		97		84	120		118
1992				92	117		118
1993	70			101	123		122
1994		100		107	126		127
1995			171	103	124		129
1996	74	96	172	97	128		117
1997			158	98	124		123
1998		96	158	100	129		121
1999	79		151	98	130	159	116
2000	86	99	155	98	126	152	126
2001	82		154	99	131	150	128
2002	76	95	159	98	147[e]	160	125
2003				103[f]	144	166	123

[a] Personal trips; population 15+
[b] 14 years and more
[c] 16–79 year-olds
[d] 16 years and older
[e] Not fully comparable with former years
[f] Increase due to methodological improvements.

■ In France, there has been an unusual evolution of short holidays; there was a gross propensity of 168 per cent in 1996, 140 per cent in the year 2000 and 152 per cent in 2002.

Simply dividing gross by net holiday propensity gives holiday frequency (travel frequency) – in other words, the average number of trips taken by those participating in tourism during the period in question. The European countries in Table 3.11 show great differences in holiday frequency, with a range of 1.3–2.5 holidays per year.

This travel frequency has been relatively stable over the last decade, with only the UK and The Netherlands being slight exceptions.

The foregoing indicators all neglect the duration of a holiday. If this is taken into account, two indicators make sense. The first is 'night participation', or the number of nights (short and long holidays) spent on holiday during one year per 100 inhabitants. Applying this to Belgium, France and The Netherlands shows two different trends: a net increase in The Netherlands, and net decreases in Belgium and, to a lesser extent, France (see Table 3.12). The absolute number of nights for the three countries cannot be compared; for Belgium, non-commercial, second and short holidays are not taken into account. In Belgium, there is a slight shift from commercial to non-commercial nights.

The second indicator is a variant – the 'overstays intensity'. This is applied in the report on the holidays of the Dutch population (NRIT, 2003), and expresses the number of nights per (short) holidaymaker. In Europe there is a strong tendency towards shorter holidays (short holidays have a very stable duration), and there is evidence for this phenomenon in precise data for Belgium, France, Germany and The Netherlands (see Table 3.13).

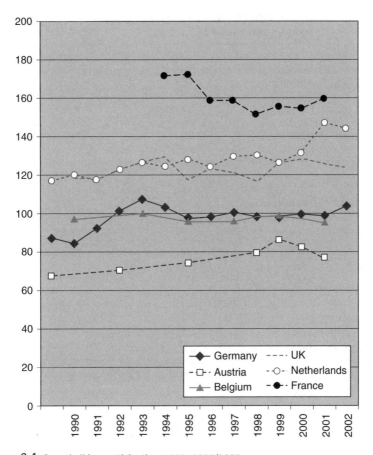

Figure 3.4 Gross holiday participation, 1990–2002/2003

A very special notion relative to holiday participation is the 'country potential generation index' (CPGI), which is measured as follows:

$$CPGI = \frac{\dfrac{N_{ci}}{N_w}}{\dfrac{P_{ci}}{P_w}} \qquad (3.2)$$

where

N_{ci} = number of holidays generated by country i;
N_w = number of holidays generated in the world;
P_{ci} = population of country i ;
P_{cw} = world population.

A CPGI greater than 1 simply means that the population of the country concerned takes relatively more holidays than its population share. This is the case in all western countries.

Table 3.11 Holiday frequency in some European countries, 1990 and 2002

	1990	2002
Austria	1.5	1.6
Belgium	1.6	1.6
France	2.5 (1995)	2.3
Germany	1.3	1.3
Netherlands	1.7	2.0
UK	1.9	2.2

Table 3.12 'Night participation' in Belgium, France and The Netherlands

	Belgium	France	The Netherlands
1990	13.0	n.a.	15.0
1996	12.2	16.9	15.5
2000	12.5	15.6	16.0
2002	11.9	15.9	17.0

Table 3.13 Average duration of holidays in Belgium, Germany, The Netherlands and France

Average duration of holidays (nights)	Belgium	Germany	The Netherlands	France
1982	15.5			
1988	14.1	16.0	12.2	
1990	13.0	15.8	11.8	
1996	11.5	13.8	11.3	10.3
2002	11.3	13.5	11.0	9.7

Seasonality

Seasonality pattern

Within most patterns of demand in tourism, there are regular fluctuations due solely to the time of the year. This is traditionally called 'seasonality'. In Chapter 1 we noted that seasonality is a typical economic characteristic of tourism, and the reasons for these annual fluctuations were indicated – climate, organization of school holidays in the generating markets, organization of annual paid leave, and psychological pressure. Chapter 1 also revealed the impact of seasonality for tourists, tourism supply and public authorities.

Seasonality varies greatly from country to country. Besides the factors mentioned in Chapter 1, national traditions are responsible for a local pattern. French and particularly Italian holidaymakers show an extremely high concentration in the month of August. On the other hand, British holidays are far less concentrated in the summer months. From that point of view, British tourists form an interesting customer group.

The seasonality pattern is highly influenced by the method of measurement:

- The measurement unit – holidays (arrivals) or nights
- Whether it includes just holidays (i.e. of four nights and more) or all holidays including short holidays
- To what extent business travel is taken into account
- Whether the pattern is based on the month of departure or the month of return
- Whether it is from the origin point of view (e.g. the British holidaymakers) or destination point of view (e.g. holidays in Wales).

Taking the origin point of view (see holiday surveys), the ideal method consists of attributing the holiday nights to the month in which they take place. In measuring the seasonality of the population of a particular country, this supposes knowledge of the date of departure and date of return of each individual holidaymaker of that country.

Figures 3.5 and 3.6 show the staggering of the holidays and short holidays in Belgium. Belgium provides comparable data for a long period. The difference between the Figures is as expected, but in both two types of holiday the summer period is dominant – albeit more markedly so for holidays than for short trips. The most striking point, however, is the growing trend towards increased staggering of holidays as well as of short breaks. Although the share of the July–August period is decreasing for both holidays and short trips, the 'winner' periods are different for both types. This evolution for Belgium (which applies to other countries as well) is mainly due to a greater fragmentation of holidays. The spectacular growth of short breaks has been a further stimulus for greater staggering of the total holiday pattern. Besides these elements, changes in the regulation of school holidays and the growing influence of early retirement have encouraged a wider spread of tourism demand.

Belgium is an example where greater staggering would be welcome. Many other countries show an even greater concentration of tourism demand, and this implies that further staggering is necessary. Several countries are making great efforts to stimulate this, and solutions should tackle the causes of concentration.

Possible instruments

Climate cannot be changed, although some tourism firms have been successful with their indoor recreation facilities or 'all weather leisure centres' (e.g. Center Parcs in several European destinations, The Sandcastle Centre in Blackpool, the Cascades in Portsmouth, Butlin's Worlds' covered pool complexes) in attracting people in off-season periods.

The reorganization of school holidays is a possible policy instrument. The best-known example is the German case. Based on long-term planning, the country is divided into five zones (each of one *Land* or a combination of *Länder*) with different dates for the beginning and end of the summer (and other) holiday periods. The German system is rotational (*das rollierende System der Ferienregelung*). Although less obvious, there are similar initiatives in France and the Netherlands.

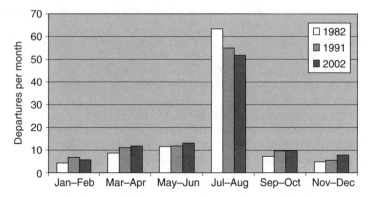

Figure 3.5 Staggering of holidays among the Belgian population based on month of departure, 1982–2002 (source: WES)

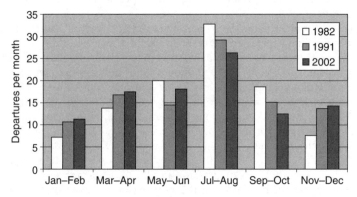

Figure 3.6 Staggering of short holidays among the Belgian population based on month of departure, 1982–2002 (source: WES)

This instrument is the most effective stimulus for increasing staggering. By defining the zones, it is possible for all members of the same family to take a holiday at the same time. There are no global solutions; each country should take initiatives in the direction of better staggering.

Improving staggering of holidays requires a two-pronged approach related to 'can' (or ability) and 'want' (or willingness) – see the 'Noordwijk' conference organized by the Dutch government in 1991 (Ministerie van Economische Zaken, 1991). 'Can' includes people who can take a holiday at whatever time they like. They are not prevented from going on holiday by poor health or disability, and are not restricted for financial reasons or by school or work regulations. Whether people *want* to go on holiday outside the peak season depends on a number of factors:

- Whether the type of holiday product they want is available (e.g. snow)
- Whether the holiday facilities are available at an affordable price
- Whether the potential holidaymaker is aware of the opportunities
- Whether holidaymakers believe they will meet other people on holiday at the same time (a deserted resort is not very attractive).

From the destination point of view, possible initiatives are:

- Price differentiation, or lower prices in shoulder and off-peak periods
- Discounts for young families with children and special offers for those aged 60+
- Choice of origin markets with better staggering of holidays
- Improvement of product supply (creating off-season products) in off-peak periods, and year-round attractions
- Greater animation in off-peak periods
- Promotion of off-peak periods
- Introduction of the 'summer time' period (as in European countries); extra daylight in the mornings is less use to tourists than longer evenings.

Local authorities and the tourism sector can do a lot to create the conditions that allow for better seasonal spread. A combination of the quoted measures should lead to:

- Better use of accommodation
- Less traffic congestion and traffic accidents
- Reduced overcrowding, leading to greater enjoyment
- Higher standards of service
- Price moderation during high season
- Less damage to the environment
- More interesting jobs in the tourism sector
- Less over booking.

With the expected further growth of tourism demand, increased staggering of holidays is the greatest challenge for demand management in the tourism sector in general in the next decade.

References and further reading

Baum, T. (1995). Trends in International tourism. *Insights*, March.

Burkart, A.J. and Medlik, S. (1981). *Tourism: Past, Present and Future*, 2nd edn. Oxford: Heinemann.

Clark, C. (2000). Changes in leisure time: the impact on tourism. *Insights*, January.

Cleverdon, R. (1990). *Tourism in the Year 2000. Qualitative Aspects Affecting Global Growth*. Discussion paper. Madrid: WTO.

Cockerell, N. (1997). Urban tourism in Europe. *Travel & Tourism Analyst*, 6.

Crouch, G. (1992). Effect of income and price on international tourism. *Annals of Tourism Research*, 19.

Crouch, G. (1993). Currency exchange rates and the demand for international tourism. *Journal of Tourism Studies*, 2.

Cuvelier, P. (2000). La fin du tourisme fordiste. *Espaces*, Décembre.

Dwyer, L., Forsyth, P. and Rao, P. (2000). The price competitiveness of travel and tourism: a comparison of 19 destinations. *Tourism Management*, 21.

Economist Intelligence Unit (1995). Real exchange rates and international demand. *Travel & Tourism Analyst, Occasional Studies*, 4.

Fayed, H. and Fletcher, J. (2002). Globalisation of economic activity: issues for tourism. *Tourism Economics*, 2.

Fayos-Solá, E. (1996). Tourism policy: a midsummer night's dream? *Tourism Management*, 6.

Frechtling, D. (2001). World population and standard of living: implications for international tourism. In A. Lockwood and S. Medlik (eds), *Tourism and Hospitality in the 21st Century*. Oxford: Butterworth-Heinemann.

Green, S. (1990). The future of green tourism. *Insights*, September.

Hawkins, R.E. (1994). Ecotourism: opportunities for developing countries. In W. Theobald (ed.), *Global Tourism. The Next Decade*. London: Butterworth-Heinemann.

Holloway, J.C. (1992). *The Business of Tourism*, 3rd edn. London: Pitman.

Koenig, N. and Bischoff, E. (2003). Seasonality of tourism in Wales: a comparative analysis. *Tourism Economics*, 3.

Krippendorf, J. (1987). *The Holidaymakers: Understanding the Impact of Leisure and Travel*. London: Butterworth-Heinemann.

Lockwood, A. and Medlik, S. (2001). *Tourism and Hospitality in the 21st Century*. Oxford: Butterworth-Heinemann.

Martin, W.H. and Mason, S. (1987). Social trends and tourism futures. *Tourism Management*, June.

Middleton, V.T.C. (1991). Whither the package tour? *Tourism Management*, September.

Middleton, V.T.C. with Clarke, J. (2001). *Marketing in Travel and Tourism*, 3rd edn. Oxford: Butterworth-Heinemann.

Ministerie van Economische Zaken (1991). *Improving Seasonal Spread of Tourism*. Noordwijk.

Müller, H. (2001). Tourism and hospitality into the 21st century. In A. Lockwood and S. Medlik (eds), *Tourism and Hospitality in the 21st Century*. Oxford: Butterworth-Heinemann.

NRIT (2003). *Trendrapport toerisme, recreatie en vrije tijd, 2002–2003*. Breda: NRIT.

Poon, A. (1993). *Tourism, Technology and Competitive Strategies*. Wallingford: C.A.B International.

Smith, S. (1997). *Tourism Analysis. A Handbook*, 2nd edn. Edinburgh: Longman.

Stäblein, F. (1994). School holidays. Presentation of an experience: rolling system of school holidays. *Conference on Staggering of Holidays*, Düsseldorf (unpublished Conference document).

Todd, G. (2001). World travel and tourism today. In A. Lockwood and S. Medlik (eds), *Tourism and Hospitality in the 21st Century*. Oxford: Butterworth-Heinemann.

Vanhove, N. (1997). Mass tourism – benefits and costs. In J. Pigram and S. Wahab (eds), *Tourism Sustainability and Growth*. London: Routledge.

Vanhove, N. (2001). Globalisation of tourism demand, global distribution systems and marketing. In S. Wahab and C. Cooper (eds), *Tourism in the Age of Globalisation*. London: Routledge.

WTO (1998). *Tourism: 2020 Vision*. Madrid: WTO.

WTO (1999). *Changes in Leisure Time: The Impact on Tourism*. Madrid: WTO.

4

Tourism supply

Tourism supply in the tourism system

The 'tourism system' is an expression often used but seldom precisely defined. The reason is quite evident. Tourism is a complex phenomenon: there are many different actors, and demand and supply are geographically separated but production and consumption take place on the same spot. A tourism system can be defined as a framework that shows the interaction between: tourism supply at the destination, the bridging elements between supply and demand, and tourism demand (see Figure 4.1). The relationship between demand and supply, via the bridging elements, is a two-way link. In the tourism system, the supply at the destination is the key element.

Suppliers provide the basic elements that together form the overall visitor experience (Ritchie and Crouch, 2003). However, according to these authors there are many resources or factors that are required by tourism and hospitality enterprises – far more than the elements cited in Figure 4.1. For them, labour is a key factor, and other supply factors include food and beverage producers, local crafts, and manufacturers of equipment (such as amusement park rides, camping equipment), etc.

Suppliers are connected to tourists through tourism marketing channels consisting mainly of intermediaries (tour operators, retail trade, meeting and convention planners etc.) and facilitators, who assist in the efficient functioning of the tourism

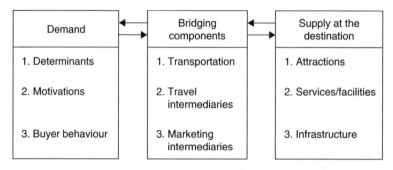

Figure 4.1 Components of the tourism system

system (e.g. flow of information, marketing, money, knowledge). Other bridging elements include the different transportation modes.

The third component of the tourism system is the customer. There is competition to serve customer needs, and it is that competition that governs the actions of the travel trade. As discussed previously, tourists are not a homogeneous group of individual travellers. There is a great variety of tourism motivations, and the range tourism segments has exploded over the last two decades.

Supply components

First, let us consider some supply elements more in detail. Without *attractions* there is no tourism. They are the key element of the tourism system, with the ability to attract people to destinations. The attractions can be of a very varied nature and are classified into three major groups:

1. Primary natural attractions
2. Primary man-made attractions
3. Purpose-built attractions.

Natural attractions include:

- Climate
- Beaches
- Landscape
- Fauna and flora
- Waterfalls
- Lakes
- Mountains.

Primary man-made attractions were not built or conceived for tourism purposes, but they have the capability to attract travellers. They can be subdivided in three groups:

1. Built attractions
   - architecture (historic and modern buildings)
   - cathedrals, churches, mosques

- abbeys
- monuments
- castles
- promenades
- archaeological sites
- natural parks
- indoor resorts
- gardens and parks.

2. Cultural attractions
   - museums
   - theatres and sports
   - art and crafts
   - religion
   - history
   - folklore
   - carnivals and other entertainment
   - festivals.

3. Social attractions
   - way of life of the destination's population
   - ethnic groups
   - language.

Purpose-built attractions were constructed or conceived especially for tourism purposes, and include:

- Theme parks
- Ski tracks
- Marinas
- Festivals
- Events
- Spas.

According to the scope, a distinction is made between three main groups. The first group consists of the 'longer-stay focused attractions', which have the ability to attract people to a destination for several days or more – beach destinations are a typical example. These attractions should have sufficient appeal or variety of attractive components to satisfy tourists for some time. The second group consists of the 'touring circuit attractions', consisting of a combination of several attractions – not necessarily of the same kind – in different locations. Typical examples include Classical Greece, historical Egypt, Italian art cities, the cherry-blossom tour in Japan, the Canadian Rockies, cruise tours and many others. The third group consists of stopover destinations, which are interesting places to visit on the way to primary destinations. A typical example is a visit to Beaune on the way to destinations in the south of France.

The next component of tourism supply is *tourism services/facilities*, also referred to as the 'superstructure' (Goeldner *et al.*, 2000). While attractions draw visitors away from home, facilities are a *conditio sine qua non* to serve these visitors away from home. They support the tourism development rather than induce it. '*L'hôtel ne fait pas le tourisme*' is a well-known expression of K. Krapf, one of the pioneers of tourism research, and indeed good accommodation and/or restaurant services are not a guarantee for successful tourism. However, a lack of facilities will make it impossible to harvest the benefits of tourism development.

The main component of tourism facilities is the accommodation sector. For successful tourism, accommodations must be available in sufficient quantity and quality to match the demand of travellers who arrive at the destination. Given access, accommodations should precede any other type of development. Accommodations can be subdivided into commercial (hotels, motels, hostels, boarding houses, bed-and-breakfasts, cruise ships, shelters, lodges, farm-based facilities, and self-catering facilities such as camping, rented apartments/cottages/houses and holiday villages) and non-commercial services (second residences, mobile homes, visits to relatives and friends, and house exchange schemes). Many of these accommodation types can be further subdivided into classes based on the quality, facilities and the available services. Most countries support a hotel classification system, although there is still no worldwide accepted system; there is not even a system at regional levels (although the Benelux system is an exception). In some countries, efforts have been made to classify camping and rented apartments or villas.

Beside accommodations, there is a need in any destination for food and beverage services (restaurants, cafés, bars, etc.). Together with accommodation, these represent an important share – quite often more than 40 per cent – of tourism expenditure.

Many further services are required by the traveller. There is a wide variety of other facilities, including shops, health services, pharmacies, banks, hairdressers, theatres, casinos, cinemas, garages, sport and leisure services, etc., that serve the tourist as well as the resident population (see the TSA in Chapter 2).

Infrastructure is the third pillar of tourism supply. Traditionally, a distinction is made between transport infrastructure at the destination, and the public utilities. The major elements of the first group are roads, railways, transport services for sightseeing tours, airports, cruise terminals, harbours, local transport network, taxis and parking facilities. It is also impossible for a destination to function without the necessary public utilities – electricity, water supply, health care, communication networks, sewage, waste disposal, water treatment etc. Although we tend to view these utilities as evident necessities, unfortunately not all destinations have them, and both the local population and tourists have to share the same lack of services.

In contrast to the two other supply components, the infrastructure does not provide receipts but costs. As Chapter 8 will demonstrate, these costs must be measured against the benefits of tourism development. Of course infrastructure facilities are seldom developed for tourists alone; the local population also needs a water supply, electricity, telecommunications, etc.

Bridging components

The bridging elements of the tourism system are very often considered as an extension of tourism supply. This is quite evident for the transport infrastructure, such as highways, roads, railways, air and sea connections, and marketing intermediaries. It is less obvious for the travel trade. Tour operators and travel agencies have their home basis in the generating markets (although this is of course not the case for incoming tour operators), and provide an essential link between supply and demand. All tour operators, however, make agreements with supply firms at the destination, and most either have many staff working in the receiving destinations or make use of the services of an incoming tour operator to support their customers at the destination.

Tourism supply, the tourist product and its lifecycle

In Chapter 1, the tourism product was considered as an amalgam of different components. From the point of view of consumers, the tourism product is the total experience from the moment they leave home until they return. The consumer makes use of many of the components mentioned in the above section. However, there are very many attractions and different types of accommodations, and this leads to thousands of possible combinations of these elements. In other words, the tourism product is not homogeneous. Even combining the same type of attraction and the same type of accommodation does not deliver the same product, so many intangible elements should be taken into account (see below).

The combination of the basic travel components – attraction, accommodation, facilities and transportation – is the work of a tour operator or a travel agent. However, many travellers compose the tourism product for themselves.

In more general terms, a consumer visits a destination that is composed of attractions, facilities, infrastructure, transportation and hospitality (Mill and Morrison, 1992). Attractions draw tourists to the destination. Facilities (e.g. hotel, entertainment) serve the needs of the traveller while away from home. Transportation and infrastructure are necessary to help ensure accessibility of the destination to the tourist. Hospitality is concerned with the way in which tourist services are delivered to the tourist consumer.

So far, we have considered the consumer viewpoint. The producer at the destination has a very different view of the tourist product. The hotelkeeper sells rooms, the restaurateur supplies food, the air carrier offers seats, etc. They all supply different elements, and are more concerned about their own product and the similar products delivered by their competitors than about products supplied by the complementary firms. That is the reason why destination management is so important – to assure a horizontal integration of the different supply components (see Chapter 5). The market structure itself is mainly determined by the suppliers of the individual components.

The above might give the impression that tourist products are composed solely of tangible elements, but the reality is very different. A tourist product is rich in intangible elements. The most important intangible elements are image, hospitality, friendliness, courtesy, ambiance, security and understanding.

Each tourist product, from the viewpoint of both the producer and the consumer, has its own lifecycle composed of five stages:

1. Introduction or launch
2. Growth or development
3. Maturity
4. Saturation
5. Decline.

For Buhalis (2000), this lifecycle also applies to a tourism destination. Some writers use the term 'tourist area lifecycle', or TALC (Butler, 1980; Cooper *et al.*,

Table 4.1 Characteristics of the tourist lifecycle

Stage	Supply	Demand
Introduction/launch/exploration	Begin	New trendy destination
Growth/development	Investment in accommodation and facilities	More people interested
Maturity	Increasing investment	Maximum visitors
Saturation/stagnation	Oversupply	Original demand changes
Decline and possibly rejuvenation	Special offer to boost visitation	Decline of demand

Source: Adapted from Buhalis (2000).

1993). The characteristics of supply and demand for each stage in the destination lifecycle are shown in Table 4.1.

Buhalis produced an interesting impact analysis for each stage of the lifecycle from the viewpoint of the destination characteristics (e.g. growth rate, price visitor type), marketing response (e.g. product, price, distribution, communication), economic impact (e.g. revenue, employment), social impact (e.g. crime at the destination, relationships between locals and tourists) and finally environmental impacts (e.g. water pollution, erosion, congestion).

TALC is, from the theoretical point of view, an appealing concept, but is of limited practical value. It is very difficult to identify the different stages and turning points, especially when there is a lack of extended series of tourist arrival data from which to assemble the curve (Cooper *et al.*, 1993). Furthermore, a destination is an aggregation of many products and different market segments, each with their own evolution. Last but not least, nothing is known about the length of the TALC. The cycle is very variable. The lifecycle of a destination is to a large extent dependent on new impulses, either by chance or intent. In any case, from time to time each destination needs to undergo radical innovations in attractions, accommodations and facilities to cope with changing demand trends and competition from newcomers.

Nevertheless, the tourist lifecycle provides a framework for understanding how products, destinations and their markets evolve.

Tourism supply and market structures

In the first section of this chapter different types of activities could be distinguished, all of which are operated by enterprises. Each of these firms supplies its own product. The market structures within which these firms operate vary from pure competition to monopoly. Looking at the variety of supply – attractions, accommodation firms, food and drink, air carriers, travel trade, cruise companies and others – four market structures can be detected in the tourism sector:

1. Perfect competition
2. Monopoly
3. Monopolistic competition
4. Oligopoly.

Sinclair and Stabler (1998) add a fifth market structure, 'contestable markets', but this is similar to perfect competition and therefore we make no further distinction here.

The need for special attention to market structures in tourism is evident from their direct impact on pricing, price policy and the strategy of the firm. In the next section, we shall discuss a number of pricing systems applied in the tourism sector.

Perfect competition

Bull (1995) defines perfect competition (or pure competition) from the seller's point of view – as the situation where the seller is faced with a market-set price level but can sell all of his or her output at that price. The firm cannot sell at a higher price than the market-set price, since buyers would immediately move to other perfect substitutes. In such a market structure it is assumed that there is a large number of firms and consumers, so that neither producers nor consumers can affect the price. It is also assumed that the product or service is undifferentiated, and that there is free entry and exit (Sinclair and Stabler, 1998). The optimal point of production from the supplier's viewpoint occurs where the marginal cost is equal to the marginal revenue or the market-set price. The many small producers are 'price takers'.

It is difficult to find instances of perfect competition in the tourism sector. Small hotels, cafés, and taxi-drivers in major cities are examples that are close to pure competition. Minor differences in location or service lead to comparative advantage of product differentiation.

Monopoly

The opposite extreme is the monopoly or quasi-monopoly situation. A monopoly signifies a single seller, and monopoly power is maintained by barriers to entry into the industry (Tribe, 1999). The monopolist is in a position to be a price-maker. Are there examples in tourism of monopolies or near-monopolies? Yes – this can be the case with unique tourist attractions (e.g. some well-known museums). Tribe refers to car ferry services to the Isle of Wight in the UK. Other examples include national railway companies and domestic air carriers.

Can a monopolist impose any price? Of course not; the monopolist will try to discover the optimum price or the price that maximizes total revenue, as indicated in Figure 4.2.

The upper graph in Figure 4.2 shows the demand curve AB, and the lower graph shows the corresponding revenue curve DE. At the price of €100 there is no demand, and of course no revenue. At zero price there is a demand of 1 million units, but no revenue. Between these two extremes is a price that maximize the total revenue, and this is €50. This price creates a demand of 500 000 units and a total revenue of 25 million euros. All other price levels lead to less total revenue. This implies that the demand curve AB is composed of two parts. In the range AC the demand curve is elastic; any decrease in the price results in an increase in demand and in revenue. In the range CB any decrease in price results in an increase of demand but a decrease of revenue: the demand is inelastic. Revenue maximization occurs where demand-elasticity equals -1.

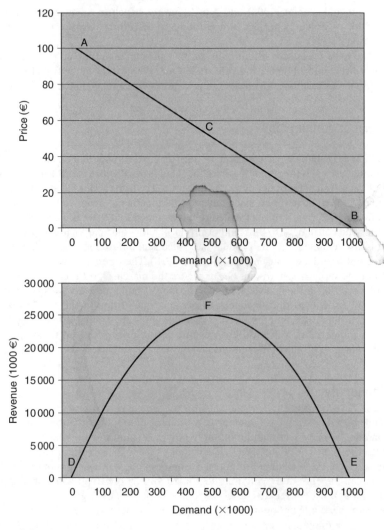

Figure 4.2 Demand, price and revenue maximization in a monopoly situation (adapted from Tribe, 1999)

Profits are maximized at a level of output where the marginal cost equals marginal revenue and the marginal cost is rising.

Monopolistic competition

Monopolistic competition is a type of market structure between perfect competition and monopoly. The characteristics of monopolistic competition are:

- Large number of suppliers and no substantial degree of concentration
- Very limited entry and exit constraints

- Limited economies of scale (unlike the cases of monopoly and oligopoly)
- Suppliers with some control over the price they sell their product.

Suppliers attempt to create market imperfections in order to have more control over pricing and market share. The hotel sector and retailing can in many cases be considered as typical examples of this market structure.

According to Sinclair and Stabler (1998), in the short run suppliers within a monopolistic competition can charge a price that provides them with a supernormal profit. In the long run, however, the higher profits combined with the low entry barriers will attract new competitors and, as a consequence, a fall in the demand for the original suppliers.

In this market structure, suppliers will attempt to minimize competition (Tribe, 1999) by:

- Product differentiation (brand loyalty via advertising, improvement to the tourism product, or adding value to tourism products along the value added chain – such as seat size or frequent flyer awards in case of an air carrier)
- Acquisitions and mergers
- Cost and price leadership.

The latter two strategies cannot be applied to all situations of imperfect competition. Here we come close to an oligopoly situation.

Oligopoly

The essential characteristic of oligopoly is that a small number of producers dominate the industry. Furthermore, there are some barriers to entry and to exit, and each actor has some control over price and output. There is a great interdependence between the producers, with each firm's price and output decisions depending, in part, on those of its competitors. This is the reason why producers operating in an oligopoly market often face the well-known 'kinked demand curve' (Figure 4.3).

In Figure 4.3, ACB is the demand curve and P_0 is the prevailing price. The demand curve is elastic in the range AB, and inelastic in the range BC. If a producer decides to increase the price to the level P_1, the competitors will not follow and he or she will lose turnover and market share; the demand falls from Q_0 to Q_1. If the producer decreases the price to the level P_2 – *ceteris paribus* – he or she knows that competitors will follow. There is only a small increase in demand from Q_0 to Q_2, and the total revenue is less than before the price reduction. Indeed, the demand curve is kinked at point C, and beyond that point the demand curve is inelastic. In other words, in the case of oligopoly the producer has no reason either to increase or to cut prices – the prevailing market price is the profit-maximum price for the producer. 'Price wars' occasionally break out if a producer believes that he or she can effectively undercut the competitors. Bull (1995) claims that in order to avoid a 'price war', oligopolists may agree not to compete on price and perhaps to restrict competition by making special arrangements. This can lead to a cartel, which is classed as illegal by most national governments and by the European Union competition regulations because a cartel is considered to restrict free trade. According to Bull, in the 1980s and beginning of the 1990s

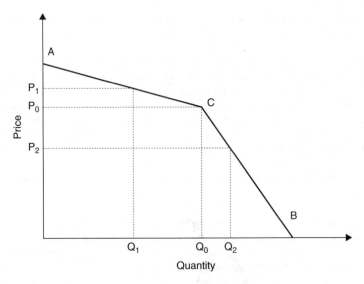

Figure 4.3 The kinked demand curve

agreement of this kind was still frequently found in the tourism sector. It should be recognized that IATA's fare-fixing cartel has disappeared in the last two decades due to deregulation of air transport, new air carriers and stronger competition legislation. Nowadays, competition between air carriers (at least on certain routes) is furious. Agreements in the tour operator business are also unlikely; non-specialized tour operators battle for market share, and consequently profit margins are very low.

Competition under oligopoly conditions is quite often based on advertising, quality and follow-the leader pricing (Tribe, 1999).

In tourism, there are many examples of oligopolistic competition. This is quite often the case with air carriers, air charters, cruise companies, tour operators, larger travel agencies (as in the UK), car rental companies, computer reservation systems, car ferry lines, holiday villages and, to a certain extent, large hotels. Destinations can also be confronted with oligopoly. It is well known that in the Mediterranean region each country keeps a close eye on the others' tourism products. The same applies to seaside destinations within the same country.

As a general conclusion, the relationship between market structures and pricing can be summarized as follows:

- Firms operating in a perfect competition (i.e. there are many buyers and sellers of homogeneous products with total freedom of entry and exit) are price-takers – they cannot influence the price
- Firms in monopolistic competition (there are still many sellers but there is also the chance for product differentiation) or in an oligopoly (few sellers) are price-shapers – in other words, they can influence the price to a certain extent
- Finally, a monopolist (only one seller) is a price-maker – he or she can set the desired price.

Key criteria in inter-firm competition

Based on theoretical models, and analysis of different tourism sectors, Sinclair and Stabler (1998) identified a number of key factors in inter-firm competition.

The first is the number and the size of firms. Where many small firms operate, the market is competitive. A small number of firms indicates an oligopolistic structure, and possibly a monopoly. Once a few large firms represent a large market share, oligopoly situations are not far away. This brings us to the second factor, the degree of concentration.

High concentration is suggestive of oligopoly or monopoly. Concentration is possible with a large number of firms – an example is the travel agency structure in the UK. A good indicator of concentration in a sector is the Gini coefficient, where a zero denotes that all firms are of the same size and a high value, approaching unity, indicates a highly concentrated market and (probably) high profits. The extent to which high concentration leads to higher profits is determined in part by ease of entry into and exit from the sector. The level of sunk costs involved in operating the firm is also important.

A third factor concerns the economies and diseconomies of scale. In the case of economies of scale, costs per unit of production decline as inputs and output increase. As long as average costs are falling, a firm will be stimulated to grow. The point at which the average costs start to rise again is where diseconomies set in. In tourism, there are several sectors where economies of scale can be realized. This is certainly the case in air travel, the cruise business, the car-ferry market and the accommodation sector. Sinclair and Stabler (1998) explain why economies of scale can be achieved, and why these economies can indicate market structure. Economies of scope, where additional products or services share common inputs, can lead to a similar situation. The authors state an important thesis:

> Evidence of unexploited economies of scale or scope, or potential for them to occur in the future through technical change, would indicate the likelihood of increased firm size and greater market power, so rendering the market less competitive. Conversely, diseconomies of scale, or supply where widely differing input proportions are possible, would enhance the long-term viability of smaller firms and create a structure which is more competitive.

All this does not preclude many small firms from being successful in the same market. They focus on particular segments or niches.

The fourth factor consists of the capital indivisibilities, fixed capacity and associated fixed costs of operations. Some sectors in tourism are confronted with high fixed costs. This is certainly the case in the transport business and, to a lesser degree, in the accommodation sector. However, tour operators who operate their own hotels and aircraft also show relatively high fixed costs. With low occupancy rates, revenues are insufficient to cover fixed and variable costs. Reduction of capacity is, in the short run, rather difficult. In such situations, firms attempt to capture trade from competitors. Price policy becomes a key element, and firms can continue to function so long as they cover their variable costs. In the long run, a firm has more alternatives. Alternative strategies include altering the product, the choice of markets and the segments served.

A fifth factor concerns price discrimination and product differentiation. The price policy practised by tourism firms provides some indication of the market structure. In the case of a large number of firms and homogeneous products or services, the prevailing price should be respected – this situation can be approximated to perfect competition. Pricing and output strategies can be applied in imperfectly competitive situations. Oligopolists should take into account the possible reaction of the competitors. Firms operating under monopolistic competition endeavour to differentiate their product from that of rival firms. It is important to note that all firms operating under imperfect competition can benefit from price discrimination. For many products and services the willingness to pay is very different from segment to segment, and price discrimination can be applied where different consumers have distinct price-elasticities of demand. A higher price can be charged for those consumers with an inelastic demand, while lower prices are charged for consumers whose demand is more elastic. Discriminatory pricing in tourism is the rule in the air business, ferry travel, rail transport and the accommodation sector. Larger hotels offer interesting discounts at weekends, but charge business people with inelastic demand higher prices during the working week. We will return to this topic in the next section.

Product differentiation is also a common practice under imperfect competition. Product differentiation can take two forms: vertical and horizontal. The first case can be based on different quality products. Horizontal product differentiation can be realized via the supply of a range of product types (e.g. for young people, special interest groups, mass tourism).

A final factor concerns pricing policies and market-share strategies. Over the past two decades, price-cutting has been the rule in tourism in many sectors working in an oligopoly situation. In the air business there has been a combination of product differentiation and price cuts. Many remember the Laker Air story, where Laker offered low prices and a low product profile. Laker went bankrupt, but its price strategy was followed by many low-cost carriers (e.g. Ryanair, Easyjet, Buzz, Deutsche BA, and Ted, JetBlue and Song in the USA). Price-cutting does not only occur among airlines; there are similar situations in other transport sectors. Where the entry of new companies is more difficult or uncommon, collusion may occur. This was the case prior to deregulation in the air business, when air fares were controlled by the IATA.

A typical example of oligopoly is the tour-operator market. In this sector, price leadership, price wars and attempts to increase market share are common practices in many European countries. Larger market share strategy leads to mergers and take-overs (for example, the Thomas Cook group and the TUI group). Integration is related to information advantages, cost savings and the possibility of increased market power.

Pricing in tourism

Each product has its price – in other words, product and price are linked to each other. From the preceding section it must be clear that price is a key element in inter-firm competition, and that is why we pay special attention to pricing in tourism. What are the objectives? What are the pricing methods or pricing approaches?

Pricing objectives

Pricing objectives can be divided into three categories. The first is of profit-oriented pricing objectives. Prices are established either to achieve a certain targeted profit or to generate the maximum profit. In the former, target profits are expressed as a percentage return on investments or sales. The Hubbart formula, which is applied in the hotel business (see below), is a typical application. In the case of profit maximization, the firm sets the price that will give the greatest profit. Yield management responds to this objective.

The second category is of sales-oriented pricing objectives, focusing on sales volumes and/or larger market share and not so much on profits. Needless to say, this is not without danger. Sales-oriented pricing can fit into the competitive strategy of a firm. An example is low-cost carriers.

Last but not is *status quo*-oriented pricing, where the position relative to the competitors is the main target. This can be called competitive pricing. A firm tries to match its competitors' prices closely (e.g. in the rent-a-car market, Budget and National follow Hertz). This is the follow-the-leader approach.

Pricing approaches

Of pricing methods or pricing approaches, three methods deserve special attention: the Hubbart formula, the break-even analysis, and yield management. Before dealing with each of these three methods in turn, let us start with the distinction made by Morrison (1989) between unsophisticated, sophisticated and multistage approaches. We limit ourselves to a general overview.

Unsophisticated approaches are based not so much on research or costs but more on the intuition of the entrepreneur. Morrison mentions four such approaches:

1. The competitive approach, where firms set prices based on their competitors' prices
2. The follow-the-leader approach, which is very similar to the competitive approach and is often applied by smaller market-share companies (e.g. Burger King may follow McDonald's price changes)
3. The intuitive approach, which is based on the entrepreneur's intuition
4. The rule-of-thumb or traditional approach. There are two well-known rule-of-thumb approaches. The first concerns the hotel sector, where it is believed that €1 should be charged per €1000 investment costs – in other words, a hotel investment of €100 000 per room should have a room rate of €100. The second concerns the restaurant sector, where multiplying the food cost of a particular dish by a factor 2.5 is still common practice. Tax inspectors might sometimes apply this rule.

All these approaches are based on little or at most one factor and do not consider the cost/profit structure of the firm and neglect the customers' expectations.

Sophisticated approaches take more factors into account. Morrison (1989) refers to the following methods:

■ Target-pricing, where the target is usually set in terms of a specific return on investment (see the Hubbart formula).

- Price discounting and price discrimination, where discounting means offering rates below the rack rate or those advertised, and discriminatory pricing means selling services to some customer groups at higher or lower prices. Discounting and discriminatory pricing can be based on criteria such as market choice, form of service provided, and place and time.
- Promotional pricing.
- Cost-plus pricing, where an amount or percentage is added to the estimated cost of a product or service.
- New-product pricing, which involves setting a different price for a new product. There are different strategies for introducing a new product; the two best known are price-skimming (an artificially high price for a new product) and penetration pricing (introducing a new product at a very low price).
- Price lining, where the firm pre-establishes prices that it feels confident will attract customers.
- Psychological pricing, where slightly lower prices are used to give customers the impression that they are receiving something extra.
- Leader pricing, where a firm offers a product for a short time at a price below its actual costs, or offers something special with the purchase of a product (e.g. a beer with the purchase of spaghetti).

In the *multistage approach*, pricing should consider nine factors (Morrison, 1989):

1. Competitors
2. Customer characteristics
3. Customer demand volumes
4. Costs
5. Channels
6. Corporate objectives
7. Corporate image and positioning
8. Complementary services and facilities
9. Consistency with marketing-mix elements and strategy.

For effective pricing, a multistage approach based on those factors is required. This will help a firm in deciding which is the best price approach and the most appropriate price level.

The Hubbart formula for determining room rates

The Hubbart formula is a typical method of determining target price in the hotel sector. This method is interesting and effective because it considers several of the factors of pricing mentioned above.

The rack rate is the result of different steps. The calculated price should be considered as an orientation rate – indeed, the Hubbart formula is cost-oriented. The method ignores the demand side and some critical supply-side variables, such as the competitive position of the company (Arbel and Woods, 1991), but the calculated price can always be adjusted to take into account the hotel positioning and the pricing policy of competitors (see Table 4.2).

Table 4.2 The Hubbart formula method

Starting point (step 1)	Desired return on investment after tax
Plus (2)	Undistributed expenses (e.g. interest, property tax, depreciation, energy costs, property maintenance)
Less (3)	Net revenues other departments
Equals (4)	Room profit
Plus (5)	Room expenses
Equals (6)	Required room revenues
Projection (7)	Projection of the number of rooms the firm expects to sell (projected occupancy rate)
Average room rate (8)	(7)/(8), or average rate per occupied room after discounts and commissions

Break-even analysis

Break-even analysis shows the relationship between costs (fixed and variable costs), demand volume and profits. The formula to calculate the break-even point is:

$$\text{Break-even point} = \frac{\text{(total fixed costs)}}{\text{(contribution margin)}} \tag{4.1}$$

The contribution margin is defined as the difference between the selling price per unit and the variable cost per unit. This formula can also be used in target pricing. In this case, the formula becomes:

$$\text{Break-even point} = \frac{\text{(total fixed costs + target profit)}}{\text{(selling price per unit − variable cost per unit)}} \tag{4.2}$$

For example, if

total fixed costs = €500 000
selling price per unit = €125
variable cost per unit sold = €40
target profit = €160 000
then the break-even point equals (500 000 + 60 000)/(125 − 40) or 7764 units.

In other words, 7764 units should be sold to achieve a target profit of €161 000.

Break-even analysis is very often used in discount pricing. For example, if the firm were to give a discount of €15 per unit, what would be the necessary sales volume to achieve the target profit? The application of the formula (500 000 + 160 000)/(110 − 40) indicates that the break-even volume increases to 9429 units. The firm can then decide whether such an increase in volume is feasible in terms of capacity and demand.

As with any method, the break-even analysis has a number of limitations. First, constant variable costs irrespective of the sales volume is assumed. Secondly, fixed costs are also supposed to be constant, which is not so evident; some fixed-cost items might increase at a certain level of turnover. Thirdly, the demand is not too sensitive to the prevailing price.

Yield management

Yield management, a method for managing capacity profitably, has its originates in the airline sector. Since then it has also gained widespread application in the hotel business and other tourism sectors. It can be defined as selling the right inventory unit to the right type of customer, at the right time and for the right price (Kimes, 1999). Yield management guides the decision of how to allocate undifferentiated units of capacity to available demand in order to maximize profit or revenue. The problem is to determine how much to sell at what price and to which segment.

As such, yield management is a method that responds to profit-oriented pricing objectives, and in particular to profit or revenue maximization. At the same time, it is an application of discriminatory pricing (see Figure 4.4).

Let us first define the term 'yield'. In the hotel business, 'yield' is equal to the occupancy rate multiplied by the average room rate:

$$\text{Yield} = \frac{\text{room nights sold}}{\text{room available}} \times \frac{\text{actual average rate}}{\text{room rate potential}} \tag{4.3}$$

Yield management concerns the first and second terms of the abovementioned formula. This method is by no means restricted to hotels.

Yield management should not be confused with pure price discrimination. The latter can be considered as a first step in the direction of yield management, but for Kimes (1999) yield management is essentially a form of price discrimination.

Figure 4.4 relates to price discrimination. The aim is revenue maximization. The total revenue with a single price P equals OPBQ. If the total demand is divided into three segments, each with its own price, the total revenue becomes $OP_1AQ_1 + Q_1EBQ + QDCQ_2$ – i.e. the total revenue with price discrimination is greater than the total revenue with a single price P_0 (OQ_1 units are sold at price P_1; Q_1Q_0 units at P_0 and O_0Q_2 units at P_2).

Tribe (1999) mentions three conditions that are necessary for price discrimination to take place. The first is that the product cannot be resold – in other words, consumer A (who is buying at a low price) cannot sell the product to customer B (at a higher price). Very often the products are not 100 per cent identical – for example, a full-fare air ticket is refundable and can be changed at no cost, unlike less expensive tickets. Tourism products as service products provide good conditions for price discrimination. The second is that the supplier should be able to identify different segments. Finally, there must be market imperfections.

According to Kimes, early yield management approaches used threshold curve methods in which a firm (for example a hotel) closed rates when demand was above a certain level and opened rates when demand was below a certain point (see Figure 4.5). By the mid-1990s, many of the major hotel chains had adopted more sophisticated mathematical programming-based methods (see Yeoman and Ingold, 1999).

Figure 4.5 shows a typical booking curve AE for a tourist product – say a hotel room. Based on historical data, the booking curve normally moves in a band between the two dotted lines. This is the expected demand pattern, and depicts the 'threshold values' (Relihan, 1989). Three months before the consumption date (say 100 days), the bookings are rather low. At point B the booking curve is outside

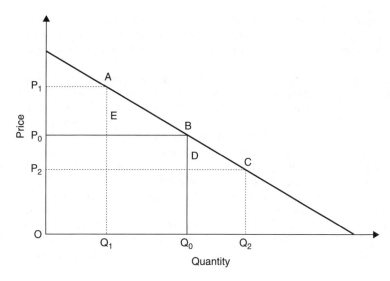

Figure 4.4 Total revenue with single pricing and price discrimination

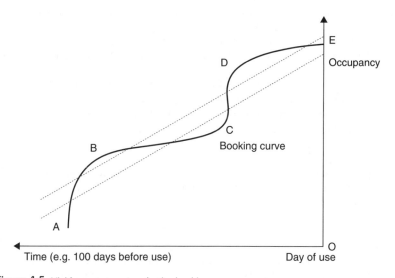

Figure 4.5 Yield management and sales booking curve

the threshold band, and prices should be adjusted upwards or discounts eliminated. At point C the actual bookings fall below the threshold, and this indicates that the management should open discount rates to encourage more reservations.

Lieberman (1993) warns of the myth that yield management is price discounting. Lieberman states:

> Raising and lowering prices dynamically for a given date, depending on demand, is a business decision … but it is not a yield-management

91

decision. Yield management focuses on how much of a product to sell at established prices. It does not tell a hotel what prices to charge or whether to change prices. But it does indicate when to open and close rate classes.

Indeed, yield management focuses on two basic elements: allocation of capacity to the right type of customer, and demand at the right price in order to maximize revenue or yield. Applied to air transport, where should the separation be made between business and economy in an aircraft on a particular scheduled flight? What is the allotment for inclusive tours? An air carrier has a lot of flexibility.

A successful yield management (system) should respond to a number of basic conditions (Kimes, 1999, Raeside, 1999). The first necessary condition is the possibility of segmenting the demand and the ability to segment by willingness to pay. This implies that the segments show different demand-elasticity (e.g. different time of use, type of traveller, early bookings with no refund restrictions). The second condition relates to a similarity of inventory units (e.g. rooms, seats). This pricing system also requires that the product can be sold well in advance, and that historical demand and booking patterns and a good information system are available.

Further conditions include:

- Fixed capacity. Many sectors in tourism are confronted with capacity constraints – once an airplane has been purchased, a cruise ship constructed or a hotel built, it is expensive and difficult to enhance its capacity.
- High fixed cost. This is related to fixed capacity; the latter is due to the high costs of enhancing capacity.
- Low variable costs. Incremental costs to a hotel or airline are very low – in other words, an additional customer is inexpensive.
- Perishable inventory. This is a characteristic of all tourist products.
- Pricing knowledge. Most firms practising yield management rely on competitive pricing methods. By offering multiple rates, firms hope to increase their revenue.
- An overbooking policy. Firms protect themselves against the possibility of no-shows. An overbooking policy cannot be developed without historical data of no-shows.

To conclude this section, a few points should be noted:

1. The application is much more complex than the text above might suggest. Air carriers and hotel chains make use of mathematical models (Raeside, 1999).
2. Consistent pricing should take into account regular customers. Even when demand is unusually heavy for an upcoming date, it would be unwise to refuse a loyal customer's request for a normally available discount rate (Lieberman, 1993).
3. The difference between working days and weekends makes the application more difficult. In case of multiple-night stays during low- and high-demand days, trade-offs need to be addressed by the yield management system.
4. Hotel managers should be aware that rooms are not the only service sold in a hotel. The restaurant, conference space and parking facilities all contribute to a hotel's profitability (Kimes, 1989).

5. Yield management can be very important at the local level when several hotels are located in the neighbourhood. Hotels within a limited vicinity are substitutes for each other, and the price at which hotel rooms are offered affects the demand for the rooms (Relihan, 1989).
6. Price-inelastic (high rate-paying) demand occurs just before arrival (e.g. business travel), and price-elastic demand occurs well in advance.

Yield management (price discrimination) is nowadays a common practice in many sectors of the tourism industry. The application is complex, and requires many data and advanced computer models. Based on contacts with yield managers in the tourism industry, revenue increases of 6–7 per cent are not unusual. However, yield management is open to all competitors. In some cases, avoiding the loss of market shares is already a positive contribution.

Supply trends

'Supply trends' could well be the title of another book; it covers a variety of items. This section is limited to a number of major trends with a great or a particular economic impact:

- More destinations
- Concentration movement in the tourism sector
- Movements in the hotel sector
- Branding
- Technological evolution affecting tourism
- New types of accommodation and attractions – timesharing, cruises, the inclusive holiday villages explosion and theme parks.

More destinations

Every year, new regions are developed as destinations. The world is becoming increasingly explored, and adventure tourism is in the picture (mountains, tourist submarines, ends of the earth, etc.). There are not only more destinations, but also the product variety in the destinations is increasing year after year (see the demand trends described in Chapter 3).

Concentration movement in the tourism sector

Concentration is probably the major trend of the tourism industry. The concentration movement started many years ago, and has accelerated in the last decade. This process is manifestly present in several sectors of the tourism industry, including air transport, hotel groups, tour operators, travel agents, theme parks, CRS's and car rental firms – considering diagonal integration.

The buying out of KLM by Air France – French interests own of 81 per cent of the shares and KLM 19 per cent – although not totally unexpected, shocked

Table 4.3 Comparison of larger air carriers in Europe

	Air France–KLM	British Airways	Lufthansa
Turnover (billion €)	19.1	10.8	12.3
Aircraft in fleet	540	348	369
Passengers (million/year)	63.4	34.0	44.0
Employed staff (1000s)	106	57	94

Europe (*Le Monde*, 2003). Air France–KLM became the largest air carrier in Europe (see Table 4.3).

By the end of the last century, four alliances dominated the world air market (WTO, 1998): the American–British Airways alliance, the Star Alliance, the Delta–Swissair Group and the Northern-Continental Group. The WTO stated in 1998: 'While their ambitions may be thwarted by regularity intervention or corporate incompatibility, if the major airlines achieve their objectives, most passenger flights will take place on one of just three airline groups before 2010'. Five years later the world map had changed completely, but there are still three big alliances:

1. The Star Alliance includes Lufthansa, United Airlines, Canada Air, Air New Zealand, All Nippon Airlines, Australian Airlines Group, British Midlands, Mexicana Airlines, Scandinavian Airlines, Singapore Airlines, Thai and Varig.
2. Oneworld includes American Airlines, British Airways, Aer Lingus, Cathay Pacific, Finnair, Iberia, Lan-Chile and Quantas.
3. The Sky Team includes Air France, Delta, AeroMexico, Alitalia, Czech Airlines and Korean Air Lines; this group is also due to be joined by KLM, Northwest and Continental.

The three alliances represent nearly 50 per cent of passengers carried (O'Toole and Walker, 2000). The air transport sector is undergoing structural changes due to the processes of liberalization, privatization, internationalization, globalization and concentration of air carriers (Fayad and Westlake, 2002).

This is a very clear example of an oligopoly situation. The danger for travellers is if the groups unofficially divide up of the world between them, creating such strong spheres of influence that competitors dare not challenge them, and thus cause possible fare rises. A distinction should be made between complementary alliances (i.e. between carriers who have separate, non-overlapping route networks which they link through an airport, coordinating flights and connections and feeding traffic to each other) and parallel alliances (i.e. between airlines who were, prior to the alliance, competitors on important routes). In the first case, alliances have not much impact on competition but do improve the airlines' economics. The situation is different for parallel alliances. These tend to impact negatively on competition, and a likely outcome is fewer flights (for example, Lufthansa has withdrawn from Australia), reduced service levels and less traffic (Morley, 2003).

However, international airline alliances also have the effect of improving the efficiency and services of airlines. The cost-reduction opportunities can be broken down into four types (OECD, 2000; Morley, 2003):

1. Finance and utilization (cost reductions due to greater asset utilization – of aircraft, lounges, inventory, IT, etc.)

2. Airline operation (such as staff and agency arrangements, sharing the expenses of marketing and promotion, flight and route efficiencies, garnered through code-sharing services)
3. External (payments to suppliers, such as airports, aircraft manufacturers, catering, maintenance, handling)
4. Risk-sharing (booking of block space on each other's flights and code-sharing).

Tourism is likely to feel positive effects (particularly complementary alliances) through tourists experiencing key service improvements – decreases in fares and total travel time, and easier connections.

The accommodation sector is following the same trend, with the consolidation of hotel groups. The effects are not always spectacular, are nevertheless multiple.

The European tour-operating sector is also experiencing a centralization of power. Since the beginning of this century, the European tour-operating map has been redesigned. Preussag, formerly an industrial group, entered the tourism business in 1997, and is taking the control of TUI, Germany's largest tour operator. In 1998, Preussag took over Thomas Cook and Carlson UK. Two years later the largest British tour operator, Thomson Travel, belonged to the Preussag group The European Union agreed with this integration provided Preussag resold Thomas Cook. In 2000, the German group acquired GTT, the leading Austrian tour operator, and took a share of 10 per cent in the largest Italian tour operator, Alpitour. In the same year, Preussag began to take control of Nouvelles Frontières, completing the process in 2002). In 2001, Preussag formed an association with the Maritz Travel Company (United States), Internet Travel Group (Australia), Protravel (France) and Britannic (UK) to establish a global network for business travel called TQ3 Travel Solutions (de Boiville, 2003). Also in 2001, Preussag decided to regroup all the tourism activities of 15 countries under the name 'World of TUI'.

At the end of the 1990s, the second largest German tour operator, C&N (from the merger in 1998 of Neckerman and Condor, affiliate of Lufthansa, formerly NUR Touristic and successor of Neckerman), began a series of take-overs. In 1999, the group acquired the French companies Aquatour, Albatros and Havas Voyages Loisirs. A year later, C&N bought Thomas Cook (which Preussag had been obliged to cede). In 2002, the group C&N Touristik changed its name to Thomas Cook. Meanwhile, Thomas Cook is also operational in Spain due to an agreement with Iberostar.

The German group Rewe and the British tour operators MyTravel (formerly Airtours) and First Choice were also active in acquiring other tour-operating companies. This short and incomplete history of take-overs in the tour-operator world illustrates a remarkable concentration movement in Europe. A major barrier for further concentration is created by the national monopoly authorities and the competition legislation of the EU (see the Thomas Cook story and Airtours' failed bid for First Choice, in Needham, 2000).

Why is there such a concentration movement in the tour-operator world? The reason can be found in an interview with J. Maillot, former president of Nouvelles Frontières, when he answered the question 'What is the interest of the British and the German tour operators to invest in France?' His reply was very clear: 'They are not so much interested to invest in France but to have a European dimension. When a company is present in several countries of the EU, one makes economies of scale'. These economies of scale are in different fields: purchase of petrol, management of the fleet, currency management etc. (de Boiville, 2003). Another phenomenon is that big integrated travel groups seek to cover all segments of the market (Needham, 2000).

This concentration movement does not exclude successful small tour operators. Not all tourism products can be 'industrialized' (e.g. Spain, the Dominican Republic, Tunisia), and many others cannot be standardized. Big tour operators concentrate on selling budget or mainstream package holidays (see Chapter 5).

In addition to horizontal and vertical integration, many travel and tourism companies are utilizing a diagonal integration strategy whereby they establish operations to offer products or services that tourists commonly purchase but which are not directly part of the tourism product (Poon, 1993; WTO, 1998) – i.e. they are diversifying. For example, airline companies are now offering insurance, etc. (see Chapter 5).

The conclusion of this subsection is clear. The concentration of airlines, hotel groups (see below), tour operators and car rental firms will lead to economies of scales and to economies of scope, which will in turn lead to lower prices. However, it also presents a danger in that large groups might gain too powerful a hold on the markets.

Movements in the hotel sector

Worldwide, the hotel sector is the backbone of the accommodation industry. In many destinations it is the dominant accommodation type. The amount of accommodation is still growing; according to Marvel (2004), the number of rooms in hotels and similar establishments (inns, boarding houses and/or guesthouses) increased from 14.7 million rooms in 1997 to 17.3 million in 2002 (these figures are only indicative) The hotel sector is also the most labour-intensive sector of tourism. with the highest value added per man/night. An employment rate of 1.5–2 persons per hotel room is not exceptional in developing countries, although the rate is much lower in developed countries, varying from nearly zero in a 'Formule 1' hotel to 0.6 in a four-star hotel (Horwath International).

The hotel sector is characterized by a growing concentration movement. Nevertheless, there is a dominance of SMEs. According to Benhamou (2000), of the 350 000 'classified' hotels in the world, about 30 000 are commercialized under the name of the 50 largest groups. Their share in terms of rooms is much higher. Table 4.4 illustrates the top six, with regard to room numbers, in 1998.

Table 4.4 The top six hotel groups, with regard to room numbers, worldwide in 1988

	Number of rooms	Number of hotels
Cendant Corporation	529 000	5980
Bass hotels & Resorts	460 000	2740
Marriott International	330 000	1690
Choice Hotels International	310 000	3670
Best Western International	300 000	3810
Accor	290 000	2670

All but one of these (Accor) are American companies; in the top 20 there are 14 American and 6 European companies. Meanwhile, a number of new acquisitions have taken place (thus Accor has acquired Frantour, CGHS and Red Roof Inns). Most of the hotels belonging to the bigger hotel groups are not affiliated via ownership, but via franchise and management contracts.

The hotel sector is characterized by increasing chain penetration (see Chapter 1) and a growing number of franchise hotels. The largest hotel group, Cendant, neither owns nor runs a single hotel. Franchising can be described as a contractual bond of interest in which the franchiser, which has developed a pattern or formula for the manufacture and/or sale of goods/services, extends to the franchisee the right to carry on the business subject to a number of restrictions, controls and consideration (Hudson, 1994). In other words, it is a licence for a specific period of time to trade in a defined geographic area under the franchiser's name, and to use an associated mark or logo. The franchisee – or a third party – is expected to make the initial investment and to pay a royalty to the franchiser. For the franchisee there are several advantages: less risks, easier access to loans, technical assistance, marketing support, training of staff and help in the operational procedure. In return, the franchisee has to pay a royalty and meet the standards of the chain and the operational-quality standards. Typical franchisers are Cendant (with the brands Day's Inn, Horward Johnson, Ramada, etc.), Bass hotels (with the brands Holiday Inn, Holiday Inn Express, Crowne Plaza, Intercontinental), Choice (with the brands Comfort, Sleep Inn, Quality, Econolodge, etc.) and Accor (with the brands Novotel, Ibis, Sofitel, Mercure, Formule 1, etc.).

The main group of franchisees consists of individuals seeking to own and operate a hotel and who can see benefits from paying franchise fees to gain access to higher levels of demand and lower costs than they could otherwise achieve.

Another form of affiliation with growing importance is the management contract, which originated in the USA. For various reasons (to depreciate freehold property assets and tax treatment), insurance companies, savings and loan institutions, banks and consortia of private investors became willing owners of hotel property although they had no experience or interest in hotel management (Slatterly and Johnson, 1993). In the 1980s there was, in the USA, a trend towards explicit separation of ownership of hotels from their management. The function of hotel brands in this context is to ease expansion and provide assurance to hotel investors of the strength of the management of any hotel. The most important hotel management companies are Marriott International, Société du Louvre (e.g. Campanile hotels), Accor, Tharaldson Enterprises, Promus Hotel Corporation, Red Roof Inns and Sol Melia.

A very special type of affiliation is 'hotel commercialization', or 'consortia'. It concerns companies specializing in commercialization (reservation systems) of independent hotels without a brand (or a franchised brand). The two largest hotel reservation systems are Rezsolutions Inc (Utell + Anasazi) and Lexington Services Corporation. In 1998 the former had 7700 affiliated hotels, and the latter had about 3000.

Another trend in the hotel sector over the last decade has been the explosion in branded budget hotel capacity. In the UK, the number of rooms in budget hotels increased from 18 155 in 1996 to 57 300 in 2002. A similar phenomenon is seen in France; in 2004 O-star hotels represented 16 per cent and 1-star hotels 12 per cent of French chain hotel rooms (Marvel, 2004).

Branding

Positioning and branding are strongly interrelated. Positioning seeks to define how a tourism firm or destination is viewed by the tourism market in terms of the benefits it is likely to provide *vis-à-vis* the many competitive firms or destinations from which the tourist may choose (Ritchie and Crouch, 2003). On the basis of the positioning chosen, the firm (e.g. a hotel) or destination seeks to project this position to the marketplace through the development of a distinctive and strong brand (for example, the 'design' of Philippe Stark for Paramount Hotel and the 'location' for Park Lane Hotel, both in New York). It is a name, symbol, logo or other graphic that both identifies and differentiates. Branding is an identifying mark for consumers who cannot see the wood for the trees. Branding is becoming increasingly important for the large tourism groups and for destinations to distinguish themselves from competitors and competing products. In the online economy, we can expect a battle of brands (Nederlands Bureau voor Toerisme, 1998).

Okoroafo (1995) emphasizes the many benefits (identification of the product or destination, assurance of product quality, limited ability for customers to make price comparisons, social visibility and product prestige), and concludes that the development of a brand name over time can offer the firm a competitive edge.

The strategies of travel groups vary from the single-brand philosophy (e.g. Club Med., Thomas Cook and the World of TUI) to a range of brands for specific markets (see the hotel group Accor). Any pan-European or global brands should take very careful account of national and local market characteristics, traditions and sensitivities (Needham, 2000).

For destinations, branding takes the form of a 'corporate identity'. It is a positioning in the form of the essential. The basic elements are isotype, logotype and baseline. The corporate identity of Spain is well known, with the sun of Miro as the isotype, España as the logotype and 'Spain marks' as the baseline (formerly 'Spain everything under the sun' and 'passion for life'). The Canary Islands use the baseline 'Canarias: warm nature'.

Technological evolution affecting tourism

Technology has two different aspects: transportation and information technology. Transport technology will lead either to further decreases in transport costs or to shorter travel times. Larger (although this is not the policy of Boeing Company) and faster aircraft are being developed; newer and faster high-speed trains are forecast (such as the 500-km/h levitational train between Hamburg and Berlin) and ever-larger cruise ships are under construction.

Air transport and air fares are (and will be) influenced by several other trends, including:

- Air deregulation and an influx of low-cost airlines.
- Further privatization of the world's national airlines, where major carriers take share holdings or acquire privatizing airlines. This phenomenon is very well phrased in the WTO report (1998): 'Privatization can be seen to be fuelling the spread of globalization'.
- Aircraft yield management by having the right type of aircraft for given routes.

Information technology is changing at an incredible pace. 'Information is the lifeblood of the travel industry' (Sheldon, 1995) – it connects tourists, tour operators, travel agents and tourism industry suppliers. For Poon (1993), information is the cement that holds together the different producers within the tourism sector – namely cruise lines, airlines, hotels, tour operators, travel agents, car rental firms and many other suppliers. It is essential to keep in mind that the links between tourism producers are provided not by goods, but by a flow of information. These information flows consist of data, services and payments. In the case of consumers, information is received in the form of advertising, promotions, counselling, bookings (e.g. airline tickets) and a matching information transaction flows from consumers to suppliers (e.g. payment).

Information technology is essential for the efficient and timely processing and distribution of all necessary information. Information technology is a generic term; in fact there are systems of information technologies. The largest and most important information systems in the tourism sector are the computer reservation systems (CRS). The US Department of Transportation defines a CRS as 'a periodically updated central data base that is accessed by subscribers through computer terminals'. CRSs have emerged as the dominant technology.

Computer reservation systems were developed by the airlines. They are primarily tools used by airlines to maintain inventory control of their seat offerings, and have played a significant role in facilitating increasing volumes of travel over the last three decades. A significant shift is now occurring towards global travel distribution systems and increased competition amongst airline groups seeking to broaden and strengthen their product distribution through developing regional global CRSs. A GDS takes the inventory from a CRS (or from many of them) and distributes it via travel agents and other distribution outlets. A GDS has no specific airline inventory control functions other than to 'report back' (French, 1998). Since the early 1990s their function has expanded to include many other travel products (e.g. accommodation, rent-a-car, etc.) and embrace alternative means of distribution to travel agents, such as the Internet (see Figure 4.6). The leading GDSs are Sabre, Galileo, Amadeus and Worldspan.

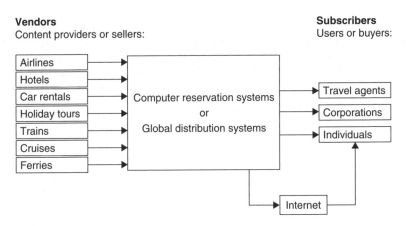

Figure 4.6 Transaction flow of global CRS/GDS industry (source: Merrill Lynch, and French, 1998)

The consequence of these supply trends is an increasing requirement for CRSs to offer more travel information, faster processing time, and more comprehensive booking and reservation functions, as well as providing enhanced management accounting information (see yield management).

CRSs are not the only form of information technology commonly used. Furthermore, CRSs are more popular with business-oriented travel agencies than with those specializing in leisure products. Nevertheless, there is a high penetration rate in all travel agencies in the largest European markets.

Other reservation systems include:

- Hotel reservation systems
- Reservation systems owned by independent companies (e.g. UTELL)
- Videotext (e.g. Prestel in the UK and Minitel in France)
- Product reservation systems owned by tour operators
- Car rental reservation systems
- National distribution systems (several of them are integrated into a GDS).

A particular form of information technology that has evolved spectacularly is the Internet. The Internet is in fact a network of networks. Two of its most used functions are electronic mail and the World Wide Web. Currently, the number of Internet users is limited in relative terms, although the USA, Canada and Finland are exceptions. However, the number of Internet users is growing very fast, and we are not too far from the point where every home in the developed world will have a personal computer and possibly a modem. Each person will be able to access many information systems all over the world. There is no doubt that this evolution is affecting travel agencies and even tour operators, and will increasing do so.

New types of accommodation and attractions

Timesharing

Timesharing is a global industry, with more than 5000 resorts and 4 million owners spanning all continents in the year 2000 (Hitchcock, 2001). It originated in Europe during the 1960s, but the real development of timesharing as a new sector took place in the USA. At the beginning of this century, the USA accounted for about one-third of all timeshare resorts and nearly 50 per cent of all timeshare owners. Within Europe, Spain has by far the largest number of timeshare resorts.

There is a good definition of timesharing in Goodall and Stabler (1990):

Timeshare, sometimes referred to as interval ownership, is a form of multi-ownership of property of which examples can be found in the business sector, as well as in the leisure sector. It is a periodic right of use or occupation where property is divided on a temporal rather than physical basis. It confers on a number of purchasers the right to the exclusive and full use of property and facilities for predetermined periods of year. In principle this right is recognized as transferable.

There are two forms of timeshare. In the first there is a real property right (e.g. weekly blocks) lasting from up to 20 years to perpetuity. However, there is a net trend for shortening timeshare validity periods. The second form concerns a contractual right (e.g. corporate share, leasehold, holiday credits or points).

Timesharing is a relatively new trend in the accommodation sector, and it only represents a marginal share of the total accommodation capacity. However, there are several destinations (e.g. resorts in the Canary Islands) where timeshare is the backbone of the accommodation supply. Furthermore, this sector shows a very high growth rate. In the 1990s, the growth rate was still 7–8 per cent (Hitchcock, 2001). The timeshare market is now sweeping the Asia-Pacific region (Dean, 1997).

In the beginning, the developers of timeshare were small, independent and very often newly formed companies. Increasingly the developers have become the construction industry and, since the mid-1980s, corporate interests from the hotel trade (e.g. Holiday Inn, Marriott or Marriott Ownership Resorts Inc., Sheraton, Hilton resorts) and even from the Walt Disney Company. Tour operators are also involved in timesharing by the acquisition of timeshare resorts or renting unsold timeshares. Club Mediterranée (buying out the French timeshare developer Club Hotel) and Tjaereborg (taking over the Club La Santa timeshare in Lanzarote, Canary Islands) have been involved in timeshare from very early on. In this way, tour operators are integrating vertically backwards into accommodation supply.

What, in fact, are the economic benefits of timesharing for a destination? Research from Joachimsthaler and Ragatz Associates (1995) highlights the economic benefits of a timeshare resort to a local community compared with conventional package holiday tourism. Case studies presented on Gran Canaria on the occasion of the AIEST Congress (AIEST, 1995) confirmed these benefits. The advantages for the destination are several, and include:

- Relatively high expenditure per man/day. Timeshare holders are considered to be high-quality customers (Hitchcock, 2001). As property owners, timeshare holders also have the illusion of buying a cheap holiday. Sometimes they benefit from seat-only charters
- Less pressure from the tour-operator business
- The improvement of holiday accommodation (very often with recreational facilities)
- Higher occupancy rates
- More responsible tourists
- An extended season in the destinations
- A stable level of employment owing to more repeat visitors and reduced seasonality.

Consumers also benefit from good accommodation and recreational facilities. They are, however, confronted with operational costs that are often much higher than they expected at the time of purchase. To be linked to a single destination is a second disadvantage, and to cope with this exchange companies have been established which provided a mechanism for timeshare owners to swap their week(s) in one resort with week(s) in another, so enabling them to take a holiday in a different place at a different time of the year. These exchanges have been a real stimulus to growth. The market leader of exchange companies is Resort Condominiums International (RCI). Other timeshare developments worldwide are affiliated to Interval International (II). These exchange companies act as tour operators for timeshare owners. Greater flexibility is also the result of the Holiday

Club concept. (Haylock, 1995). In this case, instead of laying out a capital sum to buy a period of timeshare in a resort, the buyer acquires a number of holiday credits which can be used to take a holiday of his or her choice from within the Holiday Club's owned inventory. The Swiss-based company Hapimag using this formula 35 years ago.

Timesharing has sometimes had a bad press owing to hard-sell practices and/or non-*bonafide* developers. This is the origin of the EU directive of 1994 to govern certain aspects of the sale of timeshares. This directive seeks to mitigate the worst excesses of hard sell by giving the potential buyer the right to change his or her decision and cancel the contract without financial penalty within a certain period of time ('the cooling off period'). This directive has, together with the entry of powerful brands, improved the image and credibility of timesharing. Recently, timesharing has been extended to embrace products such as cruise ships, skiing or golf holidays, villas and even caravans, rather than being restricted to the traditional beach or mountain products (Hitchcock, 2001).

Cruises

The cruise sector is showing a spectacular growth rate, and is expected to expand further in the coming decade. The excellent financial performance of the cruise sector stimulates further investment. Carnival's net income per passenger day was about $64 in 1999. While new ships were delivered at the rate of between 10 and 12 per year in the second half of the 1990s, this is now pushing up to nearer 16 per year in the early part of the twenty-first century. Cruise ships are also becoming larger; several ships on order have a tonnage of over 100 000 (Peisly, 2000). Currently the cruise ship *America World City* is under construction, with a capacity of 6200 passengers (2400 more than the present largest), and this will be operational in 2005. Table 4.5 gives the projected capacity increase in terms of berths of the top four cruise companies between 2000 and 2006 (Peisly, 2000).

Table 4.5 indicates that the top four companies are predicted growth of 75 per cent in six years.

The rapid development of cruising has also an impact on a number of destinations. Several destinations in the Caribbean are complaining of the fall in use of traditional overnight accommodation. Furthermore, several destinations are becoming the playthings of the powerful cruise companies.

All-inclusive resorts

Poon (1993) defines the all-inclusive concept as:

> holidays where virtually everything is included in one pre-paid price from airport transfers, baggage handling, government taxes, rooms, all meals, snacks, drinks and cigarettes to the use of all facilities and equipment, coaches and instructors. Even gratuities (tips and service charges) are included in this pre-paid price.

The all-inclusive concept originates from holiday camps and villages such as Butlin's in Britain and the French-based Club Méditerranée. The latter dominates this accommodation type, with more than 130 resorts by the year 2000. Other major all-inclusive chains are: Allegro Resorts (26 resorts in 1998), Robinson

Table 4.5 Projected capacity increase (berths) in the top four cruise companies, 2000–2006

	2000	2006
Carnival Corporation	63 230	104 886
Royal Caribbean International	42 989	79 888
P&O Cruises Division	26 981	50 091
Star Cruises	25 480	42 880

Clubs (24), Club Valtur (20), Super Clubs (12), Clubs International (12), Club Aldiana (10) and Sandals (10) (Page *et al.*, 2002).

In the 1990s, all-inclusive resorts in Jamaica performed better than non-all-inclusive hotels. The success was attributed to aggressive marketing, good contacts with the travel trade, psychographic market segmentation strategies (couples only, families only, health, sport etc.) and visitor satisfaction. (Poon, 1998).

Theme parks

Although there is no single agreed definition of a theme park, it is generally agreed that all theme parks are concerned with entertainment and physical experiences provided by a backbone of varied rides and attractions. Theme parks are distinguishable from amusement or other similar leisure parks by an overall themed experience which runs through all (or most) of the attractions (McEniff, 1993). The main characteristics of theme parks are as follows:

- They involve outdoor recreation
- They are visitor destinations in their own right
- They are based on rides, attractions and shows
- They are constructed around the needs of visitors, rather than relying on natural features
- They are focused on entertainment but are increasingly paying attention to education.

Theme parks are becoming ever more attractive to excursionists and tourists interested in a short break. The bigger theme parks offer a real condensed holiday product. In 2003, 14 theme parks were each visited by more than 6 million visitors (www.themata.com; see Table 4.6).

The top 50 had a total of 250.9 million visitors in 2003. The theme park world is dominated by two theme park groups; Walt Disney Attractions (89.3 million visitors in 2000) and Six Flags (48.8 million visitors in 2000). Meanwhile, the European Six Flags parks have been taken over by Palamon Capital Partners.

All over the world Disneyland has had a tremendous impact on local theme parks. In Japan, Disneyland Tokyo spurred the growth of the Japanese theme park industry, as did Disneyland Paris in Europe (Camp, 1997).

The penetration of theme parks based on the number of visits per capita is very unequal in the developed countries. The United States and Japan show the highest penetration; Europe is far behind, and within Europe the visits per capita vary from country to country (Camp, 1997). However, care must be taken in interpreting

Table 4.6 Theme parks with more than 6 million visitors in 2003

Theme park	Visitors (millions)
Magic Kingdom, Florida	15.4
Disneyland Tokyo	13.2
Disneyland Anaheim, California	12.7
DisneySea Tokyo	12.2
Disneyland Paris	10.2
Universal Studios JP	8.8
Everland (KR)	8.8
Epcot Center, Walt Disney World	8.6
Lotte World, Seoul	7.2
Disney-MGM Studios, Walt Disney World	7.9
Disney's Animal Kingdom	7.3
Universal Studios Orlando	6.8
Blackpool Pleasure Beach	6.2
Islands of Adventure at Universal Orlando	6.1

the penetration. Generally speaking, European tourists have a wider choice of tourism attractions.

The composition of receipts is also very different. In the USA, related parks' admission fees count for 40–45 per cent of income while more than 50 per cent comes from merchandise, food, drinks and other. In Europe, admission fees represent on average 55–60 per cent of total receipts, with a correspondingly lower share for merchandising.

There is also an evolution within the sector. New types of theme park are being developed away from the conventional Disneyland type of attraction. Many of the new parks focus on a particular theme (e.g. crocodiles – Jungle Crocs of the World – in Florida). There is also a trend in the existing and new parks to offer hotel and other accommodation, shopping facilities, shows and even educational activities.

References and further reading

AIEST (1995). *Real Estate Business and Tourism Development*. St-Gall: Editions AIEST.

Arbel, A. and Woods, R. (1991). Inflation and hotels: the cost of following a faulty routine. *The Cornell H.R.A. Quarterly*, February.

Benhamou, F. (2000). Mondialisation de l'hôtellerie. *Espaces*, February.

Bosselman, F., Peterson, C. and McCarthy, Cl. (2000). *Managing Tourism Growth*. Washington: Island Press.

Buhalis, D. (2000). Marketing the competitive destination of the future. *Tourism Management*, 21.

Bull, A. (1995). *The Economics of Travel and Tourism*. Sydney: Longman.

Butler, R.W. (1980). The concept of a tourist area cycle of evolution. *Canadian Geographer*, 24.

Camp, D. (1993). Theme parks in Europe. *Travel & Tourism Analyst*, 5.

Cooper, C., Fletcher, J., Gilbert, D. and Wanhill, S. (1993). *Tourism. Principles & Practice*. London: Pitman Publishing.

Daudel, S. (1991). Le yield management. *Les Cahiers d' Espaces*, 24.

Daudel, S., Vialle, G. and Humphreys, B. (1994). *Yield Management*. Paris: Institute of Air Transport.

Dean, P. (1997). The timeshare industry in the Asia-Pacific region. *Travel & Tourism Analyst*, 4.

de Boiville, G. (2003). Tour-operating Européen. Les grandes manœuvres. *Espaces*, January.

Fayad, H. and Westlake, J. (2002). Globalisation of air transport: the challenges of the GATS. *Tourism Economics*, 4.

French, T. (1998). The future of global distribution systems. *Travel and Tourism Analyst*, 3.

Goeldner, Ch., Ritchie, J.R.B. and McIntosh, R. (2000). *Tourism. Principles, Practices Philosophies*, 8th edn. New York: John Wiley.

Goodall, B. and Stabler, M. (1990). Timeshare: the policy issues considered. *Tourism Research into the 1990s*, Conference Proceedings of a Conference held at University College, Durham, 10–12 December 1990.

Haylock, R. (1994). The European timeshare market. *Tourism Management*, 5.

Haylock, R. (1995). Developments in the global timeshare market. *Travel & Tourism Analyst*, 4.

Hitchcock, N. (2001). The future of timesharing. In A. Lockwood and S. Medlik (eds), *Tourism and Hospitality in the 21st Century*. Oxford: Butterworth-Heinemann.

Hudson, T. and Webster, B. (1994). Franchising. In S. Witt and L. Mouthinho (eds), *Tourism Marketing and Management Handbook*. London: Prentice Hall.

Ingold, A. and Huyton, J. (1999). Yield management and the airline industry. In I. Yeoman and A. Ingold (eds), *Yield Management. Strategies for the Service Industries*. London: Cassell.

Kimes, S. (1989). The basis of yield management. *The Cornell H.R.A. Quarterly*, November.

Kimes, S. (1999). Yield management: an overview. In I. Yeoman and A. Ingold (eds), *Yield Management. Strategies for the Service Industries*. London: Cassell.

Kimes, S., Chase, R., Choi, S., Lee, P. and Ngonzi, E. (1998). Restaurant revenue management. Applying yield management to the restaurant industry. *The Cornell H.R.A. Quarterly*, June.

Le Monde (2003). Air France-KLM: la difficile naissance du leader européen, *Le Monde*, 1 October.

Lieberman, W. (1993). Debunking the myths of yield management. *The Cornell H.R.A. Quarterly*, February.

Lockwood, A. and Medlik, S. (eds) (2001). *Tourism and Hospitality in the 21st Century*. Oxford: Butterworth-Heinemann.

Marvel, M. (2004). European hotel chain expansion. *Travel & Tourism Analyst*, Mintel, May.

McEniff, J. (1993). Theme parks in Europe. *Travel & Tourism Analyst*, 5.

Mill, R.C. and Morrison, A.M. (1992). *The Tourism System*, 2nd edn. London: Prentice-Hall.

Morley, C. (2003). Impacts of international airline alliances on tourism. *Tourism Economics*, 1.

Morrison, A.M. (1989). *Hospitality and Travel Marketing*. New York: Delmar Publishers Inc.

Nederlands Bureau voor Toerisme (1998). *Digitale Revolutie in de Toeristenbranche*. The Hague: NBT.

Needham, P. (2000). Trends and issues in the European travel industry. *Travel & Tourism Analyst*, 6.

OECD (2000). *Airline Mergers and Alliances*. Paris: OECD.

Okoroafo, S. (1995). Branding. In S. Witt and L. Mouthinho (eds), *Tourism Marketing and Management Handbook*. London: Prentice Hall.

Origet du Cluzeau, Cl. (1996). Le yield mangement comme stade paroxystique de la loi du marché. *Revue d'Espaces*, 139.

O'Toole, K. and Walker, K. (2000). Alliance survey. *Airline Business*, July.

Page, S., Brunt, P., Busby, G. and Connell, J. (2002). *Tourism: A Modern Synthesis*. New York: Thomson.

Peisley, T. (2000). Cruising in crises. *Travel & Tourism Analyst*, 5.

Poon, A. (1993). *Tourism, Technology and Competitive Strategies*. Wallingford: C.A.B International.

Poon, A. (1998). All-inclusive resorts. *Travel & Tourism Analyst*, 6.

Raeside, R. (1999). Quantitative methods. In I. Yeoman and A. Ingold (eds), *Yield Management. Strategies for the Service Industries*. London: Cassell.

Ragatz Associates (1995). *The World Wide Resort Timeshare Industry*. American Resort Development Agency. Washington: Ragatz Associates.

Relihan, W.J. (1989). The yield-management approach to hotel-room pricing. *The Cornell H.R.A. Quarterly*, May.

Ritchie, J.R.B. and Crouch, G. (2003). *The Competitive Destination*. Wallingford: CABI Publishing.

Sawhney, S. and Lewis, R. (1992). Hotel yield management in practice: a case analysis. *Journal of Hospitality and Leisure Marketing*, 2.

Sheldon, P.J. (1995). Information technology and computer reservation systems. In S. Witt and L. Mouthinho (eds), *Tourism Marketing and Management Handbook*. London: Prentice Hall.

Sinclair, T. and Stabler, M. (1998). *The Economics of Tourism*. Routledge.

Slatterly, P. and Johnson, S. (1993). Hotel chains in Europe. *Travel and Tourism Analyst*, 1.

Tisdell, C. (ed.) (2000). *The Economics of Tourism*. Cheltenham: Edward Elgar.

Tribe, J. (1999). *The Economics of Leisure and Tourism*. Oxford: Butterworth-Heinemann.

Vogeler, C. (1995). Timesharing: a tourism and/or real estate product. *Real Estate Business and Tourism Development*, 45th AIEST Congress, Gran Canaria. AIEST.

Yeoman, I. and Ingold A. (eds) (1999). *Yield Management. Strategies for the Service Industries*. London: Cassell.

WTO (1998). *Tourism: 2020 Vision*. Madrid: WTO.

5

Competition and the tourism destination

Introduction

During the last decade there has been a growing interest in tourism literature in the notion
of the 'competitive destination'. In the preceding
decades competition in tourism was very often
identified with the price component and was frequently restricted to the micro-level (see Chapter 4).
It cannot be denied that for a destination as
well as for an enterprise, price is a vital element
of competitiveness (see Chapters 1 and 3; Dwyer
et al., 2000). However, since the beginning of
the 1990s (see AIEST, 1993; Poon, 1993; Goeldner
et al., 2000) the tourism sector and tourism
scientists have been aware that besides comparative advantages and price, many other variables
determine the competitiveness of a tourism
enterprise or destination. More and more authors
and practitioners are focusing on the competitive
destination.

The idea of the competitive destination contains two elements: destination and competitiveness.
A tourism destination is a well-defined geographical area within which the tourist enjoys various

types of tourism experiences. Ritchie and Crouch (2003) distinguish several types and levels of tourism destinations:

- A country
- A macro-region consisting of several countries (e.g. Africa)
- A province or another administrative entity
- A localized region (e.g. Flanders, Normandy)
- A city or town
- A unique locale with great drawing power (e.g. a national park, Iguaçu Falls, Disney World in Orlando, the Notre Dame in Paris).

In relative terms, very few tourists visit a macro-region or country such as Spain, USA, etc. Tourists are interested in regions and towns, such as Andalucia in Spain, the Algarve in Portugal, New York in the USA, and the Flemish art cities. These are 'tourism clusters'. Porter (1998) defines clusters as 'geographic concentrations of interconnected companies and institutions in a particular field. Clusters encompasses an array of linked industries and other entities important to tourism'. He refers to the California wine cluster as a good example. This includes hundreds of commercial wineries, thousands of independent wine-grape growers, an extensive complement of industries supporting both wine-making and grape-growing (suppliers of grape stock, irrigation and harvesting equipment, barrels, labels), advertising firms, local institutions involved with wine, and the enology program at the University of California at Davis.

Applied to tourism, we can define a cluster as a group of tourism attractions, enterprises and institutions directly or indirectly related to tourism and concentrated in a specific geographical area. Competition in tourism is mainly between clusters and not so much between countries (Bordas, 1994).

According to Ritchie and Crouch (2000), 'The fundamental product in tourism is the destination experience. Competition, therefore, centres on the destination'. For most tourists, this experience takes place in a rather small geographical area such as a town or a region. This is an entity which, from the tourism management point of view, is managerial.

'Competitiveness in tourism' can be described as the elements that make a destination competitive as defined by Ritchie and Crouch (2003):

> ... its ability to increase tourism expenditure, to increasingly attract visitors while providing them with satisfying, memorable experiences and to do so in a profitable way, while enhancing the well-being of destination residents and preserving the natural capital of the destination for future generations.

We find the same elements in the Poon (1993) and WES (1994) approaches. From this content we can derive that competitiveness in tourism has several dimensions: economic, socio-cultural and environmental. However, not all competition models dealt with in this chapter respond to this content.

Competitiveness has become a central point of tourism policy. As competition increases and tourism activity intensifies, tourism policy focuses on improving competitiveness by creating a statutory framework to monitor, control and enhance quality and efficiency in the industry, and to protect resources (Goeldner et al., 2000).

While there is some agreement about the content, the conceptual models developed to enhance competitiveness are very different. The following models will show the differences:

- The competitive forces and generic strategies of M. Porter
- The 'Porter diamond', or the determinants of competitive advantage
- The Poon concept
- The WES approach
- The Bordas demand model
- The conceptual model of destination competitiveness of Ritchie and Crouch
- The price-competitiveness approach of Dwyer, Forsyth and Rao.

These models are neither predictive nor causal. Ritchie and Crouch (2002) are right when they state that '… models should not be used to make a decision; they assist in decision making but should be no substitute for the role of the decision maker'.

Five of the above mentioned models focus exclusively on 'destination' competitiveness. Poon makes a distinction between industry players and destinations. Porter's first model – competitive forces – primarily concerns industry players, although there are applications at the destination level (see Bordas, 1994).

In the following sections of this chapter, special attention will be given to the key elements of each of these concepts. The last section will provide a synthesis of the main variables.

The competitive forces of M. Porter

In contrast to the other concepts listed above, Porter's theories about competitive forces and about determinants of competitive advantages do not originate in the tourism sector. It was only later that tourism scientists applied the theory to the tourism industry.

According to Porter, the essence of formulating competitive strategy is relating a company to its environment. In his book *The Competitive Strategy* (1980), Porter proposes the model of the 'five forces' for investigating the competitive environment (see Figure 5.1):

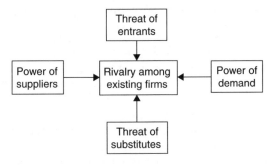

Figure 5.1 The five competitive forces of M. Porter

1. The threat of entrants
2. The power of suppliers
3. The power of buyers
4. The threat of substitutes
5. Competitive rivalry.

The state of competition in a tourism industry, as in any other industry, depends on these five competitive forces. The strength of these forces determines the profit potential of each sub-industry (e.g. tour operator, air carrier, theme park), where profit potential is measured in terms of long-run return on invested capital. Not all tourism sub-industries have the same potential, as the total profit potential is for all industries in general.

The first competitive force is the threat of *new entrants*; which can be controlled by barriers to entry such as:

- Economies of scale
- Capital requirements
- Product differentiation
- Switching costs
- Access to distribution channels
- Lack of experience (Tribe, 1999)
- Advertising barriers
- Government policies
- Expected retaliation
- Exit costs.

New entrants may stimulate more price competition, or more attention may be paid to product differentiation as they attempt to win market shares. In tourism, the threats of new entrants is quite high in most sectors, and even the threats of new destinations is very realistic. Every year, more air carriers, more hotels, new accommodation, more theme parks, more events and new tourism destinations appear on the global tourism map.

The *threat of substitutes* can take very different forms. Self-catering is an alternative to hotel accommodation; high-speed trains can substitute for short distance air carriers; direct sales can, to a certain extent, replace CRS; and the Internet is a threat to the traditional travel agent selling classical uncomplicated products. Substitutes limit the potential returns of an industry by placing a ceiling on the prices firms in the industry can profitably charge. However, there are further threats. Domestic tourism can be an excellent alternative to outbound tourism, and pure leisure activities may keep potential tourists at home. On the whole, the threat of substitutes is a reality in tourism.

The buyers' *power of demand* is great under the following circumstances:

- If a buyer group purchases large volumes relative to seller sales (the UK tour-operator business in Benidorm and other resorts in Spain relative to the local hotel sector is a typical example)
- If the products a buyer group purchases from a sector are standard or undifferentiated (e.g. hotel rooms)

- If the products a buyer group purchases from the sector represent a significant proportion of the buyer's cost or purchases (as is the case for hotel accommodation as part of a package tour)
- If a buyer group earns low profits (see low profit margins of many tour operators).

Very often a buyer is can exert a considerable power over the selling sector. The bargaining power of buyers is also influenced by the level of buyer knowledge (Tribe, 1999).

It is well known that a hotel sector (which is very fragmented and atomized) that is highly dependent on tour operators has limited bargaining power. Prices are under pressure and profit margins are reduced to nil or even below zero. Such a situation leads to lower maintenance and absence of modernization, and the vicious circle of deterioration can and will start.

The *bargaining power of suppliers* should also be considered (Porter, 1980). A supplier group is powerful if:

- It is dominated by a few companies (there is a degree of monopoly or oligopoly) and is more concentrated than the industry it sells to (e.g. air charter companies relative to tour operators)
- The industry is not an important customer of the supplying group
- The group's product is differentiated, or it has built up switching costs
- The group's product is an important input to the buyer's business (e.g. flight costs for a tour operator)
- The group poses a credible threat of forward integration (e.g. an air carrier starts a tour-operator's business)
- There are high costs of switching suppliers.

In practice, this is the case for credit card companies (Visa, American Express) and CRSs such as Sabre and Galileo supplying a booking service for hotels, airlines and car hire companies.

Backward vertical integration can be a possible solution to avoid supplier power by take-over of the supplying firm. Tribe (1999) refers to Thomson's ownership of its carrier Britannia.

Porter's last competitive force is the *rivalry among existing firms*. This rivalry can be great in a situation where:

- There is slow sector growth
- There are high storage costs or perishability
- There are high fixed costs
- There is lack of differentiation
- There is a high strategic stake (to be successful in one market)
- There are numerous or equally balanced competitors
- There is over-capacity or big changes in capacity
- There are high exit barriers.

Many sub-sectors in are susceptible to one or more of these characteristics. This is the case for air carriers, hotels and car rental firms. Strong rivalry is the logical consequence, with either a price war or a marketing-led competitive strategy.

Table 5.1 The application of competitive forces to the Caribbean

Competitive forces	Application to the Caribbean
The threat of new entrants	New seaside resorts in Caribbean countries – Cuba is only one example
The power of suppliers	Air carriers from the USA with regular flights to the different countries in the Caribbean
The power of buyers	The bargaining power of cruise carriers for mooring in the individual countries
The threat of substitutes	The Caribbean destinations have many competitive destinations in Central America and the Canary Islands
Competitive rivalry	The competition between destination is great, due to undifferentiated supply, overcapacity in several destinations and perishability of supplied products

There is a good practical application in Knowles (1994), where he relates the CRSs to the five basic competitive forces in order to determine the state of competition.

Is this theory of competitive forces applicable to tourism destinations? There can be no doubt if a destination is considered as a cluster at regional or local level. The cluster is in reality a big firm composed of hundreds of parts. There are some references to various destinations in the preceding paragraphs, but let us consider the practical example of the Caribbean area (see Table 5.1).

The combined strength of these five forces determines the profit potential (in the case of tourism destinations potential value added of the industry) and its marketing strategy. For each firm, and also for each destination, a specific competitive strategy can be developed that reflects the particular circumstances of a firm, industry or destination. For Porter, an effective competitive strategy takes offensive or defensive action in order to create a defendable position against the five competitive forces and thereby yield a superior return on investment for a firm – or in our case, value added for a destination. He formulates three potentially successful generic strategic approaches to outperforming other firms or destinations, and these are described below.

Porter's generic competitive strategies

In addition to responding to and influencing tourism structure, firms and destinations must choose a position within the industry. At the heart of positioning is competitive advantage. Porter distinguishes two basic types of competitive advantage: lower costs, and differentiation (Porter, 1990). Here, the theory is adapted to the tourism sector. Lower cost is the ability of a firm or a destination to design, produce and market a comparable service more efficiently than its competitors. Differentiation is the ability to provide unique and superior value to the buyer in terms of product quality and special features. However, there are limits to both types of advantage. A low-cost producer must offer acceptable quality of service to avoid nullifying its cost advantage. On the other hand, a differentiator may not achieve a cost position far enough above that of the competitors to offset its price premium.

Competitive advantage

		Lower cost	Differentiation
Competitive scope	Broad target	*Cost leadership*	*Differentiation*
	Narrow target	*Cost focus*	*Focused differentiation*

Figure 5.2 The generic strategies of M. Porter

Competitive scope is a third important variable in positioning. Scope is important to tourism because the sector is segmented. A firm or destination can define this scope in different terms:

- The range of tourism products
- The distribution channel
- The type of buyers
- The geographic area.

The combination of the two basic advantages and the scope advantage gives three generic strategies, or three different approaches, to arrive at a better economic performance in terms of higher return on investment or higher value added. These are illustrated in Figure 5.2.

Overall cost leadership is the first generic strategy. Achieving a position of low overall cost is not so easy; it requires a high market share or other advantages, volume production, standardized tourism products, and a management team that pays attention to cost control. The firm should possess sufficient financial means to support an aggressive price policy and cope with start-up losses.

Some big tour operators in European countries are (or were) in an overall cost leadership position. However, the profit margins are at present not very high, and far below the normal rate of 3 per cent.

Having a low-cost position defends the firm against the competitive forces:

- Powerful buyers (its price is lower than the price level of its next most efficient competitor)
- Powerful suppliers (there is more flexibility to cope with increases of input prices)
- There are entry barriers in terms of economies of scale
- It is in a favourable position *vis-à-vis* substitutes.

At destination level, several Spanish destinations and the Dominican Republic provide examples of low-cost leadership, or are the victims of the bargaining power of strong buyers. They may be successful in the short and medium term, but will not be competitive in the long term. This is not a sustainable economic development.

Differentiation is the second generic strategy. With such a strategy, a firm or destination seeks to be unique in the sector regarding some dimensions that are widely valued by customers – such as brand image, customer service, dealer network, design, technology, language knowledge, security, safety, just-in-time, etc. In the hotel business, attributes such as functional utility (e.g. type of bathroom, size of beds), symbolic utility, or being associated with a certain group and experience utility (e.g. aesthetics, knowledge, friendliness) are very efficient differentiation strategies.

Differentiation provides a certain protection against competitors because of firm or destination loyalty by customers and the resulting lower sensitivity to price. As a consequence, it creates a premium price. In many sectors of the tourism industry, differentiation is the rule. Hotel chains covering the broad scope but targeting different segments are well known. The French group Accor has a diversified brand portfolio consisting of Sofitel, Mercure, Novotel, Ibis, Formule I and Étap, ranging from five stars down to purely functional hotels. Accor has also announced the establishment of a backpacker chain, Base Backpackers, indicative of its intention to be a prominent operator across all market segments. (McVey and King, 2003).

Focused or niche strategy is the third generic strategy. Here, the firm or destination focuses on a particular buyer group, segment, market or product. In other words, the scope is narrow. In practice, there are two variants: differentiation focus and cost focus. With a niche strategy, a firm can be a big fish in a small pond. Most small tour operators apply this strategy. However, it is not without danger – for example, a tour operator specializing in the 'Egypt product' can be very successful, but a terrorist attack (as has happened in Egypt more than once) can finish the company. The demand for a specialized products can decrease, and the focus strategy can be imitated. This happens quite often in tourism.

The determinants of competitive advantage in tourism

In his book *The Competitive Advantage of Nations*, Porter (1990) developed a model that attracted much attention in the tourism sector. Taking into account the examples in his book and paraphrasing the title of his book, we can speak of 'the competitive advantage of regions'. In the context of this book, and referring to the introduction of the current chapter, a title 'The competitive advantage of tourism destination' makes sense, especially as Porter, together with Bordas (THR), applied his model to Barcelona – a city which is very successful in the short holiday and MICE market.

Porter claims that the success of a firm does not only depend on its strategy and positioning (see the five competitive forces of Porter) but also on its being embedded in the environment. Regions, destinations and clusters succeed in a particular industry or activity because their home environment is the most dynamic and the most challenging, and this stimulates firms to upgrade their advantage. This is his central thesis.

In tourism there are many clusters – groups of companies directly and indirectly related to tourism and concentrated in a specific geographical area. The tourism product as a composite product – attractions, accommodation, transport and other facilities – stimulates the clustering process (see Michael, 2003). Typical examples of tourism clusters are Bruges, Venice, Iguaçu and Ibiza.

The starting point for the development of strategies to improve the competitive position of a destination is identical to that for the determinants of competitiveness

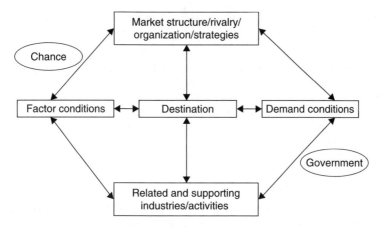

Figure 5.3 The determinants of competitive advantages of destinations

(Smeral, 1996). Based on the Porter model, competitive advantages of a destination emerge in a dynamic system consisting of four interdependent determinants, which together form a diamond – a term Porter uses to refer to these determinants (Porter, 1990; see Figure 5.3).

These determinants are:

1. Factor conditions, or the destination's position regarding factors of production necessary to compete in the tourism industry
2. Demand conditions, or the nature of (home) demand for tourism products and services
3. Related and supporting industries/activities – i.e. the presence or absence in the region of supplier industries and related industries
4. Market structure, rivalry, organization and strategies, or the conditions in the destination governing how companies are created, organized and managed, and the nature of (domestic) rivalry.

There are also two additional variables – chance and government – which can influence the system in important ways and are necessary to complete the theory.

The 'diamond' is a mutually reinforcing system. The effect of one determinant depends on the state of the others. Favourable demand conditions, for example, will not lead to competitive advantage unless the state of rivalry is sufficient to cause firms (e.g. hotels) to respond to them. Advantages in one determinant can also create or upgrade advantages in another.

What is the possible content of the determinants of a tourism cluster in general?

Factor conditions

The key elements of factor conditions are factor endowments and their permanent upgrading. Without factor endowments and attractions in particular – natural, cultural or man-made – there is no tourism activity. What do we understand by factor conditions? They include:

1. Factor endowments
   - natural resources (beaches, etc., but also population and geographical location)
   - cultural and historical resources (monuments, cultural heritage, museums, art collections, customs, handicraft, canals, events, etc.)
   - capital and infrastructure resources (accommodation, transport infrastructure, site development)
   - human resources
2. Factor prices
3. Production efficiency.

Smeral (1996) underlines an important dimension with respect to factor conditions. The factors most important to the competitive advantage of a destination are not inherited but created. The stock of existing factors is less important than the rate at which they are created, upgraded and specialized.

Demand conditions

Demand conditions (as the second broad determinant of competitive advantage), when applied to a tourism cluster, are slightly different from the original formulation in the Porter model. We can distinguish the following items:

- Size of the market
- Structure of the market (diversity in core markets, seasonality, degree of internationalization, share of long-haul travellers, etc.)
- Position in fast-growing markets
- A strengthening tourism culture of consumers and host societies (Cooper *et al.*, 2001)
- Protection of the consumer-tourist
- First-time visitors
- Sophisticated tourists (to recognize new trends).

The latter aspect is of the utmost importance. We agree with Pechlaner and Smeral (2001) that 'Quality-conscious tourists exert constant quality control, pushing suppliers towards high-quality and attractively priced market segments. Early market saturation forces suppliers to readjust quickly by instituting innovations and accessing international markets'.

Related and supporting industries/activities

The competitive position of a destination also depends on the diversity and the quality of supporting suppliers. In any destination, there is a need for many different types of suppliers to provide:

- Access to the destination (train, air, road, sea)
- Parking facilities

- Cultural, entertainment and sports facilities
- A souvenir industry
- Food and fashion (sophisticated consumer goods, high-quality food, restaurants)
- Shopping facilities
- High-quality services (e.g. taxi drivers, travel agents, tourism guides, banks, sport facilities, education, hairdressers, cleaners, ski schools, etc.)
- Competitive producers (e.g. construction industry, restoration work, etc.)
- Vocational training
- Policing
- Health care.

Market structure, rivalry, organization and strategy

The key element of this determinant is the availability of a tourism strategic plan supported by all parties involved, both public and private sector. However, this determinant involves many more aspects, including:

- A strategic tourism plan (including physical planning)
- The marketing of a destination
- An organizational structure
- A market structure with an impact on competition
- The firm size
- Cooperation among SMEs
- Public–private partnership
- Important coordinators (e.g. national air carriers such as KLM)
- Quality management (at the level of the destination as well as at the level of the individual firm)
- Destination management (e.g. information system, reservation centre)
- Image building
- Building strategic alliances.

Local government

In the prevailing economic system, tourism policy without the involvement of the public sector is not very realistic. Unfortunately, tourism policy is too often identified with public authorities. The definition of the determinants in a tourism cluster will have shown that a successful competitive policy depends on the involvement of both public and private sectors. Nevertheless, some specific public actions can stimulate or impede tourism development – for example, the hotel-stop regulation in Bruges, implementation of visitor management, traffic planning, taxation, etc.

This model can be considered as an instrument to analyse the competitive situation of a destination. It has been applied successfully in Barcelona, Bruges, Ibiza and Madrid, and probably in several other destinations. Tables 5.2 and 5.3 illustrate such an application for Bruges (Vanhove, 2002).

Table 5.2 Strengths with respect to competitiveness – the case of Bruges, 2002

Determinant	Strengths
Factor conditions	■ product policy ■ cultural patrimony ■ historic town centre recognized as UNESCO world heritage site ■ interesting museums ■ good hotel accommodation ■ price policy and price level ■ geographical location in Europe ■ language knowledge ■ small-scale atmosphere ■ professional reception infrastructure for tourists ■ security
Demand conditions	■ market size and growth potential ■ many international visitors ■ no dominance of organized group travel
Related and supporting activities	■ accessibility ■ parking facilities ■ shopping facilities ■ typical souvenirs ■ gastronomy and good food in general ■ hotel schools
Market structure, rivalry, organization and strategy	■ well-organized hotel sector, 'vzw hotels Brugge' ■ alliance between art cities in Flanders
Local government	■ Bruges: cultural capital of Europe in 2002

Table 5.3 Weaknesses or points for improvement with respect to competitiveness – the case of Bruges, 2002

Determinant	Weaknesses or points for improvement
Factor conditions	■ inadequate MICE infrastructure ■ international hotel chains (brands) ■ more active cultural experience required ■ evening activities and the hinterland as a support
Demand conditions	■ attitude of local population (a minority) towards tourism
Related and supporting activities	■ TGV connection to Lille ■ lack of a national air carrier as coordinator ■ risk of degrading quality level (prices) of services (e.g. some taxi drivers and restaurant keepers)
Market structure, rivalry, organization and strategy	■ no strategic planning (one in preparation) ■ low communication budget ■ lack of a quality plan ■ no destination management information system ■ public–private partnership ■ insufficient joining with international hotel networks
Local government	■ hotel stop

The Poon concept

Poon (1993) emphasizes the changes in tourism when she compares new tourism (flexible, segmented, diagonally-integrated, environmentally-conscious) with old tourism (mass, standardized and rigidly packaged) with respect to consumers, management, technology, production and frame conditions. For her, new tourism changes the rules of the game and calls for new strategies to ensure competitive success (Poon, 1993):

> The more rapid the changes in the firm's environment, the more important becomes strategy formulation and implementation. The travel and tourism industry is undergoing rapid and radical transformation. Therefore, competitive strategies are more important than ever for the survival and competitiveness of industry players.

Poon is rather critical with respect to Porter's generic competitive strategies. These generic strategies, although relevant, are, for her, inadequate tools to explore competitive success for tourism players. Porter's analysis is, according to Poon, more applicable to the manufacturing sector than to services. Furthermore, his strategies are more appropriate in a static environment and during the maturity stage of a product. Poon's central thesis is that 'Innovation – introduction of new products – is far more important than low cost, differentiation or focus'. We can understand this statement to a certain extent, but it is not true to say that Porter neglects the innovation factor. In his book *The Competitive Advantage of Nations* (1990), and more particularly in the chapter about determinants of national competitive advantage, he makes a distinction (with respect to factor conditions) between generalized factors and advanced and specialized factors:

> The most significant and sustainable advantage results when a nation possesses factors needed for competing in a particular industry that are both advanced and specialised. The availability and quality of advanced and specialised factors determine the sophistication of competitive advantage that can potentially be achieved and its rate of upgrading. In contrast, competitive advantage based on basic/generalised factors is unsophisticated and often fleeting.

There are also well known examples in tourism of successful applications of the generic strategies.

The Poon concept of competitive strategy has two dimensions: a micro- and a macro-level. She deals with 'competitive strategies for industry players' and 'strategies for tourism destinations'.

Competitive strategies for industry players

New tourism changes the rules of the game in the industry and calls for new strategies to ensure competitive success. The author has identified four key principles of competitive success, and for each there are a number of strategies (see Table 5.4).

Table 5.4 Competitive strategies for industry players

Principles	Strategies
Put consumer first	■ link marketing with product development ■ satisfy the consumer ■ develop a holistic approach to the holiday experience
Be a leader in quality	■ develop human resources ■ improve process continuously ■ use technology creatively
Develop radical innovations	■ don't be afraid of new ideas ■ never stop learning ■ build a capacity for continuous innovation
Strengthen your strategic position	■ seek an advantageous position in the value chain ■ integrate diagonally ■ influence the competitive environment

Source: Adapted from Poon (1993).

Some of these principles and associated strategies need further explanation, and here we emphasize five topics. The first relates to the holistic approach. A holiday experience is much more than the bed-nights at a hotel or apartment. It begins on arrival. The actions of immigration officers or customs and the attitude of taxi-drivers are all part of the holiday experience. At the destination, other critical factors in the holiday experience include the food, the behaviour of the police, the beggars on city streets, dirty streets, harassment of tourists on the beach or in restaurants, and so many other factors. Poon states that the success of certain holiday providers – Disneyland, SuperClubs, Sandals, Center Parcs – is because they have taken a holistic approach to the holiday experience.

Secondly, Poon claims that 'quality' will be the most significant factor for competitive success among industry players. Tourists want quality, flexibility and value for money. Therefore, creative recruitment of personal, the empowering of the front line, investment in education and motivation are very important.

Thirdly, radical innovation is a little bit misleading. It is not possible to develop a new holiday concept each year, but it is possible, at regular intervals, to consider exploring new markets, providing new services, developing new processes, developing a culture for innovation and encouraging new ideas.

Fourthly, what does it mean to seek an advantageous position in the value chain? A value chain is an analytical tool developed for tracing the process of value creation in an industry (Porter, 1987). The value chain can be thought of as all the interconnecting operations that make up the whole consumer experience of a product. Poon applies it to the tourism industry to provide insights into how the industry creates value. A distinction is made between primary and support activities. The primary activities in tourism consist of:

■ Transportation (e.g. baggage handling; yield management)
■ On-site services (e.g. airport transfers; tours)
■ Wholesale/packaging
■ Marketing and sales
■ Retail distribution
■ Customer service (e.g. complaint management).

Support activities for the tourism industry are very similar to those in other industries:

- Firm infrastructure (e.g. franchise and management contracts, finance; strategic alliances)
- Human-resource development (e.g. recruitment)
- Product and services development
- Technology and systems development (e.g. systems of payment; database development; access to CRSs)
- Procurement of goods and services.

According to the author, two basic principles are necessary in order to gain an advantageous position in the value chain. There is the need to influence the process of wealth creation, and also to build strategic alliances. The former requires control over two key agents: information (wealth is created through a number of information-driven activities) and consumers (getting close to the consumers and understanding them).

A final topic of great importance, and directly related to the value chain, is diagonal integration. The objective of diagonal integration is to produce a range of services (e.g. transport, insurance, holiday and personal banking) and sell them to consumers. Firms become involved in closely related activities to reduce costs and to get nearer to their consumers. Ownership may not be necessary, unlike in horizontal or vertical integration.

One of the key attractions for firms in diagonally integrating is the lower costs of production. This becomes possible through economies of scope, synergies and system gains. Economies of scope refers to lower costs associated with the joint provision of more than one product or service, rather than producing each separately. Economies of scope do not accrue from scale, but from variety. The joint provision of hotel rooms and car rentals is a good example. The cost for a hotel-keeper of adding the provision of car rentals to hotel rooms will be cheaper than two companies producing car rental services and hotel rooms separately.

Synergies are benefits that follow from the operation of interrelated activities, where each activity can generate benefits that reinforce other activities. As such, synergies can create scope economies. Thus it is possible for an air carrier to create synergy by linking its credit card to its frequent flyer programme – for example, for every euro spent on its credit card, users can earn a free mile on the frequent flyer programme.

'Systems gains' refers to economies derived from creating and engineering linkages between different activities. A bank can use its databank of customers and corresponding mailing list to market tourism products.

Strategies for tourism destinations

The second dimension of Poon's concept of competitive strategy is at the macro- or destination level. The issue is not whether to develop tourism, but rather how to develop the sector in such a way that the destination benefits. Points related to this thesis include how to use tourism to generate other sectors, how to limit tourism's negative social and cultural impacts, and how to build a dynamic private sector.

Table 5.5 Strategies for tourism destination

Principles	Strategies
Put the environment first	■ build responsible tourism ■ foster a culture of conservation ■ develop an environmental focus
Make tourism a lead sector	■ develop tourism's 'axial' potential ■ adapt strategies of development ■ develop the service sector
Strengthen distribution channels in the marketplace	■ ensure adequate air access ■ transform the role of NTOs in the marketplace ■ focus on product development at home
Build a dynamic private sector	■ don't be afraid of new tourism ■ let quality be the guide ■ build public/private sector cooperation

Source: Adapted from Poon (1993).

Similarly way to the competitive strategies for tourism players, Poon identifies four strategies that tourism destinations need in order to enhance the development of a new and sustainable tourism. The basic strategies with respect to destinations are shown in Table 5.5.

Let us focus on some of these strategies.

First, so far not all countries and destinations have respected the principle of responsible tourism. Capacity control is still an exception (as, for example, in Bermuda and The Seychelles), and comprehensive planning is not yet the rule in tourism destinations (WTO, 1992; Bosselman *et al.*, 1999). Fortunately, there are more and more examples of visitor management.

Secondly, making tourism a leading sector deserves special attention. Indeed, tourism can activate a lot of services and activities, such as car rental, food, crafts, souvenirs, construction, incoming tour operating, etc. Special attention should be paid to avoid leakages. In many destinations, local vegetable production or fruit growing can replace imported products on condition that the local producers can assure a regular supply, with the necessary quality and without too many price variations. Local architecture and local products can enhance authenticity. The implementation of the Nusa Dua project in Bali (Indonesia) is a successful illustration. A good example of manufacturing as a function of tourism is the production of fashion clothing in Togo, where the local garments are not only sold to tourists but their design and quality is also adapted to the European market so that they are sold in Paris with great success. The stimulation of authentic souvenirs can be a source of income for hundreds of families and small enterprises. Good examples include Bali, with woodcarving, stone carving, paintings and jewellery; Bruges, with lace and chocolates; the 'santons' in Aix-en-Provence, and china-works in China.

Thirdly, the plea for a transformation of the role of National (Regional) Tourist Offices from promotion to product development deserves attention.

Fourthly, public–private partnership at destination level is a necessity if an effective tourism policy is to be achieved, to encourage all efforts in the same direction and gather together the necessary financial means to implement a strategic marketing plan.

Last but not least, and also at destination level, quality management is considered to be a basic strategy. Governments must take steps to establish and enforce standards and to stimulate quality planning at the destination level.

The WES approach

The WES approach originated in a demand by the Inter-American Development Bank for the analysis of the competitive positions of a number of countries in the Caribbean area. Special attention was given to explaining the differences in the competitive positions of these Caribbean destinations and to formulating how to improve these positions. Long-term competitiveness was the focus. 'Competitiveness' was defined as a destination's capacity to reach its objectives in the long run in a more efficient way than the international or regional average. This means that a competitive destination is able to realize a higher profitability than the average, with low social costs and without damaging the environment and available resources.

From the beginning, a clear distinction was made between indicators of competitive performance, and factors that contribute to competitiveness. The former are historic measures that describe how a destination has performed in the past (e.g. international arrivals, tourist nights, accommodation capacity and occupancy rates, tourism receipts). For most of these indicators, market shares can be derived. The latter are capabilities or conditions that it is believed will contribute to or detract from the ability of a destination to be competitive in the future. The WES approach reveals a number of decisive factors of competitiveness, and these are summarized in Table 5.6.

Typical of the WES approach is the attention paid to macro-economic factors. Application of multiple regression analysis shows the impact of the income factor on the generating markets and the real exchange rate. The purchasing power indicator of generating country X against receiving country Y is defined as:

$$(\textit{Exchange rate currency X in currency units Y}) \left[\frac{\text{CPI country X}}{\text{CPI country Y}} \right] \quad (5.1)$$

where the first term is equal to the US\$ exchange rate in the currency of receiving country Y divided by the US\$ exchange rate in the currency of generating country X. (CPI stands for consumer price index).

Countries like the Bahamas and Barbados were found to be too expensive due to an over-valued currency. Fiscal policies in a number of Caribbean destinations were tourism-unfriendly. Heavy taxes on tourism necessary raw materials had a very detrimental effect. Countries that considered tourism as a milk machine were working against their own interests.

A second relevant factor – for the Caribbean – related to industrial relations. In the more traditional tourism countries of the Caribbean area, these relations were not good and were responsible for low room occupancy rates in hotels.

Another relevant factor in the competitiveness of different countries was the presence or absence of a destination management or tourism policy in general.

Table 5.6 Factors affecting the competitive position

Factors	Variables

Macro-economic factors	■ Income-generating countries
	■ Real exchange rate
	■ Availability and cost of capital
	■ Fiscal policy
	  – import taxes
	  – cost price increasing taxes
	  – taxes on profit
	  – tourism tax
	  – cruise tax

Supply factors	■ Tourist product
	  – attractions
	  – accommodation
	  – price level
	■ Labour
	  – availability
	  – cost
	  – quality and training
	■ Infrastructure
	  – transport
	  – public utilities

Transport factors	■ Availability of regular services ■ Availability of charter services ■ Availability of cruise services
Demand factors	■ Market dependence ■ Penetration in distribution channels ■ Marketing efforts ■ Presence in future growth product markets
Tourism policy	■ Institutional framework ■ Policy formulation ■ Planning capacity ■ Commercialization ■ Government budgetary support

Source: WES (1993).

Based on extensive research with American and European tour operators, it became evident that not all destinations had the ability to or were prepared to respond to future growth products such as adventure tourism, eco-tourism and all-inclusive accommodation.

The price-competitiveness approach

The preceding sections may give the impression that price is an irrelevant factor with respect to competitiveness. Most models neglect or minimize factor price.

In Chapter 1 of this book we saw that price-elasticity cannot be overlooked. This is also the policy of Dwyer *et al.* (2000) when they state that 'changing costs in particular destinations relative to others, adjusted for exchange rate variations, are regarded as the most important economic influence on destination shares of total travel abroad'. Edwards (1995) also emphasizes the role of factor price when he maintains that a fall in relative cost is linked to a rise in market share. Dwyer *et al.* (2000) define destination competitiveness as: 'a general concept that encompasses price differentials coupled with exchange rate movements, productivity levels of various components of the tourist industry, and qualitative factors affecting the attractiveness or otherwise of destination'. Consequently these authors consider two other groups of factors besides price:

1. Socio-economic and demographic factors
2. Qualitative factors.

The latter category comprises variables such as tourist appeal, image, quality of tourist services, destination marketing and promotion, cultural ties, etc.

Price factors (which affect the cost of tourism to the visitor) include the cost of transport services to and from the destination and the cost of ground content. The price factor is calculated using a series of steps:

■ Step 1: choose origin countries or generating markets
■ Step 2: choose destination markets or competitors
■ Step 3: assess expenditure pattern of tourists from different origin markets (only products and services consumed by tourists)
■ Step 4: compile relevant price data (the authors made use of the World Bank's International Comparison Programme, ICP)
■ Step 5: calculate purchasing power parities (PPP) for tourism expenditure (PPPs indicate the levels of expenditure required in different destinations to purchase the same basket of tourism goods and services)
■ Step 6: adjust PPPs by exchange rates to derive price competitiveness indices (PII).

$$Price\ competitive\ index = \frac{exchange\ rate}{PPP} \times \frac{100}{1} \qquad (5.2)$$

Let us take a practical case to interpret the price competitive index. A Japanese tourist considers Australia and France as possible destinations. A basket of goods and services consumed by a typical Japanese tourist in Australia would cost AU\$1000, but the same would cost €840 in France. The exchange rate between AU\$ and € is AU\$1 = €0.60. In this case, the price competitive index equals (0.60/0.84)100 = 71.42 – thus France is about 28.5 per cent more expensive regarding the ground component than Australia for the Japanese tourist. However, for the travel component France is 4 per cent cheaper. A similar exercise for some other destinations is illustrated in Table 5.7, and this reveals very great differences between the price levels for the different destinations – for both ground and travel components. An index of less than 100 indicates that the particular destination is less competitive than Australia with respect to the Japanese market.

These are valuable indicators, but the PII cannot be taken as the only important competitiveness factor. A visit to Australia cannot be compared with one to Italy, which offers a completely different experience. As Dwyer *et al.* are aware;

Table 5.7 Price competitive indices for various destinations, 1997 (Australia = 100; origin country Japan)

Country	Ground component	Travel component	Ground + travel component
New Zealand	95.6	83.1	88.5
USA	85.6	120.2	99.7
Italy	89.1	97.3	93.3
UK	73.6	102.2	86.2
Spain	100.7	75.3	84.4
Turkey	180.2	86.5	115.4
China	366.6	297.4	292.1
Thailand	385.6	229.5	325.6

Source: Adapted from Dwyer *et al.* (2000).

overall competitiveness is determined by both price and non-price factors. However, PPIs can be relevant in comparing identical products. They do have limitations, and the authors of the model cite several:

- Accuracy of data collection
- Comparison of airfares
- Differences of accommodation
- Prices can vary between regions in the same country
- One country can be expensive for one tourism product but far less expensive for another.

The Bordas model

The Bordas model was originally presented at the AIEST Congress in Argentina in 1993, and was further developed at the TRC meeting in Swansea in 1994. It is a typical demand (marketing) model, and does not fit into the general concept of competitiveness. Furthermore, this model was conceived for long-haul destinations, the central theme of the Bariloche AIEST Congress. It should be noted here that the model is not tested for any causal relationship, and several retained explanatory variables are difficult to express in quantitative units.

The basic relationships retained in the model are illustrated in Figure 5.4, where:

D   = long haul demand from market n to destination i
PD   = primary demand or consumers from market n interested in and preference for destination i
PC   = perceived costs
PSS = performance of sales system of destination i in market n
O   = other variables
SD   = secondary demand or consumers in market n with interest in destination i but without any preference
NDM = consumer needs, desires and motivations (perception of benefits are very important)

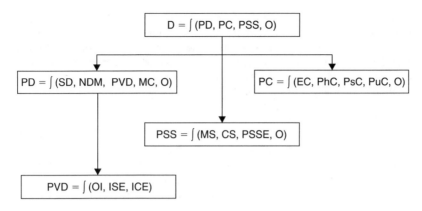

Figure 5.4 Basic relations in the Bordas model

PVD = perception of destination i by the consumers (consumer should be able to perceive the benefits)

MC = magnetism of competitors (capacity of competitors to transform SD into PD)

OI = organic image or image of destination i among the consumers who make up the SD and based on received general (very often non-tourism) information from various sources (e.g. mass media)

ISE = information from social environment (relatives and friends)

ICE = information from the trade and communication network (e.g. ads, brochures)

EC = economic/monetary cost (transportation, costs at the spot)

PhC = physical cost (tiredness and stress)

PsC = psychological cost (commercial and physical risk)

PuC = purchasing costs or cost to get access to information and to the trade)

MS = magnetism of the sales system (capacity of the sales system to create interest in the destination and capability to attract customers)

CS = conductivity of the system or the capacity to close a sale (which percentage of customers who were in contact with the sales system, decided to buy the destination)

PSSE = post-sale service efficiency (creating loyalty and recommendation).

In this marketing model for long-haul destinations there are two key elements. The first is the 'perceived value' of the destination, where image is the central point. The authentic benefits should be well known. Bordas distinguishes three types of benefits: functional, symbolic (very often associated with the need for self-esteem and belonging) and existential benefits (associated with the need for personal fulfilment, knowledge and belonging). Potential tourists have an image of the destination, and very often the image has been created independently of any tourism activity. If there is a bad image, it is difficult to change it. Tourism promotion will in most cases not be successful in changing an existing image. Only an improvement in the supply side and the creation of new and/or upgraded products can be helpful.

The second element is the 'perceived cost'. This has several facets: the economic costs, the physical effort, the psychological costs, and the difficulties in gaining access to information and what Bordas calls the sales system. The further the destination is from home, the greater the uncertainty about travel and living costs, the higher the physical cost of travel (waiting time in airports, stress, jet-lag, immobility in the aircraft, etc.), and the more significant the psychological cost (hygiene, health care and risks of all kinds). A lot can be done to reduce these costs and to enhance the competitiveness of the destination. There should be a combined effort by the tourist authority, immigration control, air carrier and others to reduce the perceived costs.

There are three important drawbacks to this model. First, it is a one-sided model – i.e. only demand-oriented. Secondly, the model is still a gross concept without any test. The use of 'other factors' in several components of the model illustrates the trial phase. Thirdly, some variables are difficult to measure. Nevertheless, the model emphasizes a number of factors neglected or underestimated in other approaches.

The Ritchie and Crouch conceptual model of destination competitiveness

The most comprehensive model is without doubt the Ritchie and Crouch model. The first test took place on the occasion of the AIEST Congress in Bariloche (AIEST, 1993), where Congress participants were members of a panel. Over the past 10 years the concept has been improved and elaborated, and has led to the publication of an interesting handbook, *The Competitive Destination* (Ritchie and Crouch, 2003). The cornerstone of the publication is the conceptual model of destination competitiveness (see Figure 5.5). It is a device that provides a useful way of thinking about a complex issue.

The authors envisage three main uses of the model:

1. As a communication tool – a lexicon for understanding, diagnosing and discussing a destination's competitiveness
2. As a framework for management in order to avoid overlooking potentially important factors
3. As an instrument for a destination audit.

Comparative and competitive advantage

The starting point of the model is the thesis that destination success is determined by two different kinds of advantages: *comparative* and *competitive*. Comparative advantages reflect the resource endowments of the destination, provided either by nature or by the overall society within which the destination resides (human, physical, historical and cultural resources; knowledge; capital; infrastructure; and tourism superstructure). Competitive advantages are those that have been established as a result of effective resource deployment (maintenance, growth and development, efficiency, effectiveness and audit) – in other words, how well the destination utilizes the available resources, or the destination's ability to add value to the available resources.

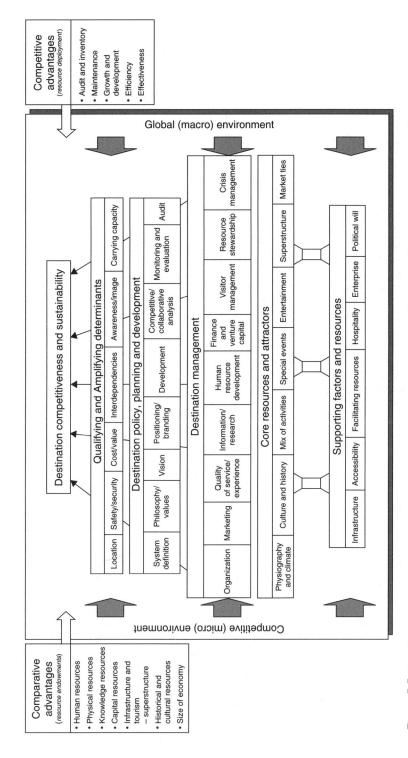

Figure 5.5 The Ritchie and Crouch conceptual model of destination competitiveness (source: *The Competitive Destination. A Sustainable Tourism Perspective*, by J.R.B. Ritchie and G. Crouch (2003), published by CABI Publishing and reproduced with kind permission)

However, for Ritchie and Crouch comparative advantage and competitive advantage are generic concepts. Greater depth is necessary. What do these concepts mean in the context of a tourist destination? So that the model would be managerially useful, they further examined the categories or components that constitute resource endowments and resource deployments in order to understand how these constructs are best made operational to determine destination competitiveness.

The components of the model

The components of the model are:

- The global (macro-) environment
- The competitive (micro-) environment
- Core resources and attractors
- Supporting factors and resources
- Destination policy, planning and development
- Destination management
- Qualifying and amplifying determinants.

Destination policy, planning and development (DPPD) and destination management (DM) can be considered as the two core components, and these will be discussed separately.

The global (macro-) environment recognizes that tourism is an open system. It is subject to many influences and pressures that arise outside the system itself. Some of them were discussed in Chapter 3. The eight global forces shaping world tourism are:

1. Economic
2. Climatic
3. Geographical
4. Environmental
5. Demographic
6. Social and cultural
7. Technological
8. Political.

All these forces create threats and opportunities. A destination manager should be aware of these challenges and opportunities and try, together with the sector, to formulate the right policy.

The competitive (micro-) environment is part of the tourism system; it concerns the actions and activities of entities in the tourism system that affect the goals of each member of the system (companies and organizations). How is destination competitiveness affected by the way in which the tourism system functions? The components are:

1. Suppliers (who supply the sector with basic factor inputs, e.g. labour, food and beverages, energy)
2. Tourism enterprises

3. Intermediaries (e.g. trade, trade shows) and facilitators (e.g. credit cards, market research consultants)
4. Customers
5. Competing destinations
6. Destination management organizations
7. Related and supporting industries (e.g. theatres, shopping facilities)
8. Other stakeholders.

An important conclusion is that there is an association between domestic rivalry among tourism enterprises (which produce the core commercial services) and the creation and persistence of competitive advantage (see also Porter, 1990).

Core resources and attractors describe the essence of the destination appeal, or the pulling force. It is these factors that are the key motivators to visit a destination. Ritchie and Crouch distinguish seven categories:

1. Physiography and climate (e.g. scenery, wildlife, beach)
2. Culture and history
3. A broad range of activities
4. Special events
5. Types of entertainment (e.g. Broadway shows in New York)
6. Superstructure (e.g. the cathedral of La Sagrada Família in Barcelona, although it was built in another era for religious reasons)
7. Market ties (e.g. religion, ethnic roots).

Most of these attractors speak for themselves. Nevertheless, the local destination management organization can do a lot to enhance the attractiveness of each of these categories and so increase the competitiveness of the destination. Indeed, competitive advantage relates to a destination's ability to employ the attractions effectively over the long term. Russia has many attractions, but is not successful in developing tourism activities. Ritchie and Crouch make an important point with respect to the factor activities:

> The real reason for visiting a destination is to do things – to actively
> participate in activities that stimulate for the moment, and then to leave
> as a participant who has vibrant memories of what he or she has done. In
> seeking to make a destination attractive and competitive, it is essential to
> ensure that it offers a broad range of activities, of memorable things to do.

Supporting factors and resources support or provide a foundation upon which a successful tourism industry can be established. This category contains elements that enhance the destination appeal. Their absence or insufficiency will be a constraint for the destination to pull tourists. The model refers to six groups:

1. Infrastructure
2. Accessibility (e.g. visas, airline access)
3. Facilitating resources (human and financial resources)
4. Hospitality (e.g. resident attitudes)
5. Enterprise (tourism enterprise contributes to destination development)
6. Political will (allocation of scarce resources).

The qualifying and amplifying determinants are described as factors of competitiveness that either moderate, modify, mitigate and filter or strengthen, enhance and augment the impact of all other factors, DPPD and DM included. They are situational conditioners on which a destination has no or little influence. However, destinations with an eye on these conditioners will be more likely to act proactively; they can foresee opportunities and threats.

Which are these qualifying and amplifying determinants for Ritchie and Crouch? They mention six situational conditioners:

1. Location
2. Destination safety
3. Destination cost level (a destination has not much influence on costs)
4. Destination interdependencies – synergistic or adversarial
5. Destination image (strong images are hard to develop and even harder to change, once formed)
6. Carrying capacity (the upper limit to the volume of demand a destination can handle).

Success factors: destination policy, planning and development, and destination management

Destination policy, planning and development (DPPD) and destination management (DM) are the other two categories of the model. In the framework of resource deployment and modern management of a region or destination, they might be considered as the key categories.

What do the authors have in mind when they talk about DPPD and DM?

> DPPD is essentially an intellectual process that uses information, judgement and monitoring to make macro-level decisions regarding the kind of destination that is desirable, the degree to which ongoing performance and related changes in the nature of visitation and the physical character of the destination are contributing to the achievement of the kind of destination that stakeholders want ... DM is more a micro-level activity in which all the stakeholders carry out their individual and organizational responsibilities on a daily basis in efforts to realize the macro-level vision contained in policy, planning and development.
>
> (Ritchie and Crouch, 2003)

A highly competitive destination does not exist by chance. It requires a well-planned environment within which the appropriate forms of tourism development are encouraged and facilitated. Tourism policy is the key to providing this environment – but what should be understood by tourism policy? According to Goeldner *et al.* (2000), it is 'A set of regulations, rules, guidelines, directives, and development/promotion objectives and strategies that provide a framework within which the collective and individual decisions directly affecting tourism development and the daily activities within a destination are taken'.

Contemporary tourism policy focuses on competitiveness and sustainability, which are also the major parameters of tourism destination management (TDM).

Successful TDM involves economic/business management skills balanced with environmental management capabilities. Economic/business skills are those related to effective resource development and deployment. Goeldner *et al.* (2000) refer to:

- Strategic planning
- The marketing of the destination
- Financial management
- Operations management
- Human resources management
- Information management
- Organization management.

Environmental management capabilities are those that are critical to effective destination stewardship, and include:

- Water quality management
- Air quality management
- Wildlife management
- Forest/plant management
- Visitor management
- Resident/community management
- Commemorative integrity.

Strategic planning is the cornerstone of DPPD. For destination purposes, strategic planning may be defined as the process whereby an organization analyses the strengths and weaknesses with respect to the supply development and demand development, decides the position it seeks to attain, and defines strategies and programmes of activity to achieve the aims (Morrison, 1989; Goeldner *et al.*, 2000). It describes the process of developing long-term plans for tourism development and marketing. It should provide a common structure and focus for all of the destination's management activities.

In a strategic planning process, there are three basic questions (see Figure 5.6):

1. Where are we now?
2. Where do we want to be in 5–10 years' time?
3. How do we get there?

There are also three concepts:

1. Mission, goals and objectives
2. Strategies
3. Projects, plans and programmes.

This scheme and also the used terminology is different from the Ritchie–Crouch presentation. However, the basic philosophy is the same.

The starting point of the planning process is a situation analysis of the present supply and market/marketing. Within the situation analysis there are two components: internal and external analysis. The elements from the above mentioned

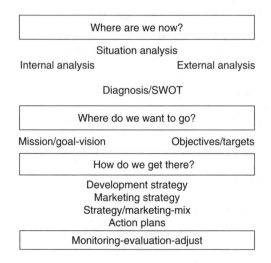

Figure 5.6 Basic questions and concepts of strategic planning

components 'micro-environment' and 'global macro-environment' provide an excellent starting point. A careful assessment (or explanation of the present situation) of the internal and external analysis leads to a SWOT analysis (Strengths, Weaknesses, Opportunities and Threats).

The first basic concept is the mission or vision or goal (not everybody considers these terms to be synonyms). Young (1966) states that this 'is a value to be sought after, not an object to be achieved'. It is a guide for all parties as to what the purpose of the organization is. The mission statement acts as a confirmation of what business the destination is in, from both supplier and consumer viewpoints. The mission statement for Belgian macro-tourism products can serve as an illustration: 'To realize a contribution to the economic development of the destinations by a rational use of the tourist production factors, and satisfy the leisure needs of the tourists with respect to the environment and the well-being of the local population'.

Next we consider the 'objective' or 'vision' as a strategic goal. With respect to destinations, there are two types of objectives. The first is objectives for regional tourism development. These objectives can take different forms, such as employment creation, better use of present supply, extension of the supply, greater revenue creation through quality improvement of the supply, diversification of the local economy, protection of natural resources, etc. The second is marketing objectives. These could include more arrivals, longer stay-overs, higher expenditure per man-day, staggering of the demand, or diversification of markets. Targets are operational objectives, and are expressed in quantitative terms (e.g. an increase of value added of 20 per cent in the next five years).

Strategy is the next basic concept. Strategy can be considered as the road to be followed to fill the gap between where we are now, and where we want to go.

With respect to regional development in general, there are several dimensions to enhance development (Vanhove, 1999). Tourism as a sector is one of these dimensions; the application of the Porter model is another. Human resources development and the stimulation of entrepreneurship are two other roads that can be followed. Physical and financial resources policies are also part of tourism destination development strategies.

Marketing strategy should in the first place be concentrated on seven core strategies:

1. Tourism scope (e.g. holidaymakers or excursionists; winter and/or summer holidays)
2. Market choice based on objective criteria
3. Formulation of product–market combinations
4. Segmentation and the choice of target markets
5. Positioning and the development of a destination brand (Crouch and Ritchie, 2004)
6. Alliances with other organizations and/or competitors
7. Communication.

We also need a strategy with respect to policy instruments. Goeldner *et al.* (2000) refer in the first place to the secondary components of tourism demand policy, or what is traditionally called the marketing mix or operational marketing: product policy, price policy, distribution policy and promotion policy. However, there are more policy instruments, such as research, training, finance and, last but not least, the macro-management organizational structure. Many of these elements belong to the action programmes.

Strategies without action programmes and implementation plans lead to a dead end. What are the facilities required to realize the strategy? Which events could support the vision? Which programmes could be encouraged (e.g. entrepreneurship programme, cultural programme, winter destination programme, etc.)?

The final stage of tourism strategic planning includes the monitoring, steering and evaluation of all the different phases of the strategic plan, and last but not least, the destination audit.

Destination management

The DPPD component creates the framework for a competitive destination. The destination management component of the Ritchie–Crouch model focuses on those activities that implement the tasks prescribed by the DPPD. As such, it seeks to enhance the appeal of the core resources, strengthen the quality and effectiveness of the supplying factors and resources, and adapt best to the constraints or opportunities imposed or presented by the qualifying and amplifying determinants.

In the model, destination management consists of nine components, each of which consists of individual destination managerial tasks that must be carefully attended to by the destination manager. They are:

1. Organization (administrative and managerial tasks)
2. Marketing (traditional marketing tasks)
3. Quality of service experiences (the destination should provide a high-quality visitor experience)
4. Information/research

5. Human resource development
6. Finance and venture capital
7. Visitor management (e.g. visitor information centre, ability to deal with crowds)
8. Resource stewardship (taking care of the tourism resource base)
9. Crisis management.

These components are all highly interdependent, and it is not obvious which should be considered first. If there is one component that must be realized before the others, it is organization – in other words, the setting up of a destination management organization (DMO). In most countries there is the need for DMOs at national, regional and local levels. For the major components of organizational development and policy, we refer to Chapter 8 of Ritchie and Crouch (2003). Tourism policy broadly defines the roles of the DMO. The latter should be functional from both strategic and operational perspectives. Ritchie and Crouch emphasize leadership and coordination as essential features of a DMO.

The other components of destination management speak for themselves. It is important to notice that the DMO should not try to carry out all these management functions itself, but should keep an overall eye on the situation.

Synthesis of the main variables

Needless to say, the analysed competition models are of a different nature. The starting point and/or the line of approach is not the same. However, each of them has the merit of emphasizing one or more particular aspects:

- The Porter (1980) model emphasizes the competitive forces of enterprises and (to a lesser extent) of destinations, and the related generic competitive strategies
- The Porter (1990) model emphasizes the home environment and related determinants
- The Poon concept emphasizes innovation, quality and making tourism a lead sector
- The WES approach emphasizes macro-economic factors and tourism policy
- The Dwyer *et al.* approach emphasizes the price component
- The Bordas approach emphasizes marketing orientation, perceived value and perceived costs
- The Ritchie and Crouch model emphasizes destination policy, planning and development, and destination management.

In order to cope with this oversimplification, the major competition variables and characteristics are summarized in a comparative table (see Table 5.8). The valuation is based on a personal interpretation of the different models. From this Table, we can draw three important conclusions:

1. Competitiveness of a destination is not a matter of just one or two factors; tourism is a complex issue, and many factors are involved. This conclusion should not be considered as a criticism of the Dwyer *et al.* approach. These

Table 5.8 The major competition variables by model

Variable/characteristic	Porter (1980)	Porter (1990)	Poon	WES	Dwyer et al.	Bordas	Ritchie–Crouch
Comparative advantage	−	+	+	+	−	−	++
Tourism policy	−	+	+	++	−	−	++
Strategic planning	++	++	+	+	−	−	++
Demand factors	−	++	−	++	−	++	+
Supply factors	−	++	−	++	−	−	++
Price	++	+	−	++	++	++	+
Innovation	−	++	++	−	−	−	+
Macro-economic factors	−	−	−	++	+	−	+
Exchange rate	−	−	−	++	++	−	−
Axis of development	+	−	++	−	−	−	+
Accessibility	−	+	++	++	−	−	++
Marketing	−	+	+	+	−	++	+
Image	−	−	−	−	−	++	++
Quality	−	++	++	+	+	−	+
Strategic alliance	−	+	++	−	−	−	+
Attractions	−	+	−	+	−	−	++
Supplying and supporting factors	−	++	+	−	−	−	++
Promotion	−	−	−	+	−	+	+
Human resources	−	+	++	+	−	−	++
Environment	−	−	++	−	−	−	++
Destination management	−	+	−	+	−	−	++
Qualifying and amplifying fact	−	−	−	−	−	−	++
Audit	−	−	−	−	−	−	++
Entrepreneur-oriented	++	−	++	−	−	−	−
Destination-oriented	−	++	++	++	−	++	++

+, important; ++, very important.

authors have tried to show the great price discrepancy between destinations and how to measure the differences in tourism purchasing power. They also recognize the role of productivity levels of various components of the tourism industry and qualitative factors affecting the attractiveness of a destination.

2. The Ritchie–Crouch concept is by far the most comprehensive model, but the Porter (1990) and WES models also contain a great variety of components. Poon's concept is based on a large number of factors, but focuses more on typical factors such as innovation, quality and the role of tourism in the development of a destination, region or country.

3. The Ritchie–Crouch, Porter and WES models have one common denominator. All emphasize strategic planning (tourism policy), attractions, supply and demand factors, and accessibility.

Meanwhile, Dwyer and Kim (2004) have developed a new model – the integrated model of destination competitiveness – which contains many of the variables identified by Ritchie and Crouch. Although this publication is not yet available, we can find the basic ideas in Dwyer *et al.* (2004) with an application of the model to Australia and Korea. The key elements of their model are:

- Core resources and supporting factors (core resources are subdivided into two categories, endowed and created, and the supporting factors relate to general infrastructure, quality of service, accessibility etc.)
- Destination management factors (public sector and private sector activities)
- Demand conditions, the three main elements being awareness, perception and preferences
- Situational conditions (economic, social, cultural, political, legal, etc.; which can be compared to the qualifying and amplifying determinants of Ritchie and Crouch).

References and further reading

Aguilo, P., Alegre, J. and Riera, A. (2001). Determinants of the price of German tourist packages on the island of Mallorca. *Tourism Economics*, 1.

AIEST (1993). *Competitiveness of Long-haul Tourist Destinations*, 43rd AIEST Congress, Bariloche. St-Gall: AIEST.

Bordas, E. (1994). *Competitiveness of Tourist Destinations in Long-distance Markets*. Paper presented at TRC Meeting, Swansea, 1994 (unpublished).

Bordas, E. (1996). *Ibiza Competitiveness Reinforcement Plan for Tourism Business*. Paper presented at the 31st TRC Meeting, Bergen, 1996 (unpublished).

Bosselman, F., Peterson, C. and McCarthy, Cl. (1999). *Managing Tourism Growth*. Washington: Island Press.

Brackenbury, B. (1993). The competitiveness of long-haul destinations – the tour operator's point of view. *Competitiveness of Long-haul Tourist Destinations*, 43rd AIEST Congress, Bariloche. St-Gall: AIEST.

Buhalis, D. (2000). Marketing the competitive destination of the future. *Tourism Management*, 21.

Cooper, C. Fayos-Solà, E. and Pedro, A. (2001). Globalisation, tourism policy and tourism education, *TedQual*, 2.

Crouch, G. and Ritchie, J.R.B. (2004). Application of the audit concept for destination diagnosis. In S. Weber and R. Tomljenovic (eds), *Reinventing a Tourism Destination*. Zagreb: Scientific Edition Institute for Tourism.

Dale, C. (2000). The UK tour-operating industry: a competitive analysis. *Journal of Vacation Marketing*, 4.

De Pelsmacker, P. and Van Kenhove, P. (1994). *Marktonderzoek. Methoden en Toepassingen*. Leuven: Garant.

Dwyer, L. and Kim, C. (2004). *Destination Competitiveness: Determinants and Indicators Current Issues in Tourism* (forthcoming).

Dwyer, L., Forsyth, P. and Rao, P. (2000). The price competitiveness of travel and tourism: a comparison of 19 destinations. *Tourism Management*, 21.

Dwyer, L., Kim, C., Livaic, Z. and Mellor, R. (2004). Application of a model of destination competitiveness to Australia and Korea. In S. Weber and R. Tomljenovic (eds), *Reinventing a Tourism Destination*. Zagreb: Scientific Edition Institute for Tourism.

Edwards, A. (1995). *Asia-Pacific Travel Forecasts to 2005*. Research report. London: EIU.

Fayos-Solá, E. (1996). Tourism policy: a midsummer night's dream? *Tourism Management*, 6.

Go, F. (2000). Integrated quality management for tourist destinations: a European perspective on achieving competitiveness. *Tourism Management*, 21.

Goeldner, R., Ritchie, J. and McIntosh, R. (2000). *Tourism. Principles, Practices, Philosophies*, 8th edn. New York: John Wiley & Sons.

Gohr, C. L., Neto, L. and Santana, E. (2002). Competitive strategies: a study of the hotel sector of Itapema/Santa Catarina. *Turismo*, 10.

Hassan, S. (2000). Determinants of market competitiveness in an environmentally sustainable tourism industry. *Journal of Travel Research*, 3.

Jacob, M., Tintoré, J., Aguil?, E., Bravo, A. and Mulet, J. (2003). Innovation in the tourism sector: results from a pilot study in the Balearic Islands. *Tourism Economics*, 3.

Knowles, T. (1994). The strategic importance of CRSs in the airline industry. *Travel & Tourism Analyst*, 4.

McVey, M. and King, B. (2003). Hotels in Australia. *Travel & Tourism Analyst*, August.

Michael, E. (2003). Tourism Economics 2. *Tourism Economics*, 2.

Middleton, V.T.C. (2001). *Marketing in Travel and Tourism*, 3rd edn. Oxford: Butterworth-Heinemann.

Morgan, M. (1996). *Marketing for Leisure and Tourism*. Hemel Hempstead: Prentice Hall.

Morrison, A.M. (1989). *Hospitality and Travel Marketing*. New York: Delmar Publishers Inc.

Pearce, D. (1997). Competitive destination analysis in Southeast Asia. *Journal of Travel Research*, 4.

Pechlaner, H. and Smeral, E. (2001). *Customer Value Management as a Determinant of the Competitive Position of Tourism Destinations*. Paper presented at the 36th TRC Meeting, Interlaken, 2001 (unpublished).

Petrillo, C. L. (2002). Position and strategic choices of Italian tour operators in European competition. *Tourism*, 1.

Poon, A. (1993). *Tourism, Technology and Competitive Strategies*. Wallingford: C.A.B International.

Porter, M. (1980). *The Competitive Strategy: Techniques for Analysing Industries and Competitors*. New York: The Free Press.

Porter, M. (1985). *Competitive Advantage: Creating and Sustaining Superior Performance*. New York: The Free Press.

Porter, M. (1987). From competitive advantage to corporate strategy. *Harvard Business Review*, 1.

Porter, M. (1990). *The Competitive Advantage of Nations*. London: The Macmillan Press.

Porter, M. (1998). Clusters and the new economics of competition. *Harvard Business Review*, Nov/Dec.

Ritchie, J.R.B. and Crouch, G. (2000). The competitive destination: a sustainability perspective. *Tourism Management*, 21.

Ritchie, J.R.B. and Crouch, G. (2002). Country and city state destinations. *TedQual*, 1.

Ritchie, J.R.B. and Crouch, G. (2003). *The Competitive Destination. A Sustainable Tourism Perspective.* Wallingford: CABI Publishing.

Smeral, E. (1996). Globalisation and changes in the competitiveness of tourism destinations. *Globalisation and Tourism,* 46th AIEST Congress; Rotorua. St-Gall: AIEST.

Tribe, J. (1999). *The Economics of Leisure and Tourism.* Oxford: Butterworth-Heinemann.

Vanhove, N. (1999). *Regional Policy: A European Approach*, 3rd edn. Aldershot: Ashgate.

Vanhove, N. (2002). Tourism policy – between competitiveness and sustainability: the case of Bruges. *The Tourist Review*, 3.

Vanhove, N. and De Keyser, R. (1997). Quality management in a resort. A practical application. *The Tourist Review*, 3.

WES (1994). *The Competitive Situation of Tourism in the Caribbean Area and its Importance for the Region's Development.* Washington/Brugge (unpublished report).

WTO (1992). *An Integrated Approach to Resort Development.* Madrid: WTO.

Young, R. (1966). Goals and goalsetting. *Journal of the American Institute of Planners*, March.

6

Forecasting tourism demand

Introduction

'Forecasting can be defined as the art of predicting the occurrence of events before they actually take place' (Archer, 1975). Forecasting is a subject that fascinates many people who are interested in the economics of tourism. Estimates of future demand at destination level are very important in managing and planning tourism development and the necessary investment. However, forecasting in the tourism sector is not an easy job. As explained in Chapter 3, many variables have an impact, and some of them are unpredictable.

Owing to the many explanatory factors, forecasting in tourism is different from forecasting in most other sectors. The aim cannot be to provide very precise predictions – for example, an increase of arrivals of, say, 5.3 per cent. Those who believe in precise estimations start with the wrong attitude. In tourism, forecasting means indicating the future direction of demand – or, in other words, getting an idea of the magnitude of the expected evolution. Knowledge of the extent of future demand should provide sufficient information for a destination management policy, allowing a limit to the range of uncertainty and thus a reduction in investment risks.

Forecasting in tourism focuses on the destination level and far less on individual enterprises. Large attractions (for example theme parks) are an exception to the general rule, but very often these are in fact visitor destinations in their own right.

Tourism forecasting requires a particular philosophy. It is often said that 'forecasting in tourism is an art'. This should not be interpreted as an aversion to forecasting methods – on the contrary. However, according to Archer (1975), sound forecasting requires a sensible amalgam of rigorous scientific analysis and sound practical experience. A 'good feeling' can be helpful. Accurate information should be the starting point (see Chapter 2), and we can learn a lot from the past – although it is a mistake to depend too much on trends. It is also wise to start from several scenarios. Consulting people from the tourism industry is a valuable complement to any forecasting method. Finally, it is recommended that forecasts be revised from time to time.

What do we forecast in tourism? There is a great variety of forecasting aims, such as expenditure, arrivals at the destination, demand for accommodation and transport services, possible product trends, etc. This variety probably explains the great interest within the tourism sector in forecasting techniques.

Forecasting in tourism poses several particular problems:

1. The development of new destinations and new types of tourism, and the marketing changes of large groups, can influence existing trends
2. The great variety of packages and independent travel leads to complex scenarios – most of which are competitive, although others are complementary
3. In a destination, decisions are made by thousands of decision-makers in public organizations and enterprises
4. Tourism suffers from a lack of sufficient reliable historic data in compatible series
5. There is a full range of economic and other variables
6. Tourism is very vulnerable to terrorism, diseases, natural disasters, political and economic changes.

It is noticeable that the forecasting literature of the last few decades is, more than for other economic subjects of tourism, to a large extent dominated by a relatively limited number of writers: Archer, Frechtling, Smeral and Witt. However, this chapter will show that other authors have also contributed to a better knowledge of forecasting in tourism.

The chapter focuses on four main topics. The first section deals with the different concepts of demand measurement, while the second pays attention to a number of qualitative forecasting methods. The quantitative methods are discussed in the third section, and the final section is dedicated to a number of interesting applications of regression analysis.

Concepts of demand measurement

Market demand can have several meanings. The first point that should be clarified is the definition of the 'market level'. Demand can be measured for:

- Product level – total product, specific tourism forms or specific item
- Geographical level – world, country, county or destination
- Time level – present, or short, medium- or long term.

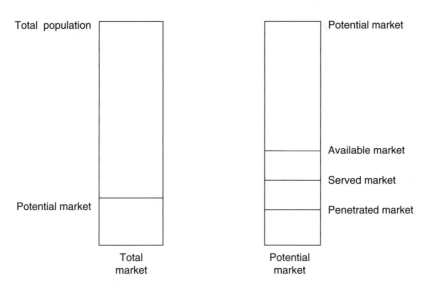

Figure 6.1 Levels of market definition (Source: Kotler, 1984)

Each type of demand measurement serves a specific purpose. A tour operator will apply short-term forecasting to determine the necessary seats and hotel rooms. A national tourist office needs more medium- and long-term forecasting to secure the necessary infra- and superstructure (accommodation) to cope with an increasing demand.

Besides the different 'market levels', a distinction should be made between total market, potential market, available market, served market and penetrated market (see Figure 6.1). A total market is the sum of the actual and potential customers of product. The potential market consists of those consumers that profess some interest in a defined product (e.g. a destination). In many surveys the customers are not only asked if there is an interest in the destination but also if they have the intention to visit the destination in the coming three or five years.

However, customers may have an interest in visiting a destination but do not have the financial means and/or access to a destination (for example, somebody may wish to visit Mombasa in Kenya, but would be unable to stand the climate). The available market therefore consists of those consumers who have the interest and the necessary income to visit a destination, along with no access constraints.

The served market is a part of the available market. The destination management can decide to pursue only well-defined segments (e.g. middle and upper classes) of a limited number of countries.

The penetrated market consists of the set of consumers who actually purchase the tourist product. From Figure 6.1, it must be clear that this is only a fraction of the total population.

Although assessment of each type of market is not an obvious measurement, it is an interesting idea and has a practical value in the framework of the marketing of a product or a destination. When the destination management is not satisfied with the present demand, a number of actions are possible: (a) a growth in the available market by lowering the price or improving access conditions; (b) extension of the served market; or (c) a promotion campaign within the potential market.

Market demand for a destination is the total volume that would be bought by a defined customer group in a defined geographical area in a defined time period in a defined marketing environment under a defined marketing programme. Several elements are relevant:

- Total volume (arrivals, nights or receipts)
- Customer group (whole market or segment)
- Time period (short, medium or long term)
- Marketing environment (e.g. business cycle, technological environment)
- Marketing programme (e.g. promotional budget).

It is important to realize that total market demand is not a fixed number but a function. For this reason it is also called the market demand function or market response function. In Figure 6.2, the horizontal axis shows increasing levels of marketing expenditure in a given period of time; the vertical axis indicates the corresponding demand level. The curve represents the estimated level of market demand as a function of varying levels of marketing effort. Some base sales would take place without any effort – the called market minimum. When marketing expenditure takes place the demand increases, but this is not infinite – beyond a certain level, increased marketing efforts not yield further demand. This suggests an upper limit of market demand, called market potential. The distance between the market minimum and the market potential shows the marketing sensitivity of demand. In an expansible market the distance between Q_1 and Q_2 is relatively large (e.g. the long-haul market for Bali), whereas in a non-expansible market the distance between Q_1 and Q_2 is relatively small (e.g. the home market of a seaside destination). It is important to note that a market demand function is not a picture of market demand over time.

The market demand corresponding to a given effort is known as the market forecast in a given marketing environment. The latter is crucial for correct interpretation of the results. If the marketing environment changes, the curve will move either upwards or downwards accordingly. In the following sections, the marketing

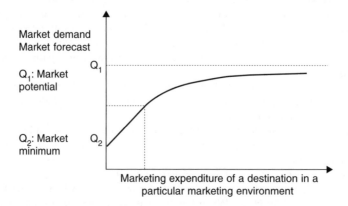

Figure 6.2 Market demand (Source: Kotler, 1984)

environment is not always the same. Assumptions are also introduced regarding the marketing environment.

Besides market demand, company demand can also be considered. A company can be a hotel, resort, or even a particular destination. Company demand is the company's share of total demand. Company demand is, like market demand, a function – the company demand function. It is subject to all the determinants of market demand plus all the other elements that influence company market share.

Qualitative methods

Quantitative methods (the subject of the next section) are based on existing (historical) data. This is less the case with qualitative methods. Qualitative approaches of assessing future demand are based on the pooled opinions of groups of experts, or simply the consumer. They can never lead to precise mathematical results, but indicate a possible range of future tourism demand. As we have seen, this is sufficient for decision-making with respect to investments, marketing and destination management. Although they have a value of their own, qualitative methods are a useful complement to more quantitative analysis. The qualitative methods can be divided into three main categories:

1. Traditional approaches
2. The Delphi method
3. Judgement-aided models.

Traditional approaches

There are in practice two traditional methods. The first is based on the holiday surveys dealt with in Chapter 2. A careful analysis of comparable surveys over a long period can provide data to distinguish emerging trends, and although this does not provide a prediction in the strict sense of the word, it can nevertheless give useful indications for certain destinations.

The second traditional method concerns surveys of travellers in the generating markets. This approach may offer useful insights about the potential markets, the attitude or the prevailing image of potential tourists towards a destination. The surveys very often include the opinion of tour operators and travel agencies. In contrast to the first traditional method, the survey approach is a type of primary market research. It can be conceived and implemented to achieve particular (forecasting) objectives. This method, which is expensive and time-consuming, can be a useful complement to demand forecasts solely based on trend extrapolation or projections starting from alternative growth rates. The survey method takes into account possible changes of causal factors, and the effects of individuals' subjective judgements about the future.

The Delphi model

The Delphi method was pioneered in the early 1960s by the Rand Corporation, and was originally used to provide long-range forecasts of technological developments.

Later the application field was extended to include economics, politics, medical developments and tourism. Archer (1976) defines the Delphi model as

> ... a systematic method of combining the knowledge and experience of experts in many disciplines to form a group consensus of opinion about the likely occurrence of specific future events. Usually the aim is to provide an indication of the degree of probability that these events will take place within specified time periods.

In essence, the Delphi technique is a special type of survey to forecast the occurrence of specified long- (or short-) term events and to generate estimates of the probability of specified conditions prevailing in the future. The technique is a means of reaching consensus among experts through administering a series of questionnaires, collating judgements and providing feedback from each series of questionnaires to all participants. The feedback is reviewed by each participant before he or she responds to a next round of the questionnaire. Comments and considerations from earlier rounds are taken into consideration, so that ultimately the most desirable solution emerges from the collective knowledge of the experts.

The Delphi method can be very helpful where data are insufficient, or where changes in a previous trend are expected or new elements might interfere, with the result that mathematical-type analysis may be inappropriate. Usually the aim is to provide an indication of the degree of probability that certain phenomena or events will take place within a specified time period.

A good application is illustrated by the Alliance Internationale de Tourisme Delphi study on the future trends of tourism (Obermair, 1998). This gives the result of an international experts' survey about long-term global tourism trends. More than 200 selected international experts from over 60 countries contributed to this study, and agreed to give their personal view of the future of tourism for the next 5–15 years and to develop this vision further in a survey of three rounds.

The technique involves several steps:

1. *Problem definition.* What should be forecast, and what are the relevant factors?
2. *Selection of panel members.* This is based on the expertise required and on the experts' willingness to participate, and is a very important step in the Delphi method. If the make-up of the panel members is basically homogeneous, 10–15 individuals is appropriate; in other cases 20 to 30 members are necessary for appropriate results (Taylor and Judd, 1989). It is, however, difficult to formulate a general rule about the minimum number of panel members, as this will be influenced by the content of the research and the geographical area covered. The 'non-response' rate must also be taken into account. An important point is the anonymity within the group of panel members.
3. *Preparation and distribution of first questionnaire.* A series of questions is prepared and tested. The wording of the questions should avoid any influence on the answers. It is important to provide each panel member with a package of background information about the topic areas, and this package can include internal and external data.
4. *Analysis and summary of questionnaire responses.* The responses for each question are statistically categorized by the median and quartile values.

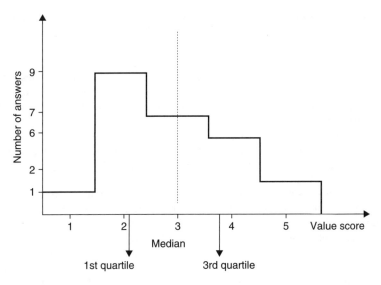

Figure 6.3 Evaluation of the recovery and growth of tourist demand in Mediterranean countries until the year 2000

Special attention might be given to relevant comments. Figure 6.3 interprets the first item of the Delphi study about the prospects for the Mediterranean coastal hotel sector (Universitat Jaume I, 1997; unpublished). Value score 1 represents stands for very improbable, very low or very negative; a score of 5 represents very probable, very high or very positive. The median is the central value of the answers in a distribution in which all the responses are valued in an increasing or decreasing order. It is the middle observation – i.e. the value above which half of the responses lie and below which half lie. The first quartile is the value score at or below which one-quarter of the answers lie; the third quartile is that value score at or below which three-quarters of the answers lie. The inter-quartile range is the difference between the first and the third quartiles, and covers (by definition) 50 per cent of the observations. A high inter-quartile value is an indication of a wide range of opinions; a low value indicates convergence.

5. *Start of the second round.* The synthesis of the first round is sent to the panel members. Each member is positioned, for each question, with respect to the other panel members. Items for which there is consensus may possibly be dropped in the second round. The panel members are invited to re-examine and reconsider their original responses in the light of the distribution of answers of the other panel members. If a participant's answer still lies outside the main range, he or she might be invited to provide reasons this point of view. It is the essence of the method that the range of responses by panel experts will decrease and converge toward the mid-range of the distribution.

6. *Analysis of the answers of the second round.* The replies to the second round are processed and summarized in a similar way to the reactions to the first round. A third or fourth round may follow, but there are unlikely to be major changes in expert opinions after the second round. It is supposed that the

147

median will move toward the 'true' answer with each succeeding round as a group consensus emerges.

7. *Development of a final report.*

Although the method takes time, there are several successful applications in the tourism sector (see Müller *et al.*, 1991; Moeller and Shafer, 1994; Frechtling, 1996; Obermair, 1998). The preparation of the questionnaire and the selection of the panel are of utmost importance to achieve a reliable result. This method makes use of the advantages of a group decision without the disadvantages. In a group decision, there is always the danger of one or two experts dominating the proceedings and of the tendency to a 'bandwagon effect'. On the other hand, this method does not allow exchange of ideas among the experts.

Delphi study results are very often expressed in the form of the probability that trends or events will occur during specific time periods. However, these results are not valid in a statistical sense (Archer, 1976).

Although used for short-term forecasts, the most common application of the Delphi technique concerns long-term forecasting (Smith, 1997; Cunliffe, 2002). We agree with Cunliffe that the Delphi method can provide information regarding the future that other conventional extrapolative techniques cannot reliably forecast.

Judgement-aided models

The most common qualitative approach is to bring together a panel of experts and ask them to achieve a consensus on a particular event or question. The aim is to generate as much debate and interchange of ideas as possible in order to reach an agreement upon forecast. Seminars are very often used in tourism. This technique can be instructive. The major danger is the 'bandwagon' effect.

A second judgement-aided method is 'scenario writing'. A scenario is an account of what could happen, given the known facts and trends. For example, in demand forecasting a hypothetical sequence of events is described showing how demand is likely to be affected by a particular causal process. In other words, this is a construction of a hypothetical sequence of circumstances in order to focus attention on the causal processes. Attention is focused both on the variables and on the decision points that occur. The intent is to indicate what actions can be taken to influence the level of demand at each stage, and what the repercussions of such actions might be (Uysal and Crompton, 2000).

Scenario-writing is not a real forecasting technique *per se*, but rather a method of clarifying the issues involved. The technique attempts to cast light on possible and plausible futures. For Archer (1975), it can form a valuable input to group forecasting such as the Delphi technique.

In the implementation of this technique there are three components:

1. A description of the current situation (baseline analysis)
2. At least one future image (a description of the potential situation in the future)
3. For each future image, at least one future path showing how the current situation could develop into the eventual future image.

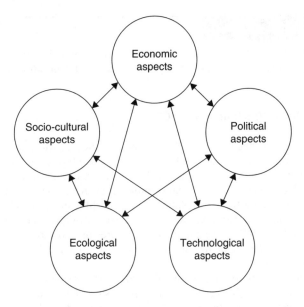

Figure 6.4 The interaction of relevant dimensions contributing to future trends in tourism (Source: Schwaninger, 1989)

Martin and Mason (1990) provide details of a good application of the scenario method. Their analysis highlights two prime areas of uncertainty about the direction of future change in the UK: the way attitudes and social values will develop, and the outlook of the economy and the future rate of growth. A particular application of scenario-writing in leisure and tourism is illustrated by Schwaniger (1989). Here, the writer analyses the interaction between economic, political, socio-cultural, ecological and technological aspects (see Figure 6.4).

A third judgement-aided method is 'morphological analysis'. Here the aim is to structure existing information in an orderly manner and so identify the probable outcome of events. The method is carried out in different steps (Archer, 1994; Uysal and Crompton, 2000):

1. The most important variables are identified (intuitively or based on multi-variate regression)
2. Each of the variables is considered in turn to assess its possible magnitude and effects
3. Parameters are placed in a multidimensional matrix (called a morphological box) to assess their interaction on demand – this process provides an indication of various attainable levels of demand under varying assumptions about the performance of each variable
4. An estimation is made of the most desirable level of demand in relation to the variables at work, followed by an assessment of how this level might be achieved.

There appear to be few applications of this method in the field of tourism.

Quantitative methods

This section deals with three different quantitative approaches: univariate time-series methods, regression analysis, and gravity and trip-generation models.

Univariate time-series methods

Univariate approaches are concerned solely with the statistical analysis of past data concerning the variable to be forecast. Univariate time-series methods start from the assumption that a variable may be forecast without reference to the factor(s) that determine the level of the variable. As such, they are non-causal techniques, or forecasting by extrapolation (Witt and Martin, 1991). Extrapolation presupposes that the factors that were the main cause of growth or decline in the past will continue to be the cause in the future. In a volatile sector such as tourism, with many influencing variables, extrapolation is a technique that should be applied with great care.

In the literature there are several univariate time-series models: moving average, exponential smoothing (single and adaptive smoothing), double exponential smoothing, trend curve analysis, decomposition methods and the Box–Jenkins approach (see also Frechtling, 1996). Most of these methods have little value for tourism.

The most widely used technique in tourism is *trend extrapolation* based on time series. A time series is a set of data collected regularly – daily, weekly, monthly, quarterly or yearly – over a period of time. Although trend curve analysis is rather simple and naïve, there are circumstances where it makes sense to make use of it. There are a number of conditions for its use:

- Time-series data must be available
- The future must be similar to the past
- It must be possible to detect trends
- It provides a short-term forecast
- It requires a stable environment.

The most common trends take a straight-line form:

$$Y = a + bT \tag{6.1}$$

where

Y = the dependent variable or the forecast variable (e.g. number of visitors)
T = time period ($t = 1$ to n)
a = a constant to be estimated using regression analysis
b = regression coefficient or slope (changes of Y in function of T).

The factor T does not represent any particular independent or explanatory variable, although it is possible that the time factor T can represent one or more independent variable(s). This can be the case with 'fashion trends' in visiting a particular destination.

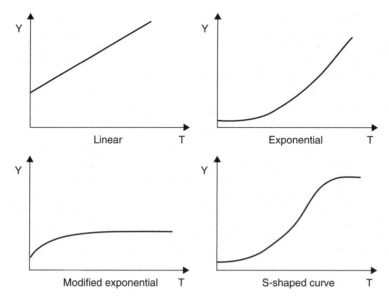

Figure 6.5 Some possible trends in tourism

However, the nature of the trend is not always linear (see Figure 6.5); there are many different trend expressions. Besides the linear trend, the most common other expressions are:

■ Exponential	$Y = ae^{bT}$ (e = 2.718) (b < 1 and b > 1)	(6.2)
■ Semi-log	$Y = a + b \log T$	(6.3)
■ Log – log or log linear	$Y = aT^b$	(6.4)
■ Hyperbola	$Y = a + b/T$	(6.5)
■ Modified exponential	$Y = ae^{b/T}$	(6.6)
■ Quadratic	$Y = a + bT + cT^2$	(6.7)
■ S-shaped curve	$Y = 1/(a + be^{-t})$	(6.8)

The exponential function can be converted into a linear equation by taking natural logarithms of both sides of the equation: $\log Y = \log a + bT$.

The S-shaped curve or the logistic curve is appropriate when there is an introduction stage, a rapid growth stage and finally a maturity stage.

Many writers also refer to *the Box–Jenkins method*, developed by G. Box and G. Jenkins (Witt and Martin 1991; Witt *et al.*, 1994; Archer, 1994; Frechtling, 1996; Witt *et al.*, 2004). This approach became popular owing to its ability to handle any time series, its theoretical foundations and its operational success. It is a highly sophisticated technique. There are two types of the Box–Jenkins approach; in its simplest form it is univariate, while in the more complex application one or more independent variables are taken into account. It is normally used in its univariate form. This method is appropriate for forecasting horizons of 12–18 months, and when there are enough observations available. According to Frechtling, 50 observations are a minimum; for others, 60–100 monthly data are required.

A good description of the method can be found in Frechtling (1996). The Box–Jenkins approach searches for the combination of two forecasting methods (autoregression and moving average) and their parameters that minimizes the error in simulating the past series. If the combination passes the statistical checks for validity, it can be used in forecasting the series. Autoregression is a forecasting model that is based upon the strong relationship between the data for one time period and the corresponding data for the preceding time period. The moving average component implies that the forecast variable depends on previous values of the error term (the actual values minus the forecast values). The use of seasonal data and the resulting relatively large number of observations permits the use of ARIMA (Auto Regressive Integrated Moving Average) (Witt *et al.*, 1994, 2004). ARIMA models can only deal with time series that are stationary in their means and variances. If this is not the case, differencing is used to achieve stationarity. A first difference is computed by subtracting the first historical value from the second, the second from the third, etc.; the results are then tested for a stationary mean. If this does not appear, then the first differenced series is differenced again. The number of times a series must be differenced to achieve stationarity is indicated by its 'integration' index.

There are five phases in applying the Box–Jenkins approach (Frechtling, 1996):

1. The preparation phase, or achieving stationarity and removing seasonality from the time series
2. The identification phase, or examining for autocorrelation and selection of model (the autoregressive method, the moving average method or the autoregressive moving average method)
3. The estimation phase (parameters are estimated in the tentative models)
4. The diagnostic checking phase (the parameters of the preceding phase are inspected for significance)
5. The forecasting phase, which implies the use of the model that produces significant parameters to forecast the transformed series. Residuals should be examined for stationarity of mean and variance, and for autocorrelation.

This is a very sophisticated method, and the forecaster should make use of the statistical packages. The Box–Jenkins method is quite often used in the airline business, and is thus sometimes called the 'airline model'.

Regression analysis or causal methods

In the preceding section there was no causal relationship between the forecast variable and an explanatory variable. Causal methods try to explain why the dependent variable or forecast variable changes as it does over time. These changes can be influenced by one or several variables. Tourism demand is so complex that in most cases several factors have an impact on the dependent variable at the same time.

There are many reasons to move to causal models. First, time-series analysis cannot predict turning points and consequently is unable to forecast accurately at the moment when an accurate forecast is most needed. Due to the introduction of one or more causal factors, a turning point can be detected and predicted. Secondly, there might be so much variation in the forecast variable that a trend cannot be detected. Thirdly, an understanding of causal relationships can be interesting and useful. Indeed, the objectives of regression models are threefold: (1) to forecast and (2) to identify explanatory factor(s), and (3) to test the efficiency of one or more variables (Crouch *et al.*, 1992).

In the literature, a distinction is made between two types of causal modelling in tourism (Frechtling, 1996). The first approach is the linear regression method, where the dependent variable is explained by one (single regression) or more explanatory factors (multiple regression). The second type is the structural model (Turner and Witt, 2001a; Smeral, 2004). Here we are confronted with a set of regression equations linked together by certain variables that are both dependent and independent variables.

This section focuses on the first type. Let us start from the following relationship:

$$Y = f(X_1, X_2, X_3, \ldots X_n) \tag{6.9}$$

This can be written as:

$$Y = a + b_1 X_1 + b_2 X_2 + \ldots b_n X_n + e \tag{6.10}$$

where

Y = dependent variable, forecast variable or variable to explain (e.g. arrivals)
$X_1 \ldots X_n$ = independent or explanatory variables
a = the intercept constant
b = slope coefficients or regression coefficients to be calculated with regression analysis
n = number of independent variables
e = error term.

Equation (6.9) can also be a multiplicative function of the type:

$$Y = aX_1{}^{b_1}X_2{}^{b_2}X_3{}^{b_3} \ldots X_n{}^{b_n} \tag{6.11}$$

which can be transformed in a log-linear function of the type:

$$\ln Y = \ln a + b_1 \ln X_1 + b_2 \ln X_2 + b_3 \ln X_3 \ldots b_n \ln X_n \tag{6.12}$$

In the latter case, the regression coefficients b_1, b_2, etc. become elasticity coefficients.

In most cases the Y and X data are time series, but this is not always the case. Y can represent a series of observations within a particular time (e.g. a year) in a number of countries, regions, segments, etc. In this case, we speak of cross-section analysis.

What are the possible independent variables? Many explanatory factors are discussed in Chapter 3. Frechtling makes a distinction between push factors (also called emissive factors – or those characteristics in the generating market that encourage people to take holidays, e.g. income); (b) pull factors (those that attract tourists to a destination, e.g. visiting friends and relatives); and (c) resistance factors such as war, prices, etc.

In any case, there should be a theoretical background or a justification of common sense to retain a possible explanatory factor. In practice, the most frequent used variables are (see also Smeral, 2003):

■ Income generating country(ies)
■ Commercial ties

- Price/relative price
- Price substitutes
- Access cost (transport price)
- Distance
- Travel time
- Exchange rate or real exchange rate (Kulendran, 1996)
- Promotion efforts or destination marketing programmes
- Population growth
- Supply capacities
- Competitive destinations
- Business cycle
- Trend factor
- Qualitative factors
- Dummy variable(s) (war, natural disaster, terrorism, etc.)
- Lagged independent variables.

In international demand equations, income, relative prices, transport costs, trend variables and exchange rate are the five most used independent variables (Smeral, 2003).

Dummy variables are specially constructed variables, and represent the presence or absence of certain effects that influence the dependent variable in the regression equation. Dummy variables can only take two values: 1 when the event occurs, and 0 otherwise. They are quite often used in tourism forecasting, and are treated as any other exogenous variable. Their coefficients are estimated from the usual least-squares formula. Measurement of the impact of mega-events on tourism flowing through the use of dummy variables has been discussed by Witt and Martin (1991).

Lagged independent variables are very often used to take account of a time lag in the relationship between a dependent and an independent factor. For example, the income of year $t - 1$ influences the number of arrivals in year t. Sometimes a lagged dependent variable is included in tourism demand functions to allow for habit persistence and supply rigidities.

All explanatory variables should be tested for significance. In the first place, the signs of the regression coefficients should conform with expectations. Secondly, the regression coefficients must be significant. Therefore we should calculate the t-ratio:

$$t = \frac{b_i}{s_{b_i}} \qquad (6.13)$$

where

t = t-ratio
b_i = regression coefficient factor b
s_{b_i} = standard error of the explanatory variable b_i.

With a confidence interval of 95 per cent, a t-ratio of 2.0 or more indicates that the regression coefficient is significantly different from zero. The critical t-values are influenced by the number of observations and the number of parameters to be estimated; they can be found in most statistical handbooks.

If the calculated regression coefficients are not sufficiently significant, the corresponding independent variable should be excluded.

It is also very important to avoid a correlation among the independent factors, called multicollinearity. The latter is responsible for inaccurate estimation of the regression coefficients (small t-ratio). A symptom of multicollinearity is a large coefficient of determination accompanied by statistically insufficient estimates of the coefficients of the independent variables. There is a further assumption that the independent variables are not affected by the dependent variable – for example, expenditures abroad (Y) can influence the exchange rate (X value).

For an accurate forecasting equation, a number of additional tests are necessary. The first question that arises is, 'does the equation accurately simulate its time series?' Therefore we have to calculate the coefficient of determination R^2 or $\overline{R}^2$ (coefficient of determination adjusted for degrees of freedom) and the F-statistic.

The coefficient of determination (R^2) indicates the percentage of the variation of the forecast variable around its mean that is explained by the independent variables; this varies between 0 and 1. A value of 1, which is exceptional, means that the explanatory variables completely explain (100 per cent) the variation in the dependent variable. $\overline{R}^2$ (coefficient of determination adjusted for degrees of freedom) is calculated by using the following formula:

$$R^2 = \frac{\text{Total variance} - \text{Residual variance}}{\text{Total variance}} \quad \text{or} \quad 1 - \frac{S^2_{y \cdot x}}{S^2_y} \quad (6.14)$$

$$\overline{R}^2 = \left(1 - \frac{\Sigma(Y - \hat{Y})^2}{\Sigma(Y - \overline{Y})^2}\right)\left(\frac{n}{n - m}\right) \quad (6.15)$$

where

$\overline{R}^2$ = coefficient of determination adjusted for degrees of freedom
$\hat{Y}$ = calculated dependent variable based on the regression equation
$\overline{Y}$ = the mean of the dependent variables
Y = dependent variable
n = number of observations in the dependent variable data series
m = number of parameters (explanatory variables plus one).

The F-test indicates whether the variance in the dependent variable explained by the independent variables is sufficiently larger than its unexplained variance. The formula is:

$$F = \frac{\overline{S}^2_{y \cdot c}}{\overline{S}^2_{y \cdot r}} \quad (6.16)$$

where

$\overline{S}^2_{y \cdot c}$ = adjusted variance of the calculated values of Y

$\overline{S}^2_{y \cdot r}$ = adjusted variance of the residuals.

Statistical textbooks give the minimum value of F to determine whether it is significant or not according to a defined level of confidence. As a rule of thumb, with a number of degrees of freedom of six and more, an F-value of 5 is significant at the 0.05 level.

A last test that is recommended is the Durbin–Watson. This test should indicate whether any relevant explanatory variables have been omitted. The regression equation based on least squares analysis assumes that the residuals or error terms are independent of one another. If this is not the case, this should be an indication that at least one explanatory variable has been left out of the equation. In time series, such a pattern is an indication of 'serial correlation' or 'autocorrelation'. The consequence is biased regression coefficients. However, serial correlation will also bias our equation's accuracy of fit, or the correlation coefficient and the F-value. Serial correlation can be tested with the Durbin–Watson test (Durbin–Watson d statistic):

$$d = \frac{\Sigma(e_{t+1} - e_t)^2}{\Sigma e_t^2} \qquad (6.17)$$

where

d or DW = Durbin–Watson statistic
e = residual
t = time period.

The DW values can vary between 0 and 4; a DW value equal to 2 indicates total absence of serial correlation. Most statistical handbooks contain tables of the critical values. It is generally accepted that there is no serial correlation with DW values between 1.5 and 2.5. If the d value falls outside this range, the best remedy is to look for the missing variable(s).

A basic question is how to use the tested equations 6.10 or 6.12 to forecast. Only significant variables should be used as the starting point. It is supposed that there are indicators for the behaviour of these retained factors for the time horizon considered, although the latter is not always the case. Often independent variables must be forecast to obtain a projection of the dependent variable. In other cases some independent variables are projected, combined with constant values for the remaining explanatory factors.

It is also recommended that two or more scenarios – pessimistic and optimistic – be considered to take account of uncertainties about the future evolution of one or more independent variables.

Gravity and trip-generation models

Gravity models focus on the effect of distance or travel-time constraints on tourism demand, and are based on Newton's Law – i.e. two bodies attract each other in proportion to the product of their masses and inversely by the square of their distance apart. Gravity models pay a lot of attention to demographic and geographic factors, push and pull factors between the origin and receiving destinations (represented by populations), and restraining (e.g. distance) variables (Crouch *et al.*, 1992).

Trip-generation models are sometimes derived from gravity models; in other cases they are merely refined forms of consumer-demand equations. They place more emphasis than do consumer models on the influence of distance as a travel constraint (Archer, 1975, 1976).

Applied to tourism, the basic gravity model normally takes the form shown in the following equation:

$$I_{ij} = G\left(\frac{P_i P_j}{D_{ij}^b}\right) \qquad (6.18)$$

where

I_{ij} = number of tourists travelling from country (region) i to country (region) j
P_i = population country i
P_j = population country j
D_{ij} = distance between i and j
b and G = parameters.

This equation can be converted into:

$$I_{ij} = GP_i P_j D_{ij}^{-b} \qquad (6.19)$$

In practice, gravity models are not used in this simplified form. Population and distance are often replaced by some more appropriate explanatory variables. Archer gives an example:

$$I_{ij} = GX_i^a A_j^c C_{ij}^{-b} \qquad (6.20)$$

or, in logarithmic form:

$$\ln I_{ij} = \ln G + a \ln X_i + c \ln A_j - b \ln C_{ij} \qquad (6.21)$$

where

I_{ij} = number of tourists travelling between country i and destination j
X_i = group of factors which generate travel in origin country i
A_j = the attractiveness of destination j
C_{ij} = the cost in terms of money and/or time in travelling from origin i to destination j.

It is really not very different from any other causal model. Forecasting follows the same procedure as with multiple regression analysis. In fact, a gravity model contains three groups of variables:

1. Those characterizing the generating market
2. Those characterizing the receiving destination

3. Those that provide the constraints between generating and receiving countries or regions.

The problem with most gravity models is the absence of a sound theoretical background. Distance alone is not an accurate measure for travel constraints. Furthermore, there is a real danger of multicollinearity.

Trip-generation models are even closer to traditional causal models. Examples of gravity and trip-generation models can be found in Labor (1969), Armstrong (1972), Crampon and Tan (1973) and Lesceux (1977). The Labor model is a typical trip-generation model, and interesting because of the independent variables used:

$$\log\left(\frac{I_{ij}}{P_i}\right) = \log G + a \log Y_i + b \log AN_i + c \log DU_i - d \log D_{ij} \quad (6.22)$$

where

I_{ij}/P_i = actual number of trips from country i to country j (per head)
Y_i = income per capita in country i
AN_i = an ancestry link; number of persons per 1000 inhabitants in origin i who were born in country j
DU = a dummy variable to measure the effect on travel of the existence of a common border between countries i and j
D_{ij} = distance factor.

Case studies of regression analysis

In the literature there are many interesting examples of the application of causal models to explain or to forecast tourism demand. This section deals with a number of illustrative cases.

Case 1: the Greek model, Dritsakis–Athanasiadis

The first case is based on a study by Dritsakis and Athanasiadis (2000). This model is built up from several explanatory factors, but is not used for any forecast.

What are the characteristics of the Greek case?

The relationship between the model's variables takes a log-linear (double log) form. This has two advantages: first, it is practical to use logarithmic transformations for non-linear functions in order to provide a linear fit so that the OLS (ordinary least squares) method can be employed; and secondly, the parameters (slope coefficients) measure the elasticity of the respective explanatory variables.

The model takes the following form:

$$\ln\frac{AR_{jt}}{P_{jt}} = a_{1j} + a_{2j} \ln\frac{Yd_{jt}}{P_{jt}} + a_{3j} \ln C_{jt} + a_{4j} \ln CON_{jt} + a_{5j} \ln N_{jt} \quad (6.23)$$
$$+ a_{6j} \ln INV_{t-2} + a_{7j} \ln AD_{jt} + a_{8j}D_t + a_9T + U_{jt}$$

where

j	$= 1, 2, \ldots, 15$ (country of origin)
t	$= 1, 2, \ldots, 34$ (1 $= 1960$)
AR_{jt}	$=$ number of tourists in Greece from country j in year t
P_{jt}	$=$ population of country j in year t
Yd_{jt}	$=$ disposable national income (1980 prices) of country j in year t
C_{jt}	$=$ average total cost for a 10-day stay in Greece including travel expenses (1980 prices) from country of origin j in year t
CON_{jt}	$=$ average cost for a 10-day stay in other competitive Mediterranean countries including travel expenses (1980 prices) from country j in year t
N_{jt}	$=$ exchange rate of the currency (current prices) of the country of origin *vis-à-vis* the Greek drachma in year t
INV_{t-2}	$=$ gross investment (1980 prices) in fixed assets in Greece, with a 2-year time lag;
Ad_{jt}	$=$ advertising expenditures (1980 prices) in the country of origin in year t
D_t	$=$ a dummy variable that measures political stability in Greece (1 in years 1967, 1974, 1980, 1982, 1983, 1989; 0 otherwise)
T	$=$ time trend
U_{jt}	$=$ error term
$a_{1j}, a_{2j}, \ldots a_{,9j}$	$=$ parameters to be estimated.

The OLS method was used in order to estimate the separate demand functions for each country of origin. What follows are the results for the origin country Germany. The first figure shows the regression coefficient, and the figures in parentheses are t values.

Yd	0.942	(1.178)
C	-0.822	(-1.302)
CON	1.712	(4.041)
N	2.965	(7.431)
INV_{t-2}	0.671	(7.612)
AD	1.297	(2.107)
D	-0.516	(-2.728)
T	0.089	(1.967)
Const.	-11.761	(-2.781)
R^2	0.973	
F	47.50	
DW	1.679	

The sign of all regression coefficients corresponds to the expectations: positive for income, exchange rate, investment in fixed assets, cost in competitive destinations and advertising expenditures; negative for cost of stay and the dummy variable.

All but two variables are significant at the level t $= 5\%$ or 95 % confidence level; this confidence level is a little bit lower for disposable income and cost of stay. It may be owing to a certain degree of multicollinearity.

The R^2 (corrected for degrees of freedom), F and DW assume very acceptable values.

The income elasticity for German tourist travelling to Greece equals 0.94; this means that an increase of disposable income in Germany will bring a 0.94 per cent increase in tourist arrivals in Greece. Price-elasticity equals -0.82, which is quite logical. Notice the very high N value. This is an indication that German tourists were very sensitive to a devaluation of the drachma. Advertising expenditure in Germany seems to be effective; the corresponding elasticity is rather high. The significant T-value is an indication of a certain preference of Germans for Greece.

Case 2: the Australian model, Crouch–Schultz–Valerio

The second case study concerns the marketing of international tourism to Australia (Crouch *et al.*, 1992). The demand model used in this study is based on conventional economic and marketing theory. The objective of the study was to measure the effect of the marketing efforts on five Australian origin markets. It is an example of an efficiency test of marketing efforts. For the same reasons – better fit to the data and direct estimates of demand elasticities – as for the first case, the Australian writers use a log-linear function. It takes the following shape:

$$\ln Ta_{it} = b_0 + b_1 \ln Y_{it} + b_2 \ln RP_{it} + b_3 \ln AF_{it} + b_4 \ln ME_{it} + b_5 T_t \\ + b_6 D_1 + b_m D_n + e \tag{6.24}$$

where

Ta_{it} = number of arrivals in Australia from country i in year t
Y_{it} = real per capita disposal personal income in origin country i in year t
RP_{it} = relative price of tourism in Australia to tourism in the origin country i in year t
AF_{it} = airfare between country i and Australia in year t
ME_{it} = marketing expenditures by the ATC in origin country i in year t
(TM = total expenditures and AD represents advertising expenditures)
T_t = time trend
$D_1 ..... D_n$ = dummy variables for disturbances
e = random error
$b_1 ..... b_m$ = regression coefficients.

Some variables need further explanation. The dependent variable is defined as the number of arrivals divided by the population, to remove the effect of population increase on arrivals. The income factor is corrected for inflation and population effects. The definition of the factor 'relative price' is important. The relative price of tourism in Australia to foreign visitors is represented as the Australian consumer price index (CPI) multiplied by the origin country/Australia exchange rate and divided by the CPI of the origin country. The airfares are converted to 'real' figures by dividing the airfare by the CPI of the origin country. Marketing efforts are measured in two different ways: total marketing expenditures of the Australian Tourist Commission (ATC), and advertising-only expenditures. The trend factor represents the 'fashionableness' of Australia over time.

The study concerns five typical markets for Australia. The results suggest that the international marketing activities of the ATC have played a statistically significant role in influencing inbound tourism. The main study results for the US market can be summarized as follows (the figures in parenthesis are not t-ratios but significance levels):

Y	2.67	(0.0002)
RP	−0.92	(0.004)
TM (lagged by 1 year)	0.11	(0.05)
D_3	0.33	(0.05)
$\bar{R}^2$	0.92	
DW	1.75	

All other variables are not significant. The retained variables in the equation with the best fit show a high confidence level. Income-elasticity is reasonably high (2.67), price-elasticity is close to unity (0.92), and the marketing expenditure shows an elasticity of 0.11.

Case 3: the EIU–Edwards model

The third case study is of a different type and with another objective. Edwards uses a multiple linear regression equation (for each country of origin), with rather limited independent variables. The main objective is a long-term forecast. At the risk of oversimplifying the many alternatives considered by the author, the basic equation takes the form:

$$Y_t = a + bX_t + cZ_t \qquad (6.25)$$

where

Y = the annual percentage growth of international tourist expenditures of origin country i (i = 1 ... 20), excluding fares, for the period 1972–1986, in national currency terms at constant relative prices

X = annual percentage growth of private consumption expenditures (income effect) at constant prices

Z = the annual percentage increase in the cost (price, exchange rate) of travel abroad relative to domestic price levels, including fares

a = a constant (annual percentage growth in Y which cannot be linked statistically to changes in X and Z)

b and c = regression coefficients (or income and cost multiplier applicable to X and Z).

The cost variable has two components: the relative rates of inflation at home and abroad, and the exchange rate. Besides the real cost, airfares are an element of variable Z. For any particular origin country a whole series of comparative cost indices can be drawn up for different destinations, showing how exchange rate-adjusted rates of inflation compare in different destinations. They can be combined into a single index, showing the overall cost of travel abroad, by weighting each destination country in terms of its relative importance (e.g. expenditures in each). For virtually all origin countries, the main six to ten destinations account for at least 80–85 per cent of total travel expenditures.

The application to the UK situation resulted in the equation (no lagging values):

$$Y = 0.79 + 2.89X - 2.14Z \qquad R^2 = 0.92 \qquad (6.26)$$

This should be read as follows: real travel expenditure of UK inhabitants grows at 0.79 per cent a year plus 2.89 times the annual percentage growth in private consumption (income), less 2.14 times the annual percentage increase in the relative costs of travel abroad (or plus 2.14 for the annual decline in this cost). Similar equations were calculated for income effect lagged, cost effect lagged and both effects lagged by one year. For most origin countries, the coefficient of determination is quite high.

Equation 6.27 is the basis on which to forecast UK international tourism expenditures:

$$Y_{t+x} = a + bX_{t+x} + cZ_{t+x} \qquad (6.27)$$

We start from the assumption that there are good estimations of the independent variables X_{t+x} and Z_{t+x}. In the EIU study, X_{t+x} are projected rises in real consumer spending (or rises in household disposable income). Z_{t+x} are projected changes in the cost of international travel relative to domestic prices, taking into account anticipated movements in real exchange rates and fares. In other words, the relative cost of travel abroad is composed of three elements:

1. The inflation rate in each origin country compared with inflation in the main destination countries from the corresponding origin country
2. The trends of exchange rates between each origin country and the destination countries for its tourists
3. Changes in costs of international air fares, including the impact of inclusive tour and concessionary fares.

The parameters a, b and c are given by equation (6.25).

A very special point in Edwards' projection is the introduction of 'ceilings'. According to the author, several major origin countries are approaching the introduced ceilings. Two possible ceilings are considered; the first stems from the annual leave and public holidays out of which the time for domestic or international tourism is taken, and the second from the share of spending on holidays in total disposable income after essential needs have been met. However for many countries there is still ample scope to absorb the ceiling effect by shifts from domestic to outbound tourism.

It should be noted that Edwards presents expenditure forecasts in eight different ways in function of national currencies or UD dollars, including or excluding fares, and constant prices and exchange rates, or relative prices and exchange rates.

Although there must be some doubts about the long-term projected values of the variable Z, the results are very acceptable and correspond retrospectively to the reality.

Table 6.1 Forecast growth rates of world travel (percentage per year)*

	Past	Forecast		
	1980–1986	*1986–1991*	*1991–1995*	*1995–1999*
Real travel expenditures at constant relative prices, including fares	3.0	4.8	4.6	5.4
Trips abroad	2.0	5.7	4.4	3.9
Nights abroad	2.0	5.8	4.4	4.4

* The forecast concentrates on the 20 main tourist origin countries which, in expenditure terms, represent 80 per cent of the world total.
Source: Adapted from Edwards (1988).

Table 6.1 illustrated Edwards' (1988) projected rates growth in world travel from 1986 to 1999.

Case 4: the WTTOUR–Smeral model

The fourth case study considers the WTTOUR – Smeral model (WTTOUR stands for World (Trade)Tourism Model). This model already has a long history, and was applied for the first time in 1992 (Smeral, 2003). The last application dates from 2003, and was presented at the TRC Meeting in Venice in the same year (Smeral, 2004). It can be considered as a typical example of a structural model. The model is composed of two parts: a tourism import function and a tourism export function (all functions are in absolute values).

The tourism imports (outbound in monetary terms) of a country k are described by the following equation:

$$M_k = b_0 + b_1 GDP_k + b_2 RMP_k + b_3 DV_k + U_k \qquad (6.28)$$

Weighted import prices (RMP) are defined by:

$$RMP_k = \sum_{i=1}^{25} g_{ik} \frac{VPI_i}{VPI_k} \qquad (6.29)$$

where

M_k = imports country k (time series 1975–1999)
k = each country in the model is both a country of origin and a country of destination
GDP_k = real GDP at 1985 prices and exchange rates
RMP_k = weighted import prices
DV = dummy variable (specific structural variables, supply factors, marketing effects)
VPI = US$ consumer price indices

GIM = imports weighted (or weighted outbound tourism in monetary terms) by country of origin

RXP = relative weighted export price indices

N = matrix of overnight stays

ROW = rest of the world

U_k = error term.

$$g_{i,k} = \frac{n_{i,k}}{n_{T,k}}$$

$$g_{j,k} = \frac{n_{j,k}}{n_{T,k}}$$

$$g_{i,T} = \frac{n_{i,T}}{n_{T,T}}$$

Matrix N gives an overview of overnight stays by countries of origin and destination for 1998. Elements n_{ij}, with $(i,j = 1, \ldots, 25)$, denote the number of overnight stays by guests from country j in country i. The sums of columns and rows (n_{Tj} and n_{iT}) denote the total overnight stays in the destination countries, and the demand for overnight stays in the country of origin. The total number of overnights in 1998 is denoted as n_{TT}.

Real tourism exports (inbound tourism in monetary terms) of a country k are described by the equations:

$$X_k = c_0 + c_1 GIM_k + c_2 RXP_k + c_3 DV_k + U_k \tag{6.30}$$

$$GIM = \sum_{i=1}^{25} g_{k,j} M_j \tag{6.31}$$

$$RXP_k = VPI_k \bigg/ \sum_{i=1}^{25} g_{iT} * VPI_i \tag{6.32}$$

$$ROW = \Sigma X_i - \Sigma M_i \tag{6.33}$$

The explanatory demand variable for each country of destination is the weighted sum of imports (GIM), weighted by the country-specific guest structure by countries of origin for country k.

The relative weighted export price indices (RXP) are made up from the consumer price indices in destination k relative to price indices of competing countries (consumer price indices of destination countries, weighted by the overall demand structure).

This structural model provides a number of interesting results:

- Income-elasticity of import functions per country
- Income-elasticity of export functions per country

Table 6.2 Forecast of real tourism imports and exports at constant prices and exchange rates, 1985 (annual changes as percentages)

	Imports			*Exports*		
	1980–2001	*2001–2010*	*2010–2020*	*1980–2001*	*2001–2010*	*2010–2020*
Japan	7.7	3.2	2.4	3.9	3.6	2.5
USA	6.8	4.0	2.8	7.8	4.6	3.1
EU-15	4.8	3.6	2.4	4.2	3.3	2.3
EU- 19	4.9	3.8	2.6	4.1	3.4	2.4
Total 25 industrialized countries	5.1	3.8	2.7	5.0	3.8	2.6

Source: Adapted from Smeral (2004).

- Price-elasticity of import functions per country
- Price-elasticity of export functions per country.

The unweighted average income-elasticity of import function equals 2.45, and the export functions show an average demand elasticity of 1.09. Smeral (2003) attributes this big difference to the structure of the model: export functions are estimated through imports, and structural effects play a major role both on the demand and the price sides. Tourism imports of a country depend on its income as generating country, whereas exports depend on the income of many different tourism importing countries.

The price-elasticity of import functions averages at -1.24, and the average price-elasticity of tourism exports equals -1.0.

Smeral uses the results of this model to forecast imports and exports up to the year 2020, and introduces assumptions concerning GDP growth and CPI. variables drawn from several available sources. Furthermore, in Smeral's basic scenario EU enlargement (only four countries) is taken into account.

Some important results are summarized in Table 6.2. One very significant conclusion that can be derived from the application of the WTTOUR model is a downward slide of annual growth rates in the industrialized countries. However, the long-term growth rates are still above the overall economic growth rates. Smeral states that 'Travel will gradually lose its character of luxury good and saturation trends will become apparent, at least in some sectors'. Smeral is aware that other explanatory factors will also play an important role. He refers to sociological and demographic factors, values, lifestyles, tastes, fashions, attractive supply, marketing communication and transport technology, political developments, etc.

Final remarks

This chapter concludes with important comments:

1. All four case studies discussed in this chapter concern international tourism at the national level. This is also the case for the contributions referred to in the

bibliography, and can be generalized to almost all quantitative forecasting applications in tourism. The explanation is quite logical – data are collected at national level. As a consequence, it is much more difficult to apply quantitative methods at a lower geographical level such as a region or a destination. For smaller areas it is recommended that quantitative methods be combined with market share analysis (Pelzer, 1977) – the position of a destination with respect to competitive power, tourism policy, supply, etc.

2. In the tourism literature, quantitative methods attract more attention than qualitative models. However, so far there is no evidence that quantitative methods are superior. It is very difficult to capture such a complex phenomenon as tourism in a limited number of variables. Although a lot of progress has been made in tourism forecasting over the last two decades, there are still many deficiencies (Prideaux *et al.*, 2003). Sociological and psychological factors are difficult to express quantitatively, and unexpected crises and disasters are impossible to forecast. Where possible, a combination of rigorous quantitative analysis with qualitative approaches or a consensus of expert opinion is recommendable.

3. Most qualitative forecasting methods are better for medium- and long-term projections than quantitative models. They are more flexible and open to more explanatory factors.

4. Multiple regression analysis in tourism is more successful in testing the significance and/or efficiency of independent factors (policy factors) than in its long-term forecasting function. The situation is different for short-term forecasts because in many cases there are reliable projections of the basic independent factors, and it can be hoped that the other explanatory variables will not change in the short run.

5. The preceding point should not be an argument for paying less attention to forecasting. We returning to the statement at the beginning of this chapter: 'Those who believe in precise estimations start with the wrong attitude. In tourism, forecasting means indicating the future direction of demand – or, in other words, getting an idea of the magnitude of the expected evolution.' Knowledge of the direction of demand narrows the range of uncertainty, and this is vital for all investment and management decisions.

References and further reading

Archer, B. (1975). *Demand Forecasting Techniques*. Paper presented to a Seminar organized by the Organisation of American States, Mexico City (unpublished).

Archer, B. (1976). Forecasting tourism demand. In S. Wahab (ed.), *Managerial Aspects of Tourism*. Cairo: Salah Wahab.

Archer, B. (1994). Demand forecasting and estimation. In B. Ritchie and C. Goeldner (eds), *Travel, Tourism and Hospitality Research*. New York: John Wiley & Sons.

Armstrong, C. (1972). International tourism: coming or going? The methodological problems of forecasting. *Futures*, June.

Arthus, J. (1972). An econometric analysis of international travel. *IMF – Staff Papers*, 19.

Costa, P., Manente, M., Minghetti, V. and van der Borg, J. (1994). *Tourism Demand to and from Italy: The Forecasts to 1995 from the TRIP Models.* Venice: Ciset.

Crampon, L. and Tan, K. (1973). A model of tourism flow into the Pacific. *The Tourist Review*, 3.

Crouch, G., Schultz, L. and Valerio, P. (1992). Marketing international tourism to Australia. *Tourism Management*, June.

Cunliffe, S. (2002). Forecasting risks in the tourism industry using the Delphi technique. *Tourism*, 1.

Dritsakis, N. and Athanasiadis, S. (2000). An econometric model of tourist demand: the case of Greece. *Journal of Hospitality & Leisure Marketing*, 2.

Edwards, A. (1988). *International Tourism Forecasts to 1999*, EIU Special Report. London: EIU.

EIU (1992). *World Travel Forecasts, 1989–2005*, EIU Special Report. London: EIU.

EIU (1995). Real exchange rates and international tourism demand. *Travel & Tourism Analyst*, 4.

Frechtling, D. (1996). *Practical Tourism Forecasting*. Oxford: Butterworth-Heinemann.

Frechtling, D. (2001). *Forecasting Tourism Demand: Methods and Strategies*. Oxford: Butterworth-Heinemann.

Huybers, T. (2003). Modelling short-break holiday destination choices. *Tourism Economics*, 4.

Kotler, P. (1984). *Marketing Management: Analysis Planning and Control.* London: Prentice-Hall International.

Kulendran, N. (1996). Modelling quarterly tourist flows to Australia using cointegration analysis. *Tourism Economics*, 3.

Labor, G. (1969). Determinants of international travel between Canada and the United States. *Geographical Analysis*, I.

Lesceux, D. (1977). *La demande touristique en Méditerranée*. Aix-en-Provence: Centre d'Etudes du Tourisme.

Lim, C. and McAleer, M. (2002). Time series forecasts of international travel demand for Australia. *Tourism Management*, 23.

Martin, B. and Mason, S. (1990). Tourism futures. The use of scenarios analysis in forecasting. Paper presented to Conference on Tourism Research into the 1990s held at University College, Durham, 10–12 December 1990 (unpublished).

Moeller, G. and Shafer, E. (1994). The Delphi technique: a tool for long-range travel and tourism planning. In B. Ritchie and C. Goeldner (eds), *Travel, Tourism and Hospitality Research*. New York: John Wiley & Sons.

Müller, H., Kaspar, Cl. and Schmidhauser, H. (1991). *Tourismus 2010. Delphi-Umfrage 1991 zur Zukunft Schweizer Tourismus*. Bern/St.Gallen, ITV-FIF.

Obermair, K. (1998). *AIT Delphi Study. Future Trends in Tourism*. Vienna, Alliance Internationale de Tourisme.

Pelzer, J. (1977). *Développement dans les méthodes de prévision de la demande touristique, basé sur l' évolution des parts de marché*. Paris: OECD.

Prideaux, B., Laws, E. and Faulkner, B. (2003). Events in Indonesia: exploring the limits to formal tourism trends forecasting in complex crises situations. *Tourism Management*, 24.

Schwaninger, M. (1989). Trends in leisure and tourism for 2000–2010: scenario with consequences for planners. In S. Witt and L. Mouthinho (eds), *Tourism Marketing and Management Handbook*. Cambridge: Prentice Hall.

Smeral, E. (1994). *Tourismus 2005*. Vienna: Wifo.

Smeral, E. (2003). *Die Zukunft des internationalen Tourismus*. Vienna: Wifo.

Smeral, E. (2004). Long term forecasts for international tourism. *Tourism Economics*, 2.

Smeral, E. and Weber, A. (2000). Forecasting international tourism: trends to 2010. *Annals of Tourism Research*, 4.

Smith, S. (1997). *Tourism Analysis. A Handbook* 2nd edn. Edinburgh: Longman.

Song, H. and Witt, S. (2000). *Tourism Demand Modelling and Forecasting: Modern Econometric Approaches*. Oxford: Elsevier.

Song, H., Witt, S. and Li, G. (2003). Modelling and forecasting the demand for Thai tourism. *Tourism Economics*, 4.

Taylor, R. and Judd, L. (1989). Delphi method applied to tourism. In S. Witt and L. Mouthinho (eds), *Tourism Marketing and Management Handbook*. Cambridge: Prentice Hall.

Turner, L. and Witt, S. (2001). Forecasting tourism using univariate and multivariate structural time series models. *Tourism Economics*, 2.

Turner, L. and Witt, S. (2001b). Factors influencing demand for international tourism: tourism demand analysis using structural equation modelling, revisited. *Tourism Economics*, 1.

Uysal, M. and Crompton, J. (2000). An overview of approaches used to forecast tourism demand. In C. Tisdell (ed.), *The Economics of Tourism*. Cheltenham: Edward Elgar.

Witt, S. (1989). Forecasting international tourism demand: univariate time series methods. In S. Witt and L. Mouthinho (eds), *Tourism Marketing and Management Handbook*. London: Prentice Hall.

Witt, S. and Martin, C. (1991). Demand forecasting in tourism and recreation. In C. Cooper (ed.), *Progress in Tourism, Recreation and Hospitality Management*, Vol. 1. London: Belhaven Press.

Witt, S. and Moutinho, L. (1999). Demand modelling and forecasting. In L. Moutinho (ed.), *Strategic Management in Tourism*. Glasgow: C.A.B. International.

Witt, S. and Song, H. (2001). Forecasting future tourism flows. In A. Lockwood and S. Medlik (eds), *Tourism and Hospitality in the 21st* Century. Oxford: Butterworth-Heinemann.

Witt, S., Brooke, M. and Buckley, P. (1991). *The Management of International Tourism*. London: Unwin Hyman.

Witt, C., Witt, S. and Wilson, N. (1994). Forecasting international tourist flows. *Annals of Tourism Research*, 21(3).

Witt, S., Song, H. and Wanhill, S. (2004). Forecasting tourism-generated employment: the case of Denmark. *Tourism Economics*, 2.

7

The economic impact of tourism

Introduction

Tourism can have a great impact on regions and, obviously, destinations. The dimension of tourism worldwide has an economical, social, cultural and environmental influence on tourism destinations (Mathieson and Wall, 1982), and the influence can be positive and/or negative. This chapter focuses on the economic impact. Some sociological, cultural and environmental impacts will be dealt with as cost elements in here and in Chapter 8.

What are the main aspects of an economic impact? They can be classified into seven major groups:

1. Income generation
2. Employment generation
3. Tax revenue generation
4. Balance of payment effects
5. Improvement of the economic structure of a region
6. Encouragement of entrepreneurial activity
7. Economic disadvantages.

Six major factors govern the magnitude of the economic impact:

1. The nature of the main facility and its attractiveness
2. The volume and intensity of expenditure

3. The level of economic development in the destination
4. The size of the economic base of the destination
5. The degree to which tourist expenditures recirculate within the destination
6. The degree to which the destination has adjusted to the seasonality of tourist demand (Mathieson and Wall, 1982).

Most of these generic advantages and disadvantages, and the factors just mentioned, will be developed in the different sections of this chapter. In the first section, 'tourism' is considered as a strategic dimension of regional and national economic development. Tourism has a number of comparative advantages relative to most other sectors in the development of backward areas. A later section examines the balance of payment effects, and will show that these effects are much more than inbound and outbound expenditures.

In tourism it is quite common to speak of direct and indirect effects, and most measurement methods make a distinction between each group of effects. To allow better understanding of those effects, we will explain the underlying mechanism. This brings us to the famous and magic 'tourism multiplier'. In fact, there is a whole variety of multipliers. Some clarification and demystification of the multiplier concept is necessary.

The main part of this chapter focuses on the measurement of income and employment generation. Special aspects concern tax-revenue generation, the impact of events, the qualitative aspects of employment in tourism, improvement of the economic structure of a region, and encouragement of entrepreneurial activity. Most of these aspects are interwoven with topics dealt with in other sections of this chapter.

Tourism as a strategic dimension of economic development

Until relatively recently, tourism was not considered to be a vehicle for economic development. The first Lomé Conference for ACP countries, in 1975, rejected tourism as a sector to be supported in the developing process of less developed countries. At that time, the attitude towards tourism was rather negative in some publications (de Kadt, 1979) – tourism provoked leakages, lack of foreign exchange, inflation, etc. Fifteen years later, on the occasion of the fourth Lomé Conference, the attitude had completely changed. Tourism had become a very important vehicle for development. Why the radical change? In the 1980s many publications proved the benefits of tourism, and gradually the attitude of international organizations changed. The second Lomé Conference paid little attention to this, but by the third Lomé Conference, in 1985, the change of attitude was noticeable. Tourism at last received the interest it deserved.

Why was it so long before tourism was recognized as a valuable component of economic development? In the 1970s, many publications – reports, books and articles – were written by authors who had never been in a developing country and/or who had an inadequate economic background. Import leakages, income transfers, foreign ownership, tourism as a factor of inflation, destruction of culture, mono-industry and social impacts were the key words in many publications. It cannot be denied that all these negative factors exist to some degree in many destinations; however, from an economic point of view it is not realistic to deny positive factors either. Mass tourism is unimaginable without economic return.

Many benefits are mentioned in the literature, but the subject is as chaotic and diverse as the Tower of Babel. Frequently mentioned variables include expenditure, income generation, employment creation, foreign exchange earnings, tax receipts, social benefits, the tourism multiplier, the transaction multiplier, and many more benefits or presumed benefits. Very often these variables are not put into their right context or relationships.

To define the role of tourism as a strategic dimension in regional and national development, and as a background for the tourism multiplier (see below), we refer first to some notions of regional (destination) economics.

Basic and non-basic activities

In regional development theory great emphasis is placed on the basic/non-basic approach, a distinction being made between basic and non-basic activities. A non-basic activity is defined as an activity that for economic reasons needs to be performed within the areas considered (e.g. shops, primary schools); a basic activity is one that, although performed within the boundaries of the area, need not to be located there (e.g. industrial plants, universities). It follows from this definition that non-basic activities are not exported to other areas; since the same holds for other areas, neither are there imports of those activities. By definition, therefore, there is no interregional trade of services or goods produced by non-basic industries. It should be emphasized that a basic industry is not necessarily an importing industry; it may export its products just as the area might import its products. In terms of a region's (nation's) balance of payments, a basic industry will reduce imports or contribute to exports (or both). It follows that basic activities generate initial income in the region. This income will be spent partly in the region, and the relationship to non-basic activities is quite evident.

However, the concept of non-basic activity is more complex than is generally presented. So far, we have linked non-basic activity to basic activities through the spending of consumers' income earned in basic activities, but there are also non-basic activities that originate in spending by the basic industries themselves. If basic industries purchase goods or services (e.g. transportation services), although part of these services may have to be performed within the area, they certainly are not non-basic in the sense used so far. These goods are produced, or these services are rendered, only because the basic industry is located in and producing within the region (Klaassen and Van Wickeren, 1975); their production is induced as a secondary production. Secondary effects can be called non-basic in so far as they must be produced within the region, and basic in so far as they need not. With the introduction of the secondary effects the distinction between basic and non-basic becomes vaguer, and a distinction between multipliers for different industries becomes necessary (see below).

Surprisingly, in regional economics, agriculture and industry are mostly classified in the group of basic activities, and tertiary activity is considered to be the non-basic group. The very term 'basic industries' illustrates that general idea; however, it is, of course, too rough a classification. Not all agriculture and industrial activities are basic, and not all services rendered are non-basic. Tourism is an excellent example of the latter, all the services rendered by the tourism sector of a region being exports to other regions. Its contribution to the balance of payments of the region is by definition positive, and tourism generates initial income in the region. Tourism is also a good illustration of an activity that by its own spending supports other branches; when the tourist sector purchases goods (for instance, a hotel buying bread from the bakery) or services (e.g. transportation services) these may be produced in the region but cannot be compared with non-basic activities in the strict sense.

As a basic activity, tourism can be a development vehicle with comparative advantages for backward regions and developing countries.

Comparative advantages of tourism

A tourist product is composed of several elements: attractions, facilities, transport, entertainment, image, etc. The basic element is the attractions, which can be of very different types. Many developing countries or developing regions in Europe are rich in natural or man-made attractions. A development based on these attractions offers the tourism sector some comparative advantages *vis-à-vis* other economic sectors.

The first comparative advantage is directly related to natural attractions (e.g. sun, beaches, mountains, etc.) and many cultural attractions (e.g. churches, castles, abbeys, museums, etc.). These attractions are raw materials that can become beneficial as attractions at limited cost, and the danger of exhaustion is more or less non-existent. As Mossé (1973) comments:

> Besides, the host country may have been endowed by nature with an abundance of readily marketable assets for whose enjoyment tourists are willing to pay: sandy beaches, picturesque sites (mountains and forests), a sunny climate, and the remnants of ancient civilizations. Out of the 20 dollars, the tourist may well have gladly spent 5–6 dollars to enjoy these 'free utilities', as Bastiat would have called them, on whose supply the host country did not have to spend a penny, either in local or in foreign currency.

The question is how to internalize these benefits. The only channels are higher value added creation in the supplying enterprises and the related taxes.

This first comparative advantage should be situated in a broader context of international trade theory. The theories of factor endowments (Heckscher–Ohlin theory) and absolute advantage (Vellas and Bécherel, 1995) can be applied. The first theory posits that the international tourism specialization of a country will be directly linked to an abundance of the resource necessary to develop the supply of tourism products for which there is a demand. Vellas and Bécherel make a distinction between three categories of factor endowments:

1. Natural resources, culture and cultural heritage
2. Human resources
3. Capital and infrastructure resources.

The theory of absolute advantage (and technological advantage) is a development of Adam Smith's analysis of international trade. Absolute advantage plays a crucial role in international tourism. As Vellas and Bécherel put it:

> Certain countries have unique tourism resources which can be either exceptional natural sites, like the Grand Canyon, or, more usually, architectural or artistic resources known all over the world. These

man-made resources motivate tourists to visit a country. Their importance
in terms of international tourism factors is determined by their
uniqueness which gives a country a monopoly or a near-monopoly.

This statement applies as well to natural attractions; the word 'countries' can
be replaced by 'destinations'. Typical examples of such unique tourism resources are
the Taj Mahal, the Borobodour Temple, the Angkor Wat, the Pyramids, the Acropolis,
the Forbidden Palace, Bali, Macchu Pichu, the Iguaçu Falls, the Norwegian Fjords,
Paris, London, Venice, Bruges, Prague and Vienna, and so many others.

The second comparative advantage concerns the import content. There are
grounds to believe that tourism on average has a lower import content than other
basic economic sectors. A number of publications support this thesis (UNCTAD,
1971; Theuns, 1975). The reason is evident: the tourists are buying services that the
local population can provide to a large extent. Furthermore, it is not too difficult – at
least in most regions – to develop the agricultural sector, in the long run, towards the
needs of the hospitality industry. Mossé supports this point of view. 'As a source of
foreign exchange, tourism is on a par with other export industries, but with one difference: they {export industries} require costly inputs' (Mossé, 1973; Vanhove, 1977).

The third advantage is the very high growth rate noted earlier. This growth,
together with the good prospects and high-income elasticity, makes tourism a
preferential sector for economic development.

Fourthly, tourism has a stabilizing effect on exports. Export markets in raw
materials are unstable, and therefore foreign earnings are uncertain. This is not the
case with tourism products (either in terms of volume or price). The price obtained
for raw materials is governed by the world market price, and is subject to terms-
of-trade conditions. To avoid a deterioration of terms-of-trade, tourism development is often a solution. Mass tourism yields important amounts of foreign
exchange, which allow the country to import manufactured goods. The counter-
part is a limited quantity of resources. To quote Mossé (1973):

> A balance of what is given and what is received should be struck not on
> the basis of the hours of work necessary, but in regard to the utility of the
> items exchanged. The utility of exports consisting of abundant wild fruit,
> stretches of sandy desert or trees growing by themselves in the forest, is
> insignificant, in contrast to the great utility of importing electrical and
> telephone equipment, transport facilities, etc.
>
> Unfortunately, there is no universally accepted measure of utility and
> use must be made of costs expressed in money or man-hours.

The tourism sector should not, however, be presented in too optimistic a manner.
Tourism is very sensitive to internal problems, political events, diseases, bad news, etc.

A fifth comparative advantage is related to the labour-intensive nature of the
sector. This high labour intensity is notable in the accommodation sector, the sub-
contracting sector, services, etc. This comparative advantage finds a lot of support
in economic theory.

Other benefits

Development of tourism on a large scale, based on mass tourism, creates external
economies. Improvements in transportation networks, water quality and sanitation

facilities may have been prompted by the tourist industry, but also benefit other sectors of the economy. An international airport – a *conditio sine qua non* for tourism development – provides improved access to other regions for locally produced goods.

Another benefit is the generation of entrepreneurial activity. According to Mathieson and Wall (1982), the extent to which the tourism sector can establish linkages with local entrepreneurs depends on:

- The types of suppliers and producers with which the industry's demands are linked
- The ability of local suppliers to meet these demands
- The historical development of tourism in the destination area
- The type of tourist development.

In terms of technical polarization, backward linkages can be identified. When a number of big hotels are located in a region, there is an immediate demand for large volumes of agricultural products and different kinds of services. Local suppliers are often unable to meet this demand in quantity and quality. After a number of years, however, the imported supplies might decrease and the local supplies increase, depending on the ability of local suppliers to meet the new demands. Entrepreneurial activity may be further stimulated by the external economies created (de Kadt, 1979; Mathieson and Wall, 1982; Krippendorf *et al.*, 1982; Vanhove, 1986; Bull, 1995; Frechtling, 1994).

Economic disadvantages

Each coin has two sides. Benefits were dealt with in the preceding section, but there is no economic activity or project without costs. A distinction is made between private costs (e.g. a hotel) and external diseconomies. The costs the latter impose are called incidental costs. The sum of private costs and incidental costs is called the social costs of an activity. There is an extensive literature dealing with benefits and costs of tourism. Some authors have emphasized the cost side (Krippendorf, 1975; de Kadt, 1979), others have stressed the benefits (Archer, 1991a), and a third category pays attention to both sides of the coin (Mathieson and Wall, 1982; Bull, 1995; Frechtling, 1994).

It is often commented that few studies have attempted to pay attention to economic costs of tourism in a systematic way. Mathieson and Wall assert that research has been limited largely to the measurement of the more obvious costs, such as investment in facilities, promotion and advertising, transportation and other infrastructure. Most studies have failed to address the indirect costs, such as the importation of goods for tourists, inflation, the transfer of the profits, economic dependence and opportunity costs (Mathieson and Wall, 1982). Nevertheless, a correct assessment of benefits takes into account a number of these qualifications.

Indeed, all transfers and imports should be eliminated. As a consequence, leakages are taken into account and the tourist income multiplier is lower. However, local inhabitants might change their buying behaviour due to a 'demonstration effect' of tourists (e.g. purchase imported products instead of local ones).

It is agreed that opportunity costs must be considered. If labour or land is used for tourism its social cost to an economy is its opportunity cost – or the cost of the opportunity of using it in the (presumably) next best activity. However, in most tourist countries or regions with a tourism vocation there is no full employment. The question is seldom 'manufacturing or tourism?' but very often 'tourism or unemployment?'. Even when an alternative activity can be retained, a tourism region with valuable resources starts from the free raw materials as a main advantage. Is it not remarkable that many objective 1 regions of Southern Europe, eligible for European Regional Development Fund support, have opted for tourism as a strategic development path?

Over-dependence on tourism can be a danger. The sensitivity of tourism demand to all kinds of external factors has been emphasized above. Tourism is susceptible to changes from within (e.g. price changes and changing fashions) and outside (e.g. global economic trends in the generating markets, political situations, religious confrontations and energy availability).

Tourism and inflation

'Tourism produces inflation' is a frequently heard saying, and a very dangerous slogan. The relationship between tourism and inflation is more complex, temporal and local.

A high inflow of tourists during a season can provoke a rise in prices of many goods and services in the tourist region. Durand *et al.* (1994) assert that it is indisputable that in cities and tourist areas the prices for products and services are in general higher than in cities or regions where there is little or no tourism, and that in holiday resorts the prices for tourist services are higher in the peak season than in the rest of the year. This upswing of prices is presumably greater in poor regions than in richer ones. Tourists can afford to buy items at high prices, so retailers increase their prices of existing products and provide more expensive goods. This has two consequences: first, local residents have to pay more for their goods; and secondly, retailers selling to tourists can afford to pay higher rents and taxes, which are passed on to the consumer (Mathieson and Wall, 1982).

How far away is the impact noticed? Tourist demand is very often concentrated in a limited number of streets or areas. Local residents change their buying behaviour and move to other points of sale. Furthermore, tourists in general are only interested in a narrow range of goods and services, such as souvenirs, sport articles, clothes, beauty products, meals and special products (e.g. chocolates and lace in Bruges).

A different aspect is the price evolution of accommodation (hotels, rented apartments) and other facilities. In the short term, supply is inelastic and an upswing of mass tourism in a region may lead to higher prices. There is not always much discipline in the tourism sector. A substantial increase in demand is followed by price increases. Regions very often forget that they are in competition with other regions, and the movement of demand from one Mediterranean country to another is a well-known phenomenon.

It is said that mass tourism makes land prices higher. Growth of tourism creates additional demand for land, and competition from potential buyers forces the price of land to rise. The local inhabitants are forced to pay more for their homes. Are the increasing land values to be considered negatively? All owners, land-owners and local residents, profit from the additional value. From the macro-economic point of view, the final result is a benefit. Furthermore, this effect is quite local.

All in all, the impact of tourism on local residents should not be overemphasized. The costs are largely compensated for by the benefits: greater wealth, more jobs and higher land values. However, there can be situations – when tourism demand is very high – where inflationary tensions in tourism spill over into the economy at large and contribute to a rise in general inflation. In some countries tourism demand represents 10 per cent and more of the GDP, and inter-sectoral linkages of tourism are intensive.

Another question is: what are the factors responsible for inflationary pressure in the tourism sector? The French authors Durand *et al.* (1994) make a distinction between demand and cost inflation in the tourism sector. First of all there is demand inflation, which results in:

- Seasonal demand
- Inelastic supply
- An insufficient market reaction (certain resorts or firms profit from an economic rent)
- Imported inflation due to international arrivals (impact of hard currencies and increase of the money mass).

Cost inflation is a consequence of a number of factors:

- Peak management
- High taxes on some tourist products and services.

However, prices cannot be increased without considering the consumer – given the law of supply and demand, which stabilizes prices. Many tourists have changed their destination from France to Spain and from Spain to elsewhere because of price differentials.

Incidental costs of tourism

The costs emphasized by de Kadt, Krippendorf and many other authors are summarized very neatly by Frechtling (1994), and covered by the term 'incidental costs' or detrimental externalities or external diseconomies.

Incidental costs, according to Frechtling, lead to quality-of-life costs and public or fiscal costs. Indeed, the local population of a region affected by external diseconomies of tourism can choose to deal with them in one of three ways:

1. They may have to accept a lower quality of life than they enjoyed without tourists
2. They may redress the decline in their quality of life through public expenditure for which they pay taxes
3. They may directly impose monetary costs on the tourists through taxes and fees.

Table 7.1 summarizes a number of important categories of incidental costs that are related to tourism import. It is not certain that a specific volume of tourists will produce costs in all categories.

Table 7.1 Possible direct incidental costs of tourism

Life-quality costs	Fiscal costs
Traffic congestion	Highway construction, police services, public transportation, port and terminal facilities
Crime	Police services, justice system
Fire emergencies	Fire protection
Water pollution	Water supply and sewage treatment
Air pollution	Police services, public transportation
Litter	Solid waste disposal, police services
Noise pollution	Police services, zoning
Destruction of wildlife	Police services, park and recreation facilities, forestry maintenance, fish and game regulation
Destruction of scenic beauty	Park and recreation facilities, police services
Destruction of social/cultural heritage	Maintenance of museums and historic sites, police services
Disease	Hospitals and other health maintenance facilities, sanitation facilities, food service regulation
Vehicular accidents	Police services, justice system

Source: Frechtling (1994).

Besides direct incidental costs, Frechtling (1994) distinguishes secondary incidental costs. Additional visitors lead to new businesses, or the extension of existing ones, which in turn require more employees and consequently a greater population. The latter imposes additional life-quality and fiscal costs on the community. Some of these costs for the additional residents are similar to those of additional visitors.

It is beyond the scope of this chapter to develop these indirect costs which are not generated directly by tourists, but indirectly. One example is very typical. Tourism demand is seasonal in many regions, and provides seasonal job opportunities. The region or country attracts a labour force that requires unemployment compensation and other income transfer programmes during the off-peak season.

Balance of payments and tourism

For a long time, earning foreign currencies was considered to be the main benefit of international tourism. For many developing countries earning hard currencies has a vital significance, and tourism is a welcome source of the foreign currencies they need to finance necessary imports. The relative importance of tourism with respect to foreign currencies is far less important for developed countries.

Nevertheless, in many western countries in the 1950s and 1960s tourism was considered to influence the international liquidity position. It is not so long ago – in the 1960s – that France and the United Kingdom took the decision to restrict their citizens taking holidays abroad in order to support their balance of payments and, more particularly, to protect the value of their own national currency. This was a kind of tourism import quota. The impact of these restrictive measures could be serious for some destinations (e.g. the Belgian Coast suffered from the British and French decision in 1967), but the overall effect on the balance of payments for the generating countries was rather limited. Some governments overestimated the role of international tourism on the value of the local currency. To get a better understanding of the role of tourism in the international liquidity position, we must define the place of the sector in the balance of payments. This is not limited to the travel account. This section should make it clear.

The balance of payments is 'an account which shows a country's financial transactions with the rest of the world. It records inflows and outflows of currency' (Tribe, 1997). It is a statement that takes into account the value of all goods, all services, all foreign aid, all capital loans and (in former days) all gold coming in and going out, and the interrelations underlying all these items (Samuelson, 1964; Bull, 1995).

The structure of the balance of payments

The basic convention applied in constructing a balance of payments statement is that every recorded transaction is represented by two entries with equal values. One of these entries is designated a credit (positive), while the other is designated a debit (negative). In principle, the sum of all credit entries is identical to the sum of all debit entries, and the net balance of all entries in the statement is zero. In practice, however, the amounts frequently do not balance. Data for balance of payments estimated are often derived independently from different sources, and as a result there may be a summary net credit or net debit (i.e. net errors and omissions in the accounts). A separate entry, equal to that amount with the sign reversed, is then made to balance the accounts.

A balance of payments (IMF standard presentation) is composed of two main parts:

1. The current account, which includes
   - goods
   - invisibles or services (travel, transportation, other services)
   - income (compensation of employees, investment income)
   - current transfers
2. The capital and financial account, which refers to capital transfers and acquisitions/disposal of non-produced, non-financial assets, and financial assets and liabilities
   - capital account (e.g. migrants' transfers, debt forgiveness)
   - financial account (direct investment abroad, direct investment in the country)
   - portfolio investment (assets, liabilities)
   - financial derivatives
   - other investments
   - reserve assets.

As described above, there is generally a third and minor part: net errors and omissions.

Let us illustrate all this with a practical case – the balance of payments for Spain, a typical tourism destination.

From Table 7.2, it can be derived that tourism is a major export item for Spain (32.7 billion US dollars). Travel represents 18.7 per cent of the total exports of goods and services and 15.7 per cent of all credits in the current account. The net

Table 7.2 The balance of payments for Spain, standard presentation, 2001 (millions of US dollars)

	Exports/credits	*Imports/debits*	*Balance*
Current account			−15082
▪ Goods	117561	−149061	−31500
▪ Services	57775	−33516	24258
▪ Travel	(32718)	(−5961)	(26757)
▪ Income	19796	−29342	−9545
▪ Current transfers	12567	−10862	1705
Capital and financial account			22186
▪ Capital account	5833	−872	4960
▪ Financial account			17226
▪ Direct investment			−6164
(abroad)		−27704	
(in Spain)	21540		
▪ Portfolio investment			−15959
▪ Assets		−43528	
▪ Liabilities	27569		
▪ Financial derivatives			47
▪ Other investment			37962
▪ Reserve assets			1340
Net errors and omissions			−7104

Source: IMF, *Balance of Payments Statistics Yearbook* (2002).

travel balance amounts to 26.7 billion US dollars. However the travel balance of Spain in Table 7.2 shows only the top of the total tourism balance (see above). Let us now pay a little more attention to the travel balance of EU countries, Australia, Japan, USA and a number of developing countries specializing in tourism.

The share of tourism exports in total exports of goods and services of the countries in Table 7.3 varies from 46.3 per cent for Cyprus and 30.4 for Greece to only 2.6 per cent for Germany and the Netherlands and 0.7 per cent for Japan. All Mediterranean countries show a share of 8.2 per cent or more; all these countries register a positive net travel balance. Notice the high net negative travel balance of Germany and the United Kingdom. The net positive travel balance of the United States is striking; this is largely due to personal travel and not business travel.

A travel deficit in itself is not bad; it must be seen in the framework of the international trade theories. Many factors can be responsible for such a deficit: tourism supply, exchange rate, climate, and economic health of the country. The thesis of a balance in the travel account, which is sometimes put forward, is a dangerous one. We fully agree with Gray (1970) when he posits:

> The idea of the desirability of balance in travel account f.o.b. might seem to argue for balance in all sub accounts of the balance of payments or particularly in the current balance. That this is a spurious doctrine which would contravene all mechanisms whereby nations gain from the exchange of goods and services needs no detailed investigation here. Such a concept, carried out to its ultimate, would debar trade in all categories

Table 7.3 Travel balance per country, 2001 (millions of U.S. dollars) *

Country	Travel credit (a)	Travel debit (b)	Travel balance (c)	Export goods and services (d)	((a/d) · 100)
Austria	10 244	−8 885	1 359	79 795	12.8
Belgium-Lux.	7 622	−10 548	−2 926	207 450	3.7
Denmark	4 624	−5 534	−970	77 856	5.9
Finland	1 437	−1 852	−415	48 776	2.7
France	30 450	−18 060	12 390	371 800	8.2
Germany	17 200	−46 120	−28 920	657 450	2.6
Greece	9 155	−4 177	4 978	30 071	30.4
Ireland	2 753	−2 869	−116	98 565	2.7
Italy	25 815	−14 210	11 605	299 978	8.6
Netherlands	6 710	−11 993	−5 283	255 875	2.6
Portugal	5 464	−2 102	3 362	34 582	15.8
Spain	32 718	−5 961	26 757	175 336	18.7
Sweden	4 253	−6 921	−2 668	98 198	4.3
United Kingdom	18 180	−37 940	−18 180	386 500	4.7
Cyprus	2 006	−427	1 579	4 329	46.3
Czech Republic	3 104	−1 386	1 718	40 496	7.7
Estonia	505	−191	314	4 981	10.1
Hungary	3 920	−1 306	2 614	35 778	10.9
Latvia	119	−224	−105	3 403	3.2
Lithuania	383	−218	165	6 046	6.3
Malta	578	−180	398	3 110	18.6
Poland	4 645	−3 495	1 150	51 419	9.0
Slovak Republic**	443	−296	147	14 317	3.1
Slovenia	1 001	−528	473	11 303	8.9
Australia	7 693	−5 807	1 886	79 909	9.6
Japan	3 310	−26 530	−23 220	448 110	0.7
Switzerland	7 509	−6 350	1 159	123 552	6.1
United states	90 090	−62 670	27 420	998 030	9.0
Kenya	308	−143	165	2 981	10.3
Morocco	2 583	−389	2 194	11 171	23.1
Mexico	8 400	−5 702	2 698	171 142	4.9
Thailand	7 075	−2 924	4 151	76 226	9.3

* Travel excludes passenger services, which are included in transportation; ** 2000.
Source: IMF, *Balance of Payments Statistics Yearbook* (2002).

except those in which two-ways trade takes place and would be even more constraining than insistence upon bilateral balancing of trade with each individual trading partner.

The real tourism external account

As noticed earlier, the travel account is only part of the story (see also the TSA in Chapter 2). To find out what tourism is worth to a country, we should include all international transactions that are in some way necessary because of tourism

Table 7.4 Tourism external account according to Baretje and Defert

Credit	Debit
Tourist receipts from abroad	Tourist expenditures abroad
Exports of goods	Imports of goods (food and equipment)
Transportation (payments by foreign companies)	Transportation (payments to foreign companies)
Foreign tourism investments	Tourist investment abroad
Dividends, interest and profit received	Dividends, interest and profit paid out
Training of foreign staff	Payments for training abroad
Income from national workers abroad	Salaries repatriated abroad
Promotion	Promotion
Other services	Other services
Balance: deficit	Balance: surplus

(Baretje and Defert, 1972; Durand *et al.*, 1994). These include not only final tourism payments, but also international payments for goods and services needed for investment in and operation of the tourism industry. The result can be termed the 'real tourism external account'. Baretje and Defert were the first to develop such a real tourism account (see Table 7.4). Later the WTO (1988) developed a standard model (see Table 7.5).

Both tables give a totally different view than the traditional balance of payments of the real significance of the international tourism transactions. However, it is not so simple to estimate all the different items.

In line with the preceding paragraphs, Airey (1978) divided the effects of tourism on the balance of payments into three categories: primary, secondary and tertiary effects. The primary effect refers to tourism receipts from abroad and payments of residents abroad. Secondary effects are the effects on the balance of payments of the direct tourist expenditures as they percolate through the economy. Secondary effects, therefore, do not require the initial visitor expenditure to have taken place in another country (Mathieson and Wall, 1982). They may appear in a number of different forms:

- Direct secondary (import hotels, marketing expenditure abroad, dividend payments to overseas investors etc.)
- Indirect secondary effects (imports of subcontractors)
- Induced secondary effects (expenditures permeate through the economy and this creates a multiplier effect).

Tertiary effects are flows of currency not initiated by tourist expenditures (purchase of travellers' requisites, export stimulus of foreign products – such as the purchase of ouzo at home after a visit to Greece). The distinction between primary, secondary and tertiary effects is interesting from the theoretical point of view, but difficult to identify in practice.

Finally, the travel account is drawn up according to two possible approaches. The first is the 'survey method', and is based on periodic surveys to measure tourist receipts and expenditures. This is the case in the United Kingdom and the United States. France, Germany and many other European countries, however, practise

Table 7.5 A model of a real tourism external account

Tourism accounts	Credit	Debit	Balance
A. Service accounts			
A.1. international travel			
1. pleasure			
2. professional			
3. other purposes			
A.2. tourism services			
1. restaurants, bars, cafés			
2. hotels, etc.			
3. international transport			
4. other tourism services			
B. Income accounts			
B.1. earnings from work in tourism			
B.2. earnings from tourism investments			
C. Transfer accounts			
C.1. private tourism sector			
C.2. public tourism sector			
I. Current account balance (A + B + C)			
D. Capital account			
D.1. direct tourism investment			
D.2. portfolio tourism investment			
D.3. investment in tourism property (real estate)			
D.4. other tourism investment			
D.5. commercial credits related to tourism			
D.6. loans to tourism enterprises			
II. Basic tourism balance = (I + D)			

Source: Adapted from WTO (1988).

the *méthode bancaire* or bank method (Durand *et al.*, 1994). This method is based on financial regulations and exchange figures from banks and other financial institutions (Bull, 1995). Both methods have pros and cons, but the bank method has the big disadvantage that the purpose of a financial transaction is not always clear. Furthermore, in a monetary zone such as the euro-zone there are no longer exchange transactions by the individual tourist.

The magic tourism multiplier

The basics of the tourism multiplier

Mathieson and Wall (1982) define the tourist multiplier 'as a number by which initial tourist expenditure must be multiplied in order to obtain the total cumulative income effect for a specific time period'. This is a dangerous definition, as it is presented as a black box process and there is a variation in multiplier values;

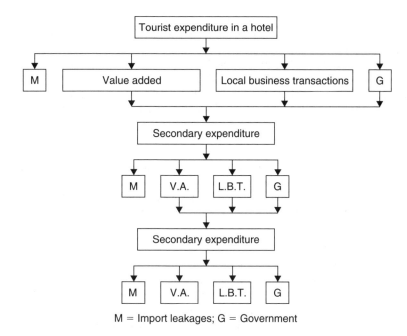

M = Import leakages; G = Government

Figure 7.1 The tourism multiplier mechanism (adapted from Cooper *et al.*, 1993)

the income multiplier is one of them. A more precise description can be found in Fletcher and Archer (1992). It is based upon the recognition that the various sectors that make up the economy are interdependent. In addition to purchasing primary inputs such as labour, imports, etc., each sector will purchase intermediate goods produced by other establishments within the local economy. Therefore, any autonomous change in the level of final demand (domestic expenditures, inbound tourism or investments) will not only affect the industry that produces that final good, but also that industry's suppliers and suppliers' suppliers, etc.

Owing to this sector interdependence, any change in final demand will bring about a change in the economy's level of output, income employment and government revenue. The term 'multiplier' refers to the ratio of the change in one of the above variables to the change in final demand that brought it about. We can illustrate the mechanism with the following scheme (see Figure 7.1).

Taking the expenditure in a hotel as a starting point, to whom does this expenditure accrue? One part creates value added or factor remuneration in the hotel. It is direct income within the region concerned. A second part leads to local business transactions – a hotelier must restock inventories to provide for future sales (bread, meat, vegetables, fruit, etc.). A third part of the expenditure is used to pay profit taxes, local taxes, etc. to local, regional or national governments. A fourth part is spent on leakages such as imports of goods (e.g. whisky) and payment of profits to people and organizations outside the region or country.

Purchases of meat, bread and vegetables provoke, in turn, the same above-mentioned effects – income creation, intermediate purchases, public transfers and import leakages – for the butcher, the baker and the farmer, etc. This process continues with a third and a fourth round. Following each round, the national or regional effects become smaller. The income created in successive rounds is called the indirect income, and the degree of magnitude of these indirect effects is governed by the extent to which business firms in the nation or region supply each other with goods.

However, a second derived impact can be noted. The more wages and profits (direct and indirect) due to the hotel expenditure rise, the more consumer expenditure increases – and this provides a further impetus to economic activity. Additional business turnover occurs, and this generates income. These are the so-called induced effects.

The indirect and induced effects together (called secondary effects – but note that this must not be confused with secondary expenditure) can be quite considerable in the absence of important leakages, such as savings (assuming that sufficient resources are available). In Figure 7.1, indirect and induced effects are presented together.

To summarize, there are three different effects:

1. The direct effect of a change in final demand refers to first-round effects
2. The indirect effect recognizes the need for an industry – subject to a change in final demand for its product – to make purchases from other industries within an economy in order to produce its output
3. The induced effect occurs as income levels rise throughout the economy as a result of the initial change in final demand, and a portion of the increased income is re-spent on final goods produced within the local economy. This additional local expenditure, arising from increased income, will generate further repercussive effects. The addition to total output, income, employment and government revenue caused by this re-spending of local income is known as the induced effect.

Two important observations should be made. First, the supplying firms should have of enough resources and spare factors of production. Secondly, there are few arguments to suggest that induced effects in tourism are different from the same effects in other sectors. The consumer behaviour of tourism earners cannot be so different from that of textile earners or other economic sectors.

Determining factors

The first factor is the size of the destination – the smaller the size of the region, the bigger the leakages. The second factor concerns inter-sector linkages. A monostructure, by definition, leads to high imports (see next section).

This brings us to the third factor, or possible leakages. There are three well-known leakages:

1. The saving quota of the population of the destination
2. The import quota, or the share of tourism expenditure that is spent to imported products
3. The tax quota, or the share going to the public sector.

A fourth possible factor is the supply constraints in the economy (see below).

Types of multipliers

There is a lot of confusion about the term 'tourism multiplier'. In reality there are several types, each with its own meaning.

The most interesting is the *tourism income multiplier* (TIM). It shows the relationship between an additional unit of tourist spending and the changes that result in the level of income in the economy. However, in theory, any income accruing to non-nationals resident in the area is usually extracted from the sum.

With respect to the income multiplier, a further distinction is made between the orthodox income multiplier (also called 'ratio' multiplier) and the unorthodox income multiplier (see Mathieson and Wall, 1982; De Brabander, 1992; Mihalic, 2002). For both income multipliers, two types are distinguished:

1. Orthodox income multipliers
   - type I – (direct + indirect income)/direct income
   - type II – (direct + indirect + induced income)/direct income
2. Unorthodox income multipliers
   - type I – (direct + indirect income)/change in final demand (additional expenditures)
   - type II – (direct + indirect + induced income)/change in final demand (additional unit of spending).

These orthodox multipliers are of little value, although they can give an idea of the degree of internal linkages in the local economy. Much more emphasis should be given to the two types of unorthodox income multipliers. The multiplier with the greatest practical value and that makes the most sense is undoubtedly the *unorthodox income multiplier type I*.

Table 7.6 lists the values of the orthodox and unorthodox multipliers of type II of a number of sources; these statistics give an idea of the great differences in function of the destination and accommodation forms.

Table 7.6 Values of various type II multipliers

	Direct income	Orthodox multiplier	Unorthodox multiplier
Gwynedd case (Archer et al., 1974)			
■ Hotel	0.23	1.43	0.32
■ Bed and breakfast	0.57	1.10	0.63
■ Caravan	0.14	1.49	0.21
■ Composite	–	1.34	0.37
Seychelles (Archer)	0.34	2.87	0.88
Edinburgh (Vaughan, 1977)			
■ Hotel	0.20	1.43	0.29
■ Bed and breakfast	0.14	1.80	0.26
■ Caravan	0.16	1.38	0.22
■ Composite	0.19	1.47	0.28
Flanders (Vanhove, 1993 – type I)			
■ Composite	–	1.30	0.57
Antwerp province (Yzewijn and De Brabander, 1989 – type I)	–	1.36	0.57

Looking at Table 7.6, an expenditure of 100 euros in Edinburgh leads to a direct income of only 19 euros and the sum of direct, indirect and induced effects amounts to 28 euros; these effects are of course higher from the point of view of Scotland or the United Kingdom – the larger the region, the lower the leakages. Notice the very different effects per accommodation type.

Archer and Fletcher (1990) have compiled a number of income multipliers (probably unorthodox income multipliers: (direct + indirect + induced income creation)/direct income creation) from reports and publications. The calculation of these multipliers is based on different methods and refers to different periods. Some of them are listed in Table 7.7 to illustrate how different they can be.

It is obvious from Table 7.7 that the larger area, the higher the corresponding tourism multiplier value. The value of the multiplier is determined by the structure of the economy, the inter-sector relations, the import content, and the nature of the tourism product etc.

As stated above, the greatest interest is in the unorthodox income multiplier of the type (direct + indirect income creation)/tourist expenditure. With the knowledge of the expenditure and the tourism income multiplier, direct and indirect income creation can be estimated. The crucial point is the knowledge of TIM, which is unknown. However, TIM-values can sometimes be used for countries and/or destinations with similar products and general economic circumstances.

One precaution should be mentioned. There is quite often confusion between the terms 'multiplier' and 'multiplicand'. The quantity of expenditure is basically the multiplicand. However, not all the expenditure is available to create income in the destination; some tourist expenditure never enters the economy at all (e.g. a rented camper van in Spain, but the camper van owner lives in Paris and thus the rental charges do not enter Spain). The same applies to package tours; a large proportion of the money paid by the holidaymaker accrues to airlines from outside the destination.

A second multiplier is the *employment multiplier*. This multiplier describes either the ratio of the direct and indirect (secondary) employment generated by additional tourism expenditure to the direct employment alone, or the amount of employment generated by a given amount of tourist spending. Similarly to the income multiplier, a distinction can be made between orthodox and unorthodox types. The tourism sector is characterized by many part-time

Table 7.7 A selection of income multipliers from reports and publications

Country/region	Multiplier value
Turkey	1.96
United Kingdom	1.73
Ireland	1.72
Egypt	1.23
Bermuda	1.17
Missouri State (USA)	0.88
Gwynedd, North Wales	0.37
East Anglia, UK	0.34
City of Winchester (UK)	0.19

workers, and therefore all jobs should be converted into full-time equivalent job opportunities.

Any tourism employment multiplier starts from three assumptions:

1. Each productive sector fully utilizes its current labour force
2. There is spare capacity in the labour force
3. There is no change in the capital/labour mix.

The next two multipliers are very similar to each other. Because most tourism products are not 'stocks', the terms 'sales' and 'output multipliers' are more or less synonyms.

The sales or transactions multiplier measures the effect of an extra unit of tourist spending on economic activity within the economy; the multiplier relates tourism expenditure to the increase in business turnover that it creates. The *output multiplier* relates a unit of tourist spending to the resultant increase in the level of output in the economy (this is very similar to the sales multiplier; see Fletcher and Archer, 1992). While the sales multiplier considers only the level of the sales that result from the direct and secondary effects of tourism spending, the output multiplier takes into account both the levels of sales and any real changes that take place in the level of stocks. The sales multiplier in the Archer study for the county of Gwynedd, North Wales, was 1.46; the corresponding income multiplier was 0.32 (Archer, 1991b). A sales multiplier, after all, is not of such great importance. Indeed, a clear distinction should be made between value added and turnover; value added (income creation) is a part of turnover creation. A destination is only interested in the generated value added and employment. However, during the 1960s the turnover effect of Clement (1961) was considered to be the real multiplier in many tourism circles. Clement's transaction multiplier was equal to 3.48, and several tourism experts and politicians used this multiplier whether it was relevant or not. The funniest thing was that in many tourism circles, this was considered to be the same in all countries and all destinations.

The government revenue multiplier demonstrates how much government revenue is created by each additional unit of tourist expenditure (taxes, charges, etc., less grants).

The import multiplier demonstrates the value of imported goods and services associated with each additional unit of tourist expenditure.

It must be clear that the various types of multipliers are intrinsically linked. Let us take an example:

Tourist expenditure	€1000
Output generation	€2500
Direct income generation	€350
Indirect income generation	€200
Induced income generation	€200

In this case the Keynesian multiplier is 0.75, the ratio multiplier (total income generated to direct income) equals 2.14, and the output multiplier is 2.5.

How can the TIM values be defined?

This section is devoted to the income multiplier – the orthodox multiplier and the unorthodox multiplier (see Bull, 1995). The traditional Keynesian multiplier formula is equal to:

$$k = \frac{1}{1 - c + m} = \frac{1}{1 - MPC} \tag{7.1}$$

where

k   = income multiplier
MPC = marginal propensity to consume
MPS = marginal propensity to save.

However, account must be taken not only of the saving quote, but also of the taxation on income and the expenditure on imports. These are two additional leakages from extra local consumption-income circulation. Equation (7.1) therefore becomes:

$$k = \frac{1}{MTR + MPS + \{[1 - MTR - MPS]MPM\}} \tag{7.2}$$

where

MTR = marginal tax rate
MPM = marginal propensity to import.

With an MPS value of 20 per cent; an MTR equal to 30 per cent and an MPM on consumption expenditure equal to one-third, the multiplier k equals 1.5.

So far the assumption has been that all the original tourism expenditure turned directly into direct and indirect income, but this may not be the case. Very often some of food and drink in a hotel is imported. There is even tourist expenditure that never enters the economy – for example, payments for transport operated by foreign carriers, foreign-owned lodging, etc. In this case, equation (7.2) becomes:

$$k = \frac{1 - L}{MTR + MPS + \{[1 - MTR - MPS]MPM\}} \tag{7.3}$$

or

$$k = \frac{1 - L}{\text{leakages}}$$

where L = the immediate leakage attributable to tourist spending not entering the economy, or the need to import goods, services and factors to provide directly for tourists' needs.

With the same parameters as for equation (7.2) and L equal to 40 per cent, the tourism multiplier k is not higher than 0.9.

The developed equation 7.3 is far too simplistic, and is unable to measure variations in the form and magnitude of sectoral linkages and leakages out of the destination's economy during each round of transactions (Cooper *et al.*, 1993). Cooper *et al.* posit that 'Even the most complex and comprehensive Keynesian models developed for some studies are unable to provide the level of detail that is required for policy making and planning'. Therefore they suggest using *ad hoc* models.

Ad hoc models

Ad hoc models are similar in principle to the Keynesian approach. They are suited to regional analysis, where it may be impractical or too expensive to undertake a full input–output analysis.

The simplest *ad hoc* model is shown in equation 7.4:

$$A \cdot \frac{1}{1 - BC} \tag{7.4}$$

where

A = the proportion of additional tourist expenditure remaining in the economy after first-round leakages – i.e. A equals the $(1 - L)$ expression in the Keynesian model

B = the propensity of the local people to consume in the local economy

C = the proportion of expenditure by local people that accrues as income in the local economy.

More advanced models have been developed to calculate tourist multipliers to estimate the effect of expenditure on income and employment. One of these models was developed by Archer and Owen (1971):

$$\sum_{j=1}^{N} \sum_{i=1}^{n} Q_j K_{ji} V_i \cdot \frac{1}{1 - c \sum_{i=1}^{n} X_i Z_i V_i} \tag{7.5}$$

where the first part of equation 7.5 is direct and indirect income generated:

j = each category of tourists, $j = 1$ to n

i = each type of business establishment, $i = 1$ to n

Q_j = the proportion of total tourist expenditure spent by the jth type of tourist

K_{ji} = the proportion of expenditure by the jth type of tourist in the ith category of business

V_i = direct and indirect income generated by unit of expenditure by the ith type of business

and the second part includes the additional income generated by re-spending of factor earnings by resident population:

X_i = the proportion of total consumer expenditure by the residents of the area in the ith type of business

Z_i = the proportion of X_i that takes place within the area

c = the marginal propensity to consume.

The multiplier and input–output analysis

Input–output analysis provides a general equilibrium approach to measuring economic impacts, rather than the partial equilibrium approach used in the methods discussed above. The input–output approach is very often used to estimate the income and employment generation; the corresponding multiplier is a derived product. It can be considered to be the best method to estimate income and employment multipliers. Input–output analysis is concerned with interrelations arising from production; the main function of inter-industry accounts is to trace the flow of goods and services from one production sector to another. Table 7.8 shows the structure of a traditional input–output table. This table, which is called a trans-actions matrix, covers all the goods and services produced in an economy (country, region, destination). It is distinguished by the fact that production activities are grouped together into a number of sectors. Tables in actual use range in size from about 25 to 100 or more productive sectors.

Each sector appears in the accounting system twice, as a producer of outputs (by row) and as a user of inputs (by column). The elements in each row of the

Table 7.8 A basic input–output table

Sales to	Intermediate demand sectors					Final demand Y	Output
	1	*2*	*3*	*4*	*... n*		
Purchases From							
Sector 1	x_{11}	x_{12}	x_{13}	x_{14}	$... x_{1n}$	Y_1	X_1
Sector 2	x_{21}	x_{22}	x_{23}	x_{24}	$... x_{2n}$	Y_2	X_2
Sector 3	x_{31}	x_{32}	x_{33}	x_{34}	$... x_{3n}$	Y_3	X_3
Sector 4	x_{41}	x_{42}	x_{43}	x_{44}	$... x_{4n}$	Y_4	X_4
...	...	...	...	...	...	...	...
...	...	...	...	...	...	...	...
Sector n	x_{n1}	x_{n2}	x_{n3}	x_{n4}	$... x_{nn}$	Y_n	X_n
Remuneration of factor labour	W_1	W_2	W_3	W_4	$... W_n$	W	W
Profits/dividends	P_1	P_2	P_3	P_4	$... P_n$	P	P
Taxes	T_1	T_2	T_3	T_4	$... T_n$	T	T
Imports	M_1	M_2	M_3	M_4	$... M_n$	M	M
Total inputs	X_1	X_2	X_3	X_4	$... X_n$		X

where:

x_{ii} = all intermediate deliveries
X = output
Y = final demand composed of private consumption, investment, government expenditure and exports
M = imports.

table show the disposition of the output of that sector during the given accounting period. It is composed of two parts: the intermediate deliveries (x_{12} shows the deliveries from sector 1 to sector 2), and the final use. With respect to tourism, the final use relates to domestic consumption, inbound tourism (or exports), tourism investment and government expenditures.

The role of a sector as a purchaser of inputs is shown in a column. Each column is composed of three elements:

1. Purchases from other sectors (e.g. x_{12} means that sector 2 purchases from sector 1)
2. Primary inputs (wages, capital returns, taxes); this comprises the value added of the sector
3. Imports.

Transactions are usually recorded at the producer's price rather than at the purchaser's cost, which means that trade and transport margins are ascribed to the using sectors.

The separation between intermediate and final use and between produced and primary inputs leads to four types of transactions, which are shown in four sections of Table 7.8.

■ Section 1 comprises the main part of the inter-sector accounts. Each entry x_{ij} indicates the amount of commodity i used by sector j.
■ Section 2 contains the final use of produced goods and services; in practice broken down by major types of use (C, I, E and G)
■ Section 3 (the bottom left-hand section) shows each sector's purchases of primary inputs (W, P and T) and imported goods and services
■ Section 4 contains the direct input of primary factors to final use (e.g. government employment and domestic service).

It is very important to notice that the 'tourism sector' is never registered as a single sector in an input–output table; tourism consumption is spread over several sectors (see Chapter 1).

The relationship between the different parts of an input–output table can be written in algebraic terms (to ease the presentation, all types of final demand are represented by a column vector Y):

$$X = AX + Y \qquad (7.6)$$
$$X - AX = Y$$
$$(I - A)X = Y$$
$$X = (I - A)^{-1}Y$$

$$\Delta X = (I - A)^{-1}\Delta Y \qquad (7.7)$$

where

X = vector of total sales of each sector
Y = vector of final demand
A = a matrix of inter-sector transactions and $(I - A)^{-1}$ is the inverse matrix of the transaction coefficients
I = unit matrix.

A change in the level of Y (ΔY) will create an increase in the level of activity in the economy (ΔX) (see output multiplier). With respect to the income multiplier, we are only interested in income generation.

Direct income creation can be calculated using the formula:

$$Y_d = \hat{B}_k \cdot b \tag{7.8}$$

where

Y_d = direct income generation
$\hat{B}_k$ = diagonal matrix of income coefficients
b   = column vector of tourist expenditure after elimination of imports and VAT.

In the next step, the indirect income generation is calculated:

$$Y_t = \hat{B}_k (1 - A)^{-1} \cdot b \tag{7.9}$$

where

Y_t = direct and indirect income creation
$(1 - A)^{-1}$ = inverse matrix.

Indirect income generation is the result of subtracting direct income (equation 7.8) from the total income generation (equation 7.9).

Now we have all the ingredients to calculate the orthodox and unorthodox income multiplier type I. We have only to apply the definition. To avoid any misunderstanding, income is sometimes only one part of the total value added; in most cases it comprises all items of value added. The same exercise can be applied for all aspects of value added and tax revenue. For the Seychelles, Archer calculated an average tourism multiplier for all value added components (direct + indirect + induced) of 0.88; the government revenue amounted to 0.28 per cent of tourism expenditure.

It is important to be aware that Table 7.8 and the abovementioned formulae are a simplification of a normal presentation and application of input–output analysis. Nevertheless, they give the basic principles. More refined methodology is beyond the scope of this publication.

Some remarks

Additional production of tourism services requires the commitment of resources that could otherwise be used for alternative activities (Cooper *et al.*, 1993). If labour is in abundance, there is no problem. The situation changes when labour or other resources are not abundant. In the latter case, meeting the tourists' demands may involve the transfer of labour from other activities to the tourism sector. This provokes an opportunity cost or income foregone (see Chapter 8) which is often not considered in the estimation of the economic impact (Archer, 1991). When there is a real shortage, there may be the need to import labour. This will result in higher import leakages, as income earned from this imported labour may, in part, be repatriated. There can be a similar situation with the use of capital resources.

A second comment is linked to the first. It concerns the displacement effect. According to Cooper *et al.* displacement can take place when tourism development occurs at the expense of other economic activities and is referred to as the opportunity cost of the development. Displacement is more commonly referred to when a new tourism investment is seen to take away tourism demand from existing firms – for example, a successful big new hotel complex may reduce the turnover of existing hotels. As a consequence, the overall tourism activity may not (or may only partly) have increased (see Chapter 8).

A third remark is of a completely different nature. The use of input–output analysis poses the problem of insufficient correspondence between the sector in an input–output table and the data derived from visitor expenditure surveys. As a consequence, the tourist expenditure has to be deconstructed to fit the sectors defined in the existing input–output table. A loss of accuracy is the logical result.

The final comment concerns the static character of most multiplier methods. They assume that production and consumption functions are linear, and that intersector expenditure patterns are stable (Cooper *et al.*, 1993). Furthermore, they assume that all sectors are able to respond to additional demand (supply capacity condition; availability of factor resources). The models are also based on constant relative prices, and they suppose no change in technology (Archer, 1991).

It must be clear that multiplier analysis does not measure the long-term benefits for a destination due to the growth of tourism (Archer, 1991; Cooper *et al.*, 1993).

Measurement of income generation

The preceding section is a good introduction to measuring the impact of tourism on income. The two basic driving forces for the tourism sector are expenditure and investment, both of which are essential elements of final demand in an input–output table. Receipts in foreign exchange are a component of expenditure, and as such the export element of final demand. Foreign exchange earnings in tourism can be of great importance in certain countries – Spain is a good example.

The key elements of the final demand, tourism expenditure (tourism export included) and tourism investment, are the basis of two major benefits: income and employment. In other words, what does tourism create in terms of income and employment generation? As such, there is a relationship between the four key variables in the tourism sector: expenditure and investment on the one side, and income and employment on the other.

Between these four key variables there are special links. For example, investments depend on the expenditure in the present and the future. In turn, investments can stimulate expenditure.

There is also a linkage of the key components with other aggregates. Government receipts in tourism are a derivative of expenditure and investments. In principle, each economic activity yields returns to the public sector, such as direct taxes, VAT, company taxes, social security receipts etc. These returns are a function of the key variables, as is the case for any other economic sector.

To measure income generation, different methods have been developed. The most commonly applied are:

- The national accounts method (simplified)
- The Henderson–Cousins method
- The input–output approach

- The tourism satellite account approach
- The multiplier method.

Each of these methods has pros and cons; the choice of a method is very often influenced by the availability of data or instruments (e.g. an input–output table for the destination) and the financial resources. The best-performing method is undoubtedly input–output analysis. However, all methods start from expenditure and investments, and all but one are related to the multiplier mechanism.

All these methods have one drawback in common: they assume that factors of production (such as labour) flow freely to the tourism sector. These resources are assumed not to be used elsewhere (see Chapter 8 and Dwyer *et al.*, 2004). This is the case in most developing countries. In destinations where there is full employment, the net effect can be lower. This applies to all possible economic effects, such as income, value added and employment. Therefore, Dwyer *et al.* suggest the use of Computable General Equilibrium (CGE) models. The latter, however, are time-consuming, and very complicated to use.

The national accounts method (simplified)

The national accounts method is used when the destination cannot make use of an up-to-date input–output table and does not have of a Tourism Satellite Account. In this case, a 'simplified national accounts method' can be a substitute. The application requires several steps:

1. The available expenditure data are broken down into subgroups which are very close to sectors of the national accounts, such as food, drinks, accommodation, transport, etc.
2. VAT is eliminated from the gross receipts and these adjusted expenditures are the basis to measure the gross value added creation for each subgroup, based on ratios derived from national accounts
3. Indirect income generation is the next step.

As we saw in the previous section, indirect value added generation is linked to intermediate deliveries. The latter are equal to:

$$\text{Intermediate deliveries} = \text{turnover} - \text{VAT} - (\text{imports} + \text{direct income}) \quad (7.10)$$

All the elements of this 'equation' are known or can be derived via national accounts ratios. Intermediate deliveries in turn are composed of value added, imports and inter-sector deliveries, and can be measured via average national accounts ratios. This provides the first round indirect value added, and first round intermediate deliveries. The latter are the starting point of second, third, fourth and possibly fifth rounds. We have only to total all the calculated indirect value added in the successive rounds to obtain the total indirect value added. Gross value added (direct and indirect) less depreciation provides us with net value added.

This method is not the most refined one, but it is after all logical in its conception, and is quite simple to apply.

The Henderson–Cousins method

The original version of this method was developed by Archer and Owen (1971) and improved by Henderson and Cousins (1975) in the well-known Greater Tayside study. The method requires a tremendous volume of fieldwork, and is therefore only applicable for small destinations.

The starting point of this method is an injection of tourist expenditure. It has the further practical advantage that the multiplicand depends upon the number of days spent in the destination by tourists and their daily expenditure, the number and size of which are estimable by survey methods. The business unit is taken as the basic element of this analysis, and the objective is to measure for each business the contribution to regional income (and employment) out of receipts from tourism. Furthermore, the method is built on the principles of the tourism multiplier.

The multiplier process may be expressed as follows:

$$k = a + b + c \tag{7.11}$$

where

k = multiplier

a = direct regional income generation per € of tourist expenditure, i.e. factor incomes generated within businesses which directly receive tourist expenditure

b = indirect regional income generation per € of tourist expenditure, i.e. factor incomes generated in other businesses whose turnover is indirectly augmented with purchases made by the original businesses

c = induced regional income generation per € of tourist expenditure, i.e. factor incomes generated as the result of expenditure by residents of the region whose income has previously been increased through direct or indirect income generated by tourism.

For a better understanding, the following may be helpful.

	ith type of business		
jth type of tourist	*Accommodation*	*Restaurant*	*Shopping*
Hotel Camping Holiday village Rented apartment			

More formally:

$$a = \sum_{j=1}^{n} \sum_{i=1}^{n} K_{ji} Y_{di} \tag{7.12}$$

where

a = direct regional income generation

K_{ji} = the proportion of €1 expenditure spent by the jth type of tourist in each type of business

Y_{di} = the increase in factor incomes in the region per €1 of turnover to the ith type of business generated exclusively within that type of business which directly receives tourist expenditure.

If b = indirect regional income generation:

$$b = \sum_{j=1}^{n} \sum_{i=1}^{n} K_{ji}(Y_i - Y_{di}) \qquad (7.13)$$

where Y_i = the increase in factor incomes per €1 of turnover to the ith type of business generated within that type of business and in all other types which participate in the subsequent flow of transactions.

If c = induced income generation:

$$c = (a + b)\frac{1}{1 - L\sum_{i}^{n} X_i Z_i Y_i} \qquad (7.14)$$

where

L = average propensity to consume with disposable income (see former c in Keynesian expression)

X_i = the proportion of total consumer spending by residents in the ith type of business

Z_i = the proportion of consumer spending by residents in the ith type of business within the region.

The complete model to measure regional income generation can be expressed as follows:

$$G_r = \sum_{j=1}^{n} \sum_{j=1}^{n} N_j Q_j K_{ji} Y_i \left(\frac{1}{1 - L\sum_{i=1}^{n} X_i Z_i Y_i} \right) \qquad (7.15)$$

where

G_r = total income generation

N_j = the numbers of days in the region spent by the jth type of tourist

Q_j = the total daily expenditure by the jth type of tourist.

N_j and Q_j together represent the multiplicand, while the remainder of the expression specifies the consequent multiplier.

The input–output approach

Earlier in this chapter we dealt with the structure of an input–output table and how it can be used to measure various multipliers. However, the main function of input–output analysis with respect to tourism is to calculate the value added and employment generation.

In the application of the procedure, five steps are crucial:

1. First, determine whether the destination has an up-to date input–output table or a useful reference table. This is a preliminary condition.
2. Next, the final demand or net tourism expenditure must be defined – this implies corrections for VAT and imports.
3. The tourism expenditure must then be broken down in such a way that the expenditure can be attributed to the sectors contained in the available input–output. This step is far from straightforward. Tourism expenditure is spread over different sectors, and several typical tourism sub-sectors (such as accommodation and retail trade) are not used in national input–output tables. Furthermore, the transactions are expressed in producers' prices and not market prices. On the other hand, tourist expenditure is defined in market prices. The differences between consumption price and producers' prices are called distribution margins (distribution and transport). Therefore it is necessary to define the corresponding distribution margins for each product and/or service group. The margins are in fact the output of the retail trade and transport sectors, and the corresponding amounts should therefore be attributed to the retail trade and different transport sectors. In a number of cases, the distribution margin is equal to zero. This applies when the producing sector sells directly to the consumer (e.g. repair of cars, hotel and restaurant).
4. Direct income generation is estimated by multiplying the real production of the different sectors with the corresponding income coefficient, defined as NVA_{mpj}/P_j. In input–output notation:

$$Y^d = \hat{B}_k \cdot b \tag{7.16}$$

where

NVA_{mpj} = net value added at market prices of sector j
P_j = output sector j
Y^d = direct income generation
$\hat{B}$ = diagonal matrix of income coefficients
b = column vector of tourist expenditure (final demand f_j) after elimination of imports and VAT:

$$b_j = f_j - f_j^{imp} - VAT_j \tag{7.17}$$

5. Next, the indirect income generation is estimated:

$$Y^t = \hat{B}_k (1 - A^n)^{-1} \cdot b \tag{7.18}$$

where

Y^t = direct + indirect income creation
$(1 - A^n)^{-1}$ = inverse matrix based on national inter-sector relations.

To obtain the indirect income generation, Y^d is subtracted from Y^t.

It is possible to go one step further and relate the induced effects. This is possible by including an additional column and row in the matrix of production coefficients. This column is that part of the final demand that constitutes consumer expenditure; the row is income payments to the personal sector (Archer and Fletcher, 1996).

The Tourism Satellite Account approach

The basic methodology underlying the estimation of the value added requires the TSA Tables 5 and 6 (see Chapter 2), and equation (7.19) (OECD, 2000):

$$TVA_{ij} = (GO_{ij} - II_{ij}) \cdot TS_{ij} \qquad (7.19)$$

where

TVA_{ij} = tourism value added for the ith commodity of the jth industry
GO_{ij} = gross output of the ith commodity of the jth industry
II_{ij} = intermediate inputs for the ith commodity of the jth industry
TS_{ij} = tourism share of the output of the ith commodity of the jth industry.

The TSA Table 6 shows the domestic supply and internal consumption by products. The rows detail output by tourism characteristic product and enhancing services. Total output of an activity (in a column) is obtained as the sum of its outputs by product. The rest of the block of rows shows intermediate consumption by product, and a total. The difference between total output (at basic prices) and total input (at purchaser's prices) provides value added at basic prices. The last block of rows presents the components of value added.

The columns are first organized by productive activities, with emphasis on the tourism industries. The supply by domestic producers is first added over activities to obtain the aggregate value of total output of domestic producers at basic prices. This column is then added to imports, which represent supply within the domestic economy of imported products, and a column recording taxes less subsidies on products concerning domestic output and imports to obtain 'total domestic supply at purchaser's price'. This total domestic supply is systematically compared to internal tourism consumption product by product (on each row). For most of the variables presented in columns, a column for tourism share is presented (how much of the value of the variable is attributable to internal tourism consumption).

How do we establish tourism shares? This is based on direct information from suppliers or visitors (surveys of expenditure by product) and the opinion of experts. With the tourism shares established for output, it is possible to estimate, for each activity, a tourism share to be applied to the components of intermediate consumption. From the difference between the values of output attributable to visitor consumption and to intermediate consumption, the value added generated by visitor consumption can be computed. For each activity, an estimate of value added can be established. Adding across all activities, it is possible to obtain the total value corresponding to that variable.

The calculation of tourism GDP is more problematic: the difference between TVA and tourism GDP consists mainly of taxes and subsidies. These items are not necessary as connected to the production of tourism products as in the case with intermediate consumption and output. To obtain the GDP generated by internal tourism consumption, to the value added we must add taxes less subsidies on products and imports related to tourism products, whose value corresponds mathematically to the difference between this variable valued at purchaser's prices and at basic prices, since distribution margins have already been given the appropriate treatment.

It is very important to notice that equation (7.19), and the TSA approach in general, provides only the direct income effect and not the indirect effect. The latter should be estimated with the input–output method.

In Table 2.3 (see Chapter 2), the tourism value added – direct effects and inclusive business trips – for Austria was estimated at 182 462 million Austrian schillings for exclusive business travel, and 194 416 million Austrian schillings for inclusive business trips. This is the sum of the value added of all the tourism industries and the connected and non-specific industries (Franz *et al.*, 2001). Total tourism value added – direct and indirect effects – for Austria (exclusive business travel) amounted in 1999 to 235 billion Austrian schillings.

The distinction made in the Austrian case between inclusive or exclusive 'business travel' has its reasons. In the TSA approach, business travel is considered in total tourism demand and has an impact on value added on the satellite level. When comparing TSA value added with the value added of the whole economy, it has to be adjusted. Indeed, on the macro-economic level the intermediate consumption – in this case business trips of residents – is considered as input and has to be deducted from the residents' tourism consumption calculated in the TSA. In other words, double counting should be avoided (Smeral, 2002).

The multiplier method

The final method is the multiplier method. This consists of a simple multiplication of tourism expenditure with the income multiplier (type II). The problem is that this multiplier is unknown. Sometimes, the multiplier of a similar region is applied. This can only be justified when the economic structure of the reference region is very similar to and of the same size as the region concerned. However, such a situation is exceptional, and the result can only be a very approximate estimation of the income generation.

Measurement of employment generation

Employment is, together with income generation, the most important benefit of tourism development. The measurement of the employment impact can be divided in two groups:

1. The supply approach
   - tourism-related sectors
   - minimum requirement method

2. The demand approach
   - the national accounts method
   - the tourism satellite account approach
   - the Henderson–Cousins method
   - the input–output approach
   - the multiplier method.

The supply approach

In tourism research, two supply approaches are quite often applied. The first can be called 'employment in tourism-related sectors', and is simply an addition of the employment (self-employed and employee) in sectors that are considered to be tourism-related, such as accommodation, restaurant, cafés, etc. The result is an overestimation of the number of jobs. Many of the firms working in these sectors supply not only tourists but also, and sometimes almost only, local residents. Therefore this method has neither a scientific nor a practical value.

The second supply approach, the minimum requirement method, can be more relevant, particularly in smaller areas or destinations. It should be implemented in different steps. First, the relevant sectors for tourism must be defined. The choice of the sectors is less important (e.g. retail trade) than in the preceding supply approach, and the reasons will become clear as we advance to the next steps. Once the relevant sectors have been defined, the employment in those sectors can be registered.

In the following stage, a region without tourism activities and without regional distribution function is defined; this is known as the reference region. In the reference region, the employment in the relevant sectors per 1000 inhabitants should be noted. This ratio is considered to be the 'minimum requirement'.

Finally, the tourism share in the relevant sectors of the tourism destination of step 1 is calculated. This is the total employment per sector minus the minimum requirement based on the ratios obtained in the reference region.

With respect to this method, two points should be noted. First, there might be underestimation of the tourism employment due to unregistered jobs in the tourism destination. Second, the tourism destination itself should be free of any distribution function outside the region.

Most measurements of employment generation are based on the demand approach. The methods are the same as for the calculation of the income impact. Therefore, we limit the following paragraphs to the essential items and make abstractions for the TSA approach and the Henderson–Cousins method. Currently, the TSA procedure for the employment table is not available (see also Heerschap, 1999). The Henderson–Cousins method is not very suitable for the measurement of employment.

The national accounts method

The use of the national accounts method is quite simple. Based on income (value added) generation, we can derive the employment by dividing the income generated by the average gross salary of the employed and self-employed (gross income plus the employer's social security contribution). This leads to the number of 'standardized' employed persons. This approach can lead to an underestimation owing to the fact that the salaries in the tourism sector are below the national average. On the other hand, an overestimation can be the result of neglecting profits in the tourism firms. This approach – and this applies to all demand methods – does not take into account employment in the public sector related to tourism.

Sometimes a destination authority is only interested in the direct effect. In this case, it is sufficient to divide the income generated, adjusted for VAT, by the average gross salary of an employed person.

The input–output approach

Employment generation can be calculated, based on the input–output approach, in a similar way to income generation:

$$E_d = \hat{A}k \cdot b \qquad (7.20)$$

$$E_t = \hat{A}k(1 - A^n)^{-1} \cdot b \qquad (7.21)$$

where

E_d = column vector of direct sectoral employment
E_t = vector of direct and indirect employment
$\hat{A}k$ = diagonal matrix of employment coefficients; the employment coefficient or labour coefficient is defined as the employment in sector i divided by the production in sector i
b = column vector tourist expenditure.

The application of this approach to Flanders (Vanhove, 1993), with a tourism expenditure of 159 billion Belgian francs, resulted in direct income generation of 74.5 billion Belgian francs, 26.2 billion Belgian francs in indirect income, direct employment of 54 900 and indirect employment of 19 000 people (reference year, 1990). This employment effect is of the same magnitude as in the most important industrial sectors in Flanders.

With the same method, it was relatively easy to calculate the direct and indirect government receipts for Flanders:

	Direct + indirect effects (billions of Belgian francs; 1 € = 40.34 Bfr)
Direct taxes	7.1
Profit taxes	5.6
Indirect taxes	4.0
Related to production VAT	14.2
Social security	10.8
Total	41.7

In other words, an expenditure of 159 billion Belgian francs created 41.7 billion Belgian francs in government receipts.

A similar and interesting piece of research was carried out by Archer and Fletcher for the Seychelles (Archer and Fletcher, 1996), also based on the input–output method. However, in their application, induced effects were also retained. This study proves how important tourism is in terms of income and employment creation. The reference year was 1991, and the case is relevant for the impact tourism might have on a country.

The major data of economic impact for the Seychelles were:

Visitor arrivals	97 668
Tourist nights	938 000
Tourism expenditure	527 million SEYRs (or 99 million US$)
Income creation	466 million SEYRs (direct, indirect and induced)
Government revenue	148 million SEYRs
Direct employment generated	3772
Total employment generated	8312 (direct, indirect and induced)

The contribution of tourism to the GDP was 18.4 per cent. With the secondary effects resulting from the multiplier effect, tourism contributed approximately 23.5 per cent to the GDP.

About 24 tourists created one direct job, but with secondary jobs (indirect and induced) taken into account as well, only 10.8 tourists were needed to support one job. In terms of nights, 248 nights contributed to a direct job and with secondary jobs 113 nights were sufficient for one job. A similar figure for Bruges (948 nights for a direct job; reference year 1992) shows the very labour-intensive character of tourism in the Seychelles.

Archer and Fletcher (1996) also calculated the number of tourists needed in the Seychelles to create one job for a number of countries of residence:

	Direct	Direct, indirect and induced
UK/Eire	22.4	10.3
France	25.5	11.6
Germany	18.7	8.4
Italy	22.4	10.0
Switzerland	20.8	9.2
Africa	29.3	13.5

These data stress the relative importance of German tourists for the Seychelles. The impact on employment of these tourists is about one-quarter greater than that of tourists from Africa.

Of course, the results for Flanders and the Seychelles cannot be generalized to any country or region. It all depends on leakages, economic structure, tax systems, etc. Nevertheless, by and large the impact of tourism on income and employment generation is important. This conclusion also holds for most developing countries.

The multiplier method

Above, we defined the employment multiplier either as the ratio of the direct and indirect (secondary) employment generated by additional tourism expenditure to the direct employment alone, or as the amount of employment generated by a given amount of tourist spending. The latter formulation has the greatest practical value.

$$E_k = (\text{direct} + \text{indirect employment})/\text{expenditure}. \qquad (7.22)$$

For the province of Antwerp, E_k amounted to 0.54 jobs per million Belgian francs expenditure; in the Flanders study, E_k was equal to 0.49.

Similar to the income generation, this method is only valuable if one disposes of an employment multiplier of a region with more or less identical characteristics. It is important to be aware that knowledge of direct and indirect employment per million expenditure in similar regions leads to a rough estimation.

Special characteristics of employment

So far the quantitative employment effect of tourism has been emphasized, but attention should also be paid to the qualitative aspects.

First, tourism is a growth sector, and all predictions for the next decade (EIU and WTO) are very optimistic. Even in developed countries, tourism is a sector with promising job opportunities. However, Thomas and Townsend (2001) warn against having too optimistic a perspective. The exceptionally rapid growth of the 1980s, relative to employment in all other sectors, was no longer the case in the 1990s. Smeral (2001) sounds the same warning.

Secondly, tourism is a sector with a high degree of semi-skilled and so-called unskilled workers. This can be seen as an opportunity for the large number of unskilled workers without jobs, especially in developing countries (Cucker, 2002).

Tourism is also a sector with a high percentage of part-time jobs. Hudson and Townsend reveal that in Great Britain, 38 per cent of the men and 56 per cent of the women working in the horeca sector (hotel, restaurant and cafes) are part-time workers (Hudson and Townsend, 1992). According to Wood, there is a tendency in advanced industrialized societies towards increased part-time employment and the casualization of work (Wood, 1992). Thomas and Townsend (2001) show that in 1998, UK hotels and restaurants employed as many part-time (not standardized) as full-time workers.

A fourth characteristic of employment in tourism is the high share of female workers. According to Hudson and Townsend, in Great Britain women amount to 45 per cent of full-time workers and take 73 per cent of the part-time jobs. The study for the Antwerp province reveals that 50 per cent or part-timers are female workers (Yzewijn and De Brabander, 1989).

The sector also has many small firms and self-employed. For the Antwerp province, in the horeca sector the ratio of employee to employer is no higher than 2. Moreover, British sources indicate the increasing number of young workers in the tourism sector (The Host Consultancy, 1991; Wood, 1992).

A final characteristic is the seasonality of employment. The intensity of seasonality is different per country and tourism region, but where it exists it makes tourism employment less attractive.

All in all, employment in tourism is growing, but most characteristics indicate that the sector has a low image (Smeral, 2004).

The impact of events

The demand methods dealt with in the two preceding sections can be applied to events; however, cost–benefit analysis (see Chapter 8) is a better approach. In economic impact studies of events, expenditure is the key element. Therefore it is important, especially with major events, to define expenditure in the right way. Furthermore, it is necessary to make a distinction between the result for the event organizer and that for the host city (Baade and Matheson, 2004).

Major events always involve 'crowding-out' effects, expenditure switching and retained expenditure. Big events are very often confronted with crowding-out effects, when traditional visitors prefer not to visit the region where the event takes place for reasons of over occupation, higher prices, etc. (Scherly and Breiter, 2002). These effects can take different forms:

- Geographical diversion – people avoid the place of the event and visit another region
- Temporal substitution – traditional visitors come before or after the event
- Monetary substitution – visitors abstain from coming to the region and spend the money on other products or services.

Cost–benefit analysis takes these crowding-out effects into account through the application of the 'with and without' and not the 'before and after' principle (Vanhove, 1976).

Mules and Faulkner (1996) cite several examples of what they call expenditure 'switching':

- Local people might participate in the event and reduce their expenses for other goods and services. This is a pure substitution effect. Ryan (1998) uses the term 'displaced expenditure'.
- Visitors may switch their expenditure in time. They planned a trip to the region regardless, and simply arrange the timing of their visit to coincide with the event. Their expenditure cannot be attributed (or only partially) to the event (see also Dwyer and Forsyth, 1997).
- Visitors may switch their expenditure in terms of location within a country.
- Local, regional or national governments may switch public expenditure from other public works to infrastructure in favour of the event.

A special case is retained expenditure (Ryan, 1998), which occurs when residents strongly support the event and would have travelled out of the city or region anyway in order to attend it. In other words, the spending is not lost to other destinations. In that sense, the event does contribute to the economy of the destination.

References and further reading

Airey, D. (1978). Tourism and balance of payments. *Tourism International Research-Europe*, third quarter.

Archer, B. (1991a). Tourism and island economies: impact analyses. In C. Cooper (ed.), *Progress in Tourism, Recreation and Hospitality*. London: Belhaven Press.

Archer, B. (1991b). The value of multipliers and their policy implications. In S. Medlik (ed.), *Managing Tourism*. Oxford: Butterworth-Heinemann.

Archer, B. (1995). Importance of tourism for the economy of Bermuda. *Annals of Tourism Research*, 4.

Archer, B. (1996). The economic impact of tourism in the Seychelles. *Annals of Tourism Research*, 1.

Archer, B. and Fletcher, J. (1990). Tourism: its economic importance. In M. Quest (ed.), *Horwath Book of Tourism*. London: MacMillan.

Archer, B. and Owen, C. (1971). Towards a tourist regional multiplier. *Regional Studies*, 5.

Archer, B., Shea, S. and de Vane (1974). *Tourism in Gwynedd: An Economic Study*. Cardiff: Wales Tourist Board.

Baade, R. and Matheson, A. (2004). The quest for the Cup: assessing the economic impact of the World Cup. *Regional Studies*, 4.

Baretje, R. and Defert, P. (1972). *Aspects économiques du tourisme*. Paris. Berger-Levrault.

Baum, T. (1995). Trends in international tourism. In *Insights*. London: English Tourist Board.

Bosselman, F., Peterson, C. and McCarthy, Cl. (1999). M*anaging Tourism Growth*. Washington: Island Press.

Bull, A. (1995). *The Economics of Travel and Tourism*. Sydney: Longman.

Eurostat, OECD, WTO and UN Statistics Division (2001). *Tourism Satellite Account: Recommended Methodological Framework*: Luxembourg: Eurostat.

Clement, H. (1961). *The Future of Tourism in the Pacific and the Far East*. Washington, DC: US Department of Commerce.

Cooper, C. (ed.) (1991). *Progress in Tourism, Recreation and Hospitality*. London: Belhaven Press.

Cooper, A. and Wilson, A. (2002). Extending the relevance of TSA research for the UK: general equilibrium and spillover analysis. *Tourism Economics*, 1.

Cooper, C., Fletcher, J., Gilbert, D. and Wanhill, S. (1993). *Tourism. Principles & Practice*. London: Pitman Publishing.

Cucker, J. (2002). Tourism employment issues in developing countries: examples from Indonesia. In R. Sharpley and D. Telfer (eds), *Tourism and Development. Concepts and Issues*. Clevedon: Channel View Publications.

De Brabander, G. (1992). *Toerisme en Economie*. Leuven: Garant.

de Kadt, E. (1979). *Tourism Passport to Development*. Oxford: Oxford University Press.

Durand, H., Gouirand, P. and Spindler, J. (1994). *Economie et Politique du Tourisme*. Paris: Librairie Générale de Droit et de Jurispridence.

Dwyer, L. and Forsyth, P. (1997). Impacts and benefits of MICE tourism: a framework for analysis. *Tourism Economics*, 1.

Dwyer, L., Forsyth, P. and Spurr, R. (2004). Evaluating tourism's economic effects: new and old approaches. *Tourism Management*, 3.

Ferri, J. (2004). Evaluating the regional impact of a new road on tourism. *Regional Studies*, 4.

Flechter, J. and Archer, B. (1992). The development and application of multiplier analysis. In C. Cooper (ed.), *Progress in Tourism, Recreation and Hospitality Management*, Vol. 3. London: Belhaven Press.

Franz, A., Laimer, P. and Smeral, E. (2001). *A Tourism Satellite Account for Austria*. Vienna: Statistik Austria and WIFO.

Frechtling, D. (1994). Assessing the economic impacts of travel and tourism. In J. Ritchie and C. Goeldner (eds), *Travel, Tourism and Hospitality Research*. New York: John Wiley & Sons.

Getz, D. (1991). *Festivals, Special Events and Tourism*. New York. Van Nostrand Reinhold.

Gray, H.P. (1970). *International Travel International* Trade. Lexington: Heath Lexington Books.

Heerschap, N. (1999). The employment module for the Tourism Satellite Account of the OECD. *Tourism Economics*, 5.

Henderson, D. and Cousins, R. (1975). *The Economic Impact of Tourism. A Case Study in Greater Tayside*. Edinburgh: Tourism and Recreation Research Unit, University of Edinburgh.

Hudson, R. and Townsend, A. (1992). Tourism employment and policy. Choices for local government. In P. Johnson and B. Thomas (eds), *Perspectives on Tourism Policy*. London: Mansell Publishing.

Keller, P. and Bieger, T. (eds) (2003). *Sport and Tourism*. AIEST Congress, Athens, 2003. St-Gall: AIEST.

Klaassen, L. and Van Wickeren, A. (1975). Interindustry relations; an attraction model. In H.C. Bos (ed.), *Towards Balanced International Growth*. Rotterdam: North Holland Publishing Company.

Krippendorf, J., Messerli, P. and Hänni, H. (eds) (1982). *Tourismus und Regionale Entwicklung*. Diesüsenhofen: Verlag Rüegger.

Mathieson, A. and Wall, G. (1982). *Tourism: Economic, Physical and Social Impacts*. London: Longman.

Mihalic, T. (2002). Tourism and economic development issues. In R. Sharpley and D. Telfer (eds), *Tourism and Development. Concepts and Issues*. Clevedon: Channel View Publications.

Mossé, R. (1973). *Tourism and the Balance of Payments*. Geneva: IUOTO.

Mules, T. and Faulkner, B. (1996). An economic perspective on special events. *Tourism Economics*, 2.

NRIT (2003). *De macro- ekonomische betekenis van toerisme en recreatie in Nederland in 2001*. Breda: NRIT.

OECD (2000). *Measuring the Role of Tourism in OECD Economies. The OECD Manual on Tourism Satellite Accounts and Employment*. Paris: OECD.

Py, P. (1996). *Le tourisme. Un phénomène économoque*. Paris, La Documentation Française.

Ryan, C. (1996). Event impact measurement in Auckland, New Zealand. *Tourism Economics*, 2.

Ryan, C. (1998). Economic impacts of small events: estimates and determinants – a New Zealand example. *Tourism Economics*, 4.

Ryan, C. and Lockyer, T. (2001). An economic impact case study: the South Pacific Masters' Games. *Tourism Economics*, 3.

Saarinen, J. (2003). The regional economics of tourism in Northern Finland: the socio-economic implications of recent tourism development and future possibilities for regional development. *Scandinavian Journal of Hospitality and Tourism*, 2.

Samuelson, A. (1964). *Economics*. New York: McGraw-Hill.

Scherer, R., Strauf, S. and Bieger, T. (2002). Die wirtschaftlichen Effekte von Kulturevents. Das Beispiel Lucerne Festival. In *Schweizerische Tourismuswirtschaft, Jahrbuch 2001/2002*. St Gallen: Universität St Gallen.

Scherly, F. and Breiter, M. (2002). *Impact économique des grandes manifestations sportives en Suisse. Etude de cas 'Athletissima' Lausanne 2001*. Lausanne: HEC Lausanne.

Schmidhauser, H. (1979). The Employment Effect of Tourism in the Tertiary Sector, Demonstrated by the Example of Switzerland. Bern: AIEST.

Smeral, E. (2001). Beyond the myth of growth in tourism. In T. Bieger and P. Keller (eds), *Tourism Growth and Global Competition*. St-Gall: AIEST.

Smeral, E. (2002). *A Tourism Satellite Account for Austria. The Economics, Methodology and Results*. 37th TRC Meeting, Barcelona 2002.

Smeral, E. (2004). Quandaries of the labour market in tourism exemplified by the case of Austria. *Tourist Review*, 3.

The Host Consultancy (1991). *Jobs in Tourism and Leisure – A Labour Market Review*. London: ETB.

Theuns, H. (1989). *Toerisme in ontwikkelingslanden*. Tilburg, Tilburg University Press.

Thomas, B. and Townsend, A. (2001). New trends in the growth of tourism employment in the UK in the 1990s. *Tourism Economics*, 3.

Tisdell, C. (ed.) (2000). *The Economics of Tourism*, Vol. 2, Part 1. Cheltenham: Edward Elgar Publishing.

Tribe, J. (1997). *The Economics of Leisure and Tourism*. Oxford: Butterworth-Heinemann.

UNCTAD (1971). *Elements of Tourism Policy in Developing Countries*. Geneva: UNCTAD.

Vanhove, N. (1976). Cost–benefit analysis. Theory and techniques applied to tourism. In S. Wahab (ed.), *Managerial Aspects of Tourism*. Turin: Salah Wahab.

Vanhove, N. (1977). Fremdenverkehr und Zahlungsbilanz der EG-Länder und der Mittelmeerländer. In R. Regul (ed.), *Die Europäischen Gemeinschaften und die Mittelmeerländer*. Baden-Baden: Nomos Verlagsgesellschaft.

Vanhove, N. (1986). Tourism and regional economic development. In J. Paelinck (ed.), *Human Behaviour in Geographical Space, Essays in Honour of L.H. Klaassen*. Cheltenham: Gower.

Vanhove, N. (1993). Sociaal-economische betekenis van het toerisme in Vlaanderen. In U. Claeys (ed.), *Toerisme in Vlaanderen*. Leuven: Acco.

Vanhove, N. (1997). Mass tourism – benefits and costs. In S. Wahab and J. Pigram (eds), *Tourism, Development and Growth*. London: Routledge.

Vanhove, N. (2003). Externalities of sport and tourism investments, activities and events. In P. Keller and T. Bieger (eds), *Sport and Tourism*. AIEST Congress, Athens, 2003. St-Gall: AIEST.

Vaughan, R. (1977). *The Economic Impact of the Edinburgh Festival*. Edinburgh: Scottish Tourist Board.

Vellas, F. and Bécherel, L. (1995). *International Tourism*. London: MacMillan Press.

Williams, A. and Shaw, G. (eds) (1988). *Tourism and Economic Development: Western European Experiences*. London: Belhaven Press.

Wood, R. (1992). Hospitality industry labour trends: British and international experience. *Tourism Management*, 3.

WTO (1988). *Economic Review of World Tourism*. Madrid: WTO.

WTO (2000). *Tourism Satellite Account, Measuring Tourism Demand*. Madrid: WTO.

Yzewijn, D. and De Brabander, G. (1989). *De economische betekenis van het toerisme en de recreatie van de Provincie Antwerpen*. Antwerp: Provincie Antwerpen.

8

Micro- and macro-evaluation of projects in the tourism and hospitality industry

Introduction

So far we have dealt with various aspects of demand and supply in tourism, and the impact of tourism on value added creation, employment generation and the balance of payments. There is still one economic aspect missing. There cannot be a tourism industry without projects. These projects can take different forms, such as development of attractions, accommodation, entertainment, transport, congress centres, events, etc. They all involve serious investment. The investor – public or private sector – always has a great financial responsibility, and therefore a preliminary investment appraisal is a must.

Long experience in the tourism sector has taught us that many investment decisions are very emotional; sometimes projects by physical planners are taken for granted, wrong investment appraisal methods are applied and/or the right method is used incorrectly.

Therefore, special attention to investment appraisal has its place in a book dealing with various economic aspects of tourism. To a large extent the methods dealt with in this chapter are not unique for the tourism sector. However, any responsible person in tourism should have knowledge of the right approach to evaluating a tourism project. Probably the responsible person – public or private – will not carry out the investment appraisal; nonetheless, he or she should be able to understand the results of such a study.

Most projects in the tourism sector are the initiative of individuals or companies – tourism or financial – and here the classic investment appraisal methods apply. However, in tourism, more than in any other sector, the investor (or what we call the 'paymaster') is not a company or a tourism entrepreneur but the public sector. Indeed many projects belong to the general tourism infrastructure, and the benefits do not only accrue to the paymaster, who may not consider the negative effects. In other words, externalities must be taken into account. In such a case, the classic methods of investment appraisal are insufficient.

The latter consideration justifies the title of this chapter. A project can be appraised from the micro point of view or from the macro point of view. In the first case, only benefits (receipts) and costs for the investor (private or public) come into the picture. In the second case, the benefit and cost items are large in number and of different natures. The total impact of the project for the destination should be taken into account. Application of cost–benefit analysis is the correct method.

This chapter focuses on five topics. First, we focus on the nature of investment appraisal and will explore the difference between micro and macro approaches. Secondly, attention will be paid to externalities in tourism. A third section deals with the conventional and the more scientific methods of investment appraisal, while in a fourth section we proceed with the content of a feasibility and business plan related to the hotel sector. A major part of this chapter is focused on the cost–benefit analysis applied in the tourism sector.

The nature of a tourism investment appraisal

This section focuses on two major topics; the basics of investment appraisal, and an exploration of the difference between micro- and macro-evaluation.

An investment comprises a planned series of capital expenditures undertaken in anticipation of their generating a larger series of cash flows at various times in the future. The main problem of investment appraisal is quite clear from this definition: it is the evaluation of uncertain future cash flows in relation to cash outlays (possibly also uncertain) in the immediate or near future. The solution of this general problem involves an understanding of the basic techniques of discounting and compounding.

The basic assumption of discounting and compounding is that money has a time value – that a given sum of money now is normally worth more than an equal and certain sum at some future date. Why? Because it permits profitable investment or consumption in the interval. This means that a given sum today is worth more than the same sum in 10 years, because it can be invested and earn additional money in the intervening period. For this reason, economists have learned to discount receipts expected in the future. The opposite site of the coin is the time preference of individuals for present consumption over present savings (or future consumption). For postponing consumption, people need to be rewarded. The reward per unit of savings, in the form of interest, will depend on several factors, and we shall deal with this further in this chapter.

Discounting is the ascertainment of present values; compounding is the ascertainment of terminal values. The basic equations are:

$$S = P(1 + r)^n \tag{8.1}$$

$$P = \frac{S}{(1 + r)^n} \quad \text{or} \quad S(1 + r)^{-n} \tag{8.2}$$

where

P identifies a sum at the present time
S identifies a sum arising in the future
r = rate of discount.

Most investment problems involve more than the comparison of a future sum with a present sum; usually the problem is relating a series of future cash flows to a present investment outlay or a series of outlays. Equation (8.2) becomes:

$$P = \sum_{i=1}^{i=n} \frac{A_t}{(1 + r)^n} \tag{8.3}$$

where A_t = cash flow in year t.

In the case when the cash flows vary from year to year in an irregular manner, there is no formula that will enable the present value of the series to be computed in one embracing calculation. Where the series of cash flows follow a regular pattern, shortcut formulations can be used. Three situations arise in practice.

The first is constant periodic cash flows or annuities. In this case, equation (8.3) can be transformed into:

$$P = \frac{A[1 - (1 + r)^{-n}]}{r} \tag{8.4}$$

when A = 1

$$a_{n/r} = \frac{1 - (1 + r)^{-n}}{r} \tag{8.5}$$

and $a_{n/r}$ = present value of an annuity of €1 a year for n years at r per cent per annum.

The second case is constant periodic cash flows – perpetuity. A perpetuity is an annuity that goes on for ever. If in equation (8.5) n goes to infinity, so that the annuity becomes a perpetuity, then the $(1 + r)^{-n}$ term becomes zero, and the present value of the perpetuity equals 1/r (Bierman and Smidt, 1990).

The third possible situation is when cash flows grow at a compound rate. The shortcut formula becomes:

$$P = \frac{A_{a_{n/r_0}}}{1 + b}$$ (8.6)

where

$r_0 = (r - b)/(1 + b)$
b = growth rate of the cash flows.

An investor is after all interested in the return of an investment project. Therefore we return to equation (8.3) to define the yield rate, which is the solution r in equation (8.3); it is the rate that equates capital outlays and their resultant cash flows. The yield rate is that rate of interest that discounts future cash flows to the present value.

Although the ascertainment of the terminal values is of less importance with respect to investment appraisal, two formulae should be mentioned. The first relates to a series of cash flows:

$$S = \sum_{i=1}^{i=n} A_i (1 + r)^{n-1}$$ (8.7)

In the case of constant periodic cash flows, a shortcut formula can be applied:

$$S = \frac{A[(1 + r)^n - 1]}{r}$$ (8.8)

Where A is a series of 1, equation (8.8) becomes:

$$S_{n/r} = \frac{[(1 + r)^n - 1]}{r}$$

where $S_{n/r}$ is the conventional symbol for the terminal value of an annuity of €1 per year, for n years at r per cent per annum.

These basic notions and formulae are the fundamentals of the discounting (or scientific) methods of investment appraisal that we deal with in the third section of this chapter.

We have explained the difference between micro- and macro-evaluations. The discounting methods mean that we take into account the revenues and cash costs over the life of the project, discounting them to a base year and subtracting the capital costs of the project (also discounted). The discounted cash flow approach takes account only of the advantages of the project to the investor (i.e. it is a micro-evaluation).

For many tourism projects, the discounted cash flow approach is insufficient. Social cost–benefit analysis (CBA) is more useful. Referring to Prest and Turvey (1967), CBA can be defined as:

> a practical way of assessing the desirability of projects, where it is
> important to take a long view (in the sense of looking at repercussions in
> the further as well as in the nearer future) and a wide view (in the sense

of allowing for side effects of many kinds on many persons, industries, regions etc.) i.e. it implies the enumeration and evaluation of all the relevant costs and benefits.

In addition to the cash flows, the calculations take account of all the changes in social benefits and social costs that result from the project, reducing them to monetary terms and discounting them to a present value from which the capital cost may be subtracted in order to obtain the net present value. CBA is by definition a macro-approach. We set the macro-economic costs and benefits against each other. Costs are defined in a special way – what level of output would have been reached if the factors of production were utilized in the rest of the economy? – i.e. costs of the project are measured in terms of its opportunity costs. Benefits are the additional benefits to the community that result from the realization of the project. The fundamental objective of a CBA is to complete the private economic calculations with figures for the economic benefits and costs of a project to its consumers and the society as a whole.

CBA is directly related to the externalities. 'External benefits' is a frequently used term in tourism. What do we understand by external benefits, and are there also external costs? This the subject of the next section.

Externalities in tourism: what does it mean?

Definition

'Externalities' is one of the vaguest and most ambiguous terms in economic science. Webster's Dictionary defines 'externality' as 'the state or quality of being external'. This definition is of course not very helpful. We find a more useful description in Boardman *et al.* (2001), who describe an *externality* as an effect that production or consumption has on third parties – people not involved in the production or consumption of a good. It is a by-product of production or consumption for which there is no market. 'No market' is not an essential part of the definition, and to our view is not always correct.

Other authors use the expression 'external effects' instead of 'externalities' (Sugden and Williams, 1988; Mishan, 1994). They consider the social costs and benefits of a (private or public) project rather than the financial outlays and receipts that would be considered by decision-makers in private (or public) firms. There are several reasons for expecting social costs and benefits to be different from private (public) outlays and receipts. Indeed, externalities or external effects may occur for a wide variety of reasons. Some result because a particular type of technology is used (e.g. deterioration of the landscape caused by transport of electricity). Others result because of interdependencies or synergies between producers and consumers of different groups of producers (e.g. my neighbour is a beekeeper who provides pollination services for the fruit in my orchard). A third group of externalities occurs because of networking (e.g. a convention centre stimulates the turnover of hotels and restaurants). Others arise because of negative effects on competitive projects, companies or events.

It is clear from the above that there are positive and negative externalities. The first group produces benefits, while the latter imposes social costs.

'Externalities' is a generic term that is used, rightly or wrongly, to justify many projects. Furthermore, in many studies several terms are used to cover externalities – indirect effects, spillover effects, induced effects, stemming effects, pecuniary effects, side effects, etc. Many consultants in the tourism sector abuse externalities to inflate the so-called benefits of a project. Therefore, to avoid such abuses it seems appropriate to start with identification of the types of externalities.

In this section we make a distinction between three types of negative and three types of positive externalities: 'unpaid' costs and benefits; 'underpaid' costs and benefits; and positive and negative side effects.

Negative externalities

The first category of negative externalities is *unpaid costs*. Any project or event is the initiative of a person, firm or public body. Who pays for or finances the project is not important; we call the investor the paymaster. At this level the paymaster is responsible for the investment costs and the running costs of the project, but he also cashes in the direct payments of the consumer (e.g. entrance fees to participate in an event, the use of a ski-lift etc.). We call this the 'project' or 'micro-' level. It does not matter if the investor belongs to the private or the public sector.

However, in most cases the paymaster does not pay for all the costs of the project or event. Many projects provoke a lot of economic, social and/or environmental costs for which the investor does not pay. There is no free lunch. A third party will pay the bill or suffer inconvenience (Vanhove, 2003).

Typical examples of unpaid costs include:

- Water pollution
- Air pollution
- Noise pollution
- Traffic congestion
- Security costs of events
- Destruction of landscape
- Extension of an airport
- Sight pollution of windmills.

In the case of *underpaid costs*, some costs are taken into account, but not at the full price. A typical example is the expropriation of land for a big event at a price below the market value – in other words, the price of the land retained in the investment costs at the micro-level is lower than the real value. This brings us to the notion of opportunity costs. Cost should be measured at opportunity costs.

'Opportunity costs' is another economic term that leads to a lot of interpretation problems and misunderstanding. Any tourism project (e.g. an event) requires resources that could be used to produce other goods or services instead. Tourism projects such as festivals, sporting events, theme parks, winter sports infrastructure, for example, require labour, land, capital and/or equipment. The resources used for these purposes cannot be used to produce other goods or services. Almost all public or private projects incur opportunity costs. Conceptually, these costs equal the value of the goods and services that would have been produced had the resources used in carrying them out been used instead in the best alternative way (Boardman *et al.*, 2001). In other words, production elsewhere is foregone.

As we said, cost items should be measured at the opportunity costs. In efficient markets, opportunity costs are equal to market prices. However, markets are not always efficient. Let us suppose that the Olympic Games is to take place in a region or country with very high unemployment. In the construction phase of the necessary infrastructure (e.g. new stadia, new sport infrastructure) and in the running of the games, hundreds or thousands of unemployed find jobs. All of them are paid a normal salary. These salaries are included in the investment and running costs at the micro-level.

However, costs should be measured at opportunity costs. What are the opportunity costs of an unemployed person? His or her best alternative is probably unemployment. The corresponding contribution of unemployed people to the national product is zero (unemployment benefit is a pure transfer). There is no production (goods or services) foregone. This type of underpayment of costs is quite often a very important item in project appraisal from a macro point of view. This might be even more the case in a tourism than in an industrial region. Many tourism regions have high unemployment.

A third group of negative externalities relates to *side effects* on competitive projects or events. We all know of situations where a new tourism project is competing with an existing production unit in the same region – for example, a seaside resort with a famous beach festival is confronted with a similar new production in a neighbouring resort, or a new congress centre is built in a place close to a city which already has good congress facilities.

In such circumstances, a reduction in the turnover of the existing product can be expected. The corresponding reduction of value added should be considered as a cost item for the new event or congress centre.

Positive externalities

Again, *unpaid benefits* are the first category of positive externalities. The paymaster does not pay all the costs of a tourism project and, similarly, not all benefits of a project or an event accrue to the investor. In tourism there are many possible unpaid benefits, such as:

- Image effect
- Promotion effect
- Improvement of international liquidity position
- Increase of property value
- Free fees.

However, in other cases the consumer does not always pay the full price of a product or service, or we are confronted with *underpaid benefits*. If the consumer pays less than the market price for a service (e.g. a performance) – benefits are measured in terms of market prices – it seems obvious that there is an underpayment of benefits.

The situation becomes more complicated when we consider the consumers' willingness to pay. This brings us to the notion of consumer surplus. The latter is one of the foundations of cost–benefit analysis (Pearce, 1983; Boardman *et al.*, 2001).

215

A demand curve indicates the quantities of a good or service that individuals purchase at various prices. In Figure 8.1, a downward-sloped demand curve is illustrated as line P_1F.

The key is the link between demand schedules and the willingness to pay (WTP). Figure 8.1 illustrates that there is at least one consumer who is willing to pay a price of P_1 for one unit of service X. Similarly, there is at least one person who would pay a price of P_2 for the second unit of X, and there is someone who would pay P_3 for the third unit of X, and so forth. The message from this exercise is that the area under the demand curve, or the sum of all the unit-wide rectangles, closely approximates the WTP for X by all members of society. In other words, the triangle P_1P_4C and the rectangle P_4CX_3O in Figure 8.1 approximate society's WTP for a given amount of X, in this case the amount X_3. Thus the sum of the triangle and the rectangular approximates the total gross benefits society would receive from consuming X_3 units of service X. The consumers pay P_4 to the producers of the tourism service. In this case, the net benefits from consuming X_3 units equal the area below the demand curve but above the price line P_4C. This triangle P_1P_4C is called the consumer surplus. When demand curves are known, consumer surplus is one of the basic concepts in CBA to value impacts. The reason why consumer surplus is so important to CBA is that changes in consumer surplus can be used as reasonable approximations of society's WTP policy changes (Boardman *et al.*, 2001).

To show how the concept of consumer surplus can be used in CBA, consider a project that results in a price change. We take a price reduction in Figure 8.1 from P_4 to P_5. This would result in a benefit to consumers equal to the area of the trapezoid P_4CFP_5. It follows both because consumers gain from paying a lower price for the X_3 units they previously purchased, and because they gain from the consumption of $X_3 - X_4$ additional units.

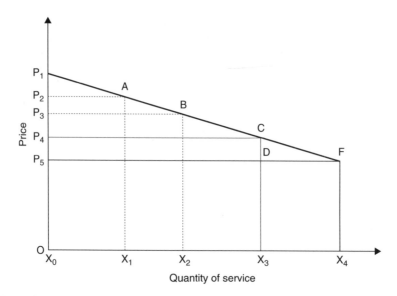

Figure 8.1 Consumer surplus

216

If there is an increase in the price, there is a loss of consumer surplus. However, if the price increases results from an imposed tax, there is no loss but a simple transfer – money is transferred from consumers to the government. From the perspective of society as a whole, its net impact is zero.

Changes in consumers' surplus are measures of the effects on the welfare of individuals of changes in the prices of goods that they consume. Individuals may be affected in a very similar way if there are changes in the costs of 'factor prices' (such as labour, the use of capital and land) that they supply.

Such changes are said to lead to changes in producers' surplus (Sugden and Williams, 1988). Producer surplus is the supply-side equivalent to consumer surplus. To define producer surplus, we refer to Figure 8.2. At a price of P_1, the producers receive revenues equal to the area represented by the rectangular area OP_1BX_1. The difference between this rectangular area and the area of the rectangle under the supply curve S, that is the area AP_1B, is called producer surplus. Indeed, some producers are willing to produce at a price lower than P_1.

Thus, producer surplus equals the revenues from selling X_1 less the variable costs required to produce X_1 – or the sum of total producer surplus and opportunity costs (that is areas $AP_1B + OABX_1$) corresponds to total revenues.

Price changes that are due to a project result in impacts on producers that can be valued in terms of changes in producer surplus. An increase in price to P_2 increases producer surplus (or economic profits) by P_1P_2CB (Boardman *et al.*, 2001).

Most tourism projects or events have a positive impact on the turnover of many other production units such as hotels, restaurants, pubs, souvenir shops, etc., known as the *side effects* on complementary activities. It is not the turnover that counts but the additional value added created. Quite often the additional value added in complementary activities is many times greater than the value added at the micro-level.

Those complementary activities have in their turn an impact on intermediate deliveries. We call them indirect effects (indirect income).

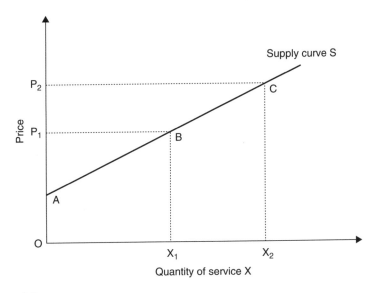

Figure 8.2 Producer surplus

Care must be taken with secondary effects due to spending of earned direct and indirect income, or induced effects (induced income). Should we take into account the portion of incomes resulting from an event spent by the recipients? This brings us to the famous multiplier effects, more particular the induced effects (see below. We have to be careful with induced effects).

The discounting methods

The unscientific conventional methods of investment appraisal

Before dealing with the discounting methods, we will briefly discuss the conventional methods that are very often applied in tourism.

The most conventional is undoubtedly the 'rate of return method', or the 'average-profit method'. This method can be defined as the ratio of profit, net of depreciation, to capital. This method has three significant shortcomings:

1. It fails to allow for the incidence of capital outlays and earnings. In other words, this method neglects one of the basic principles of investment appraisal: money has a time value.
2. It neglects the pre-production period. The latter has a great impact on the results of big projects with a long preparation and construction phase.
3. It strongly discriminates against short-term projects and projects that pay off heavily in the early than the later years.

A variant of the rate of return method is the 'peak-profit method'. The basis of this method is to take the level of profit in the best year and express it as a rate of return on the sum invested. The assumption behind this method is that the peak-profit rate of return is in some way a guide to the average profitability of the project. It is evident that the same shortcomings apply to this variant. Furthermore, having similar profit streams every year is an additional assumption.

A third, and quite often applied, conventional method is the 'payback method'. This method does not calculate a return, but the time period it takes (T) for an investment to generate sufficient incremental cash to recover the initial incremental capital outlay in full. If A (cash flow) is constant,

$$T = \frac{C}{A} \tag{8.9}$$

This method is applied for sectors and projects subject to rapid technological changes, and is useful in assessing risk and liquidity.

Owing to the significant shortcomings or the special character of the conventional methods, discounting methods are far more suitable in appraisal of tourism projects. There are three basic discounting methods:

1. The net present value method (NPV), which has two derived methods:
   ■ Benefit–cost ratio (B/C)
   ■ NPV per unit of outlay
2. The yield method, or the internal rate of return (IRR)
3. The annual capital charge method (ACC).

Taking into account that the underlying conditions of the ACC method are never fulfilled in tourism, in the following paragraphs we will discuss the other discounting methods.

Net present value method

The NPV can be defined as the sum of the annual net benefits (gross benefits minus gross costs) of an investment discounted by the opportunity costs of capital. The latter is the rate of return that capital can earn on its best alternative uses. In other words, it is the sum of the present values of the cash flows for all the years during the projects' life. Cash flows can be categorized into positive and negative.

Positive cash flows (receipts) can take different forms:

- Gross receipts (or net profit)
- Rent
- Net changes in working capital
- Net residual asset values
- Depreciation provision less replacement expenditure.

Negative cash flows (expenditures) are:

- Capital outlays
- Operational expenditure (or operating losses)
- Terminal expenditure.

In mathematical terms, NPV can be written as:

$$\text{NPV} = \sum_{i=1}^{i=n} \frac{A_i}{(1 + r)^i} \quad \text{or} \quad \sum_{i=1}^{i=n} \frac{B_i}{(1 + r)^i} - \sum_{i=1}^{i=n} \frac{C_i}{(1 + r)^i} \tag{8.10}$$

where

A_i = net cash flow at the end of year i
B_i = positive cash flows
C_i = negative cash flows
r = cost of capital or discount rate
n = project life.

The minimum NPV value acceptable for an investor is zero; a value lower than zero means that the present value of the costs exceeds the present value of the benefits.

Three important points should be noted with respect to the application of equation (8.10):

1. The NPV value is strongly influenced by the value of the discount rate; the higher the r value the lower the NPV.
2. Although depreciation is a cash flow, depreciation is never included as a cost in discounted cash flow (dcf) analysis. Its function in conventional accounting – to allow for recovery of the initial capital outlay – is taken care of in the dcf techniques by entering the original capital outlay into the cash flow.

3. Financial charges such as interest and repayment of capital (amortization) are not normally taken into account in the cash flow because the discounting techniques themselves allow for the return on capital as well as the return of capital – assuming the capital outlay has been entered into the cash flow as a cost item, which is the normal practice.

Internal rate of return

The IRR of a tourism investment project is defined as the rate of 'interest' which discounts the future net cash flows of a project into equality with its capital cost; it is the r value that results in a zero NPV.

$$\text{IRR} = \sum_{i=1}^{i=n} \frac{A_i}{(1+r)^i} - C = 0 \quad \text{or} \quad \sum_{i=1}^{i=n} \frac{B_i}{(1+r)^i} = \sum_{i=1}^{i=n} \frac{C_i}{(1+r)^i} \quad (8.11)$$

Without using software the calculation of IRR can be time consuming, owing to the successive discounting approximations (successive interpolations). A shortcut formula can be helpful:

$$\text{IRR} = L_r + (H_r - L_r) \frac{\text{NPV at } L_r}{|\text{NPV at } L_r + \text{NPV at } H_r|} \quad (8.12)$$

where

L_r = an interest rate that results in a positive NPV
H_r = an interest rate that results in a negative NPV.

The expression $|\text{NPV at } L_r + \text{NPV at } H_r|$ is the absolute difference between the two NPVs.

Benefit–cost ratio

A variant of the NPV, often used in project appraisal, is the 'benefit–cost ratio' – or the present value of the benefits over the present value of the costs:

$$\frac{B'}{C'} = \frac{\displaystyle\sum_{i=1}^{i=n} \frac{B_i}{(1+r)^i}}{\displaystyle\sum_{i=1}^{i=n} \frac{C_i}{(1+r)^i}} \quad (8.13)$$

Any B/C ratio over 1.00 should be accepted. However, the ratio can vary as a function of the degree of 'grossness' (i.e. lack of detail) in the project presentation. A simple example may be an illustration. Table 8.1 presents the same project in three different forms of 'grossness'.

In other words, the same project can be presented with several B/C ratios and all ratios are correct. Needless to say, this means that a project evaluator can present

Table 8.1 The benefit–cost ratio for the same project presented with different levels of detail, A, B and C

	A	B	C
Present values			
■ Capital outlay	100	100	100
■ Marketing costs	100	–	100
■ Administrative costs	100	100	–
■ Maintenance	1000	1000	–
■ Other costs	1500	–	–
Total costs	2800	1200	200
Benefits	3100	1500	500
NPV	300	300	300
B/C ratio	1.11	1.25	2.50

the same project in a more positive or a less positive way. This method also makes it difficult to compare different projects because each project can have a different degree of 'grossness' of the cost items.

Net present value per unit of outlay

The NPV per unit of outlay is simply the NPV divided by the total investment outlay, with the latter being discounted at the same rate used to get the NPV. In the context of a fixed development budget, this is considered by many authors of cost–benefit analysis to be the best approach for the ranking of projects. We start first with the project with the highest NPV pet unit of outlay; then comes the project with the second highest ratio, etc. If the budget is limited, the project with the lowest ratio should be dropped first.

However, the definition of 'investment' itself contains some arbitrary elements. In some projects, 'current' outlays may be just as important as 'capital' outlays. For this reason, it is probably desirable to define the denominator in this measure to include all outlays subject to the rationing process, rather than just the 'investment' expenditure alone. The formula can be written as:

$$R = \frac{\text{NPV}}{C'} = \frac{B' - C'}{C'} \tag{8.14}$$

where

R = NPV per unit of outlay
B' and C' are expressed in present values.

In relating NPV or dcf to total costs, we automatically arrive at the most acceptable criteria to be applied.

Accept/reject decisions

As a formal accept or reject criterion, NPV and IRR lead to the same selection of single projects. However, the ranking can be different (see Figure 8.3).

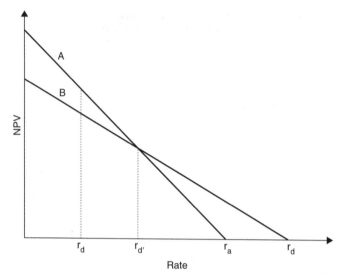

Figure 8.3 Comparison of NPV and IRR methods

What are now the advantages and disadvantages of the NPV and IRR? The advantages of IRR are threefold:

1. It is most familiar to people
2. There is no dispute about the cost of capital; nevertheless, *ex-post* the IRR should be related to a reference base
3. There is no discussion about what to include in the denominator.

The IRR also has a number of disadvantages:

1. The rate of discount cannot be changed during the lifetime of the project (this disadvantage has only theoretical significance)
2. It works in favour of short-term projects
3. It can yield multiple and meaningless results
4. It may provide a different project ranking to the NPV approach.

In Figure 8.3, the IRR of project A is equal to r_a and of project B is equal to r_b. As long as the discount rate is lower than $r_{d'}$, project A is superior to project B; beyond the $r_{d'}$ rate we reach the inverse situation.

The NPV has one major drawback. NPV is an absolute quantity – a money value expressed in absolute terms – and as such it is difficult to interpret the result. What is the meaning of an NPV of 100 million euros? This value can be high, but also rather marginal. Comparison of the result with the amount of investment is necessary, which gives the NPV per unit of outlay.

The necessity for a feasibility study

A project evaluation is more than an application of a discounted cash flow method. It is necessary to investigate in advance the possibility of selling the tourism products and the cost of their production, so that the anticipated profit may be foreseen before taking a decision in favour of or against the venture. The detailed process of this investigation and measurement is known as a feasibility study. Pandit (1986) describes a feasibility study as follows:

> The literal meaning of the word feasibility is possibility, practicability etc., but its application in the present context covers a wider range. Feasibility in this case would cover necessity, practicability and profitability, based on which a decision can be taken on the justifiability of the investment.

According to Ward (1991), 'a feasibility study might be defined as an appraisal of a development proposal providing a measurement of the return on investment'.

In these descriptions there are three basic elements. First, *necessity* means there is a demand in the market. In the case of a hotel project, this implies the following demands:

- General market conditions (e.g. geo-economic situation)
- Project market conditions (the performance of existing hotels, sales composition)
- Specific demand factors (type of economic activities, characteristics of existing hotels)
- A segment of customers and growth perspectives.

Secondly, *practicability* indicates that the implementation of the project is technically practicable. Many facets should be considered and investigated, including:

- Architecture (what will make the hotel superior to the ones in the competing market, attractive and acceptable to the guests, suitable for efficient operation, etc.)
- Basic architectural plans (site plans, typical floor plan, etc.)
- Budgetary constraints, quality level and size
- Available sites – examining them evaluating their suitability (suitability of location and various aspects of the plot of land such as size, soil conditions, visibility of the site, shape of the site, availability of water, electricity and other public utilities, etc.)
- Factors relevant to the preference of the clientele (e.g. entrance, size of the bedrooms, view from the rooms, facilities, garden and landscape)
- Investment costs.

Thirdly, *profitability* relates to the NPV or IRR and financial obligations – in other words, will the project meet all its operating expenses, debt refunding, depreciation and tax payments and earn profit? All this implies that attention should be paid to the tariff structure, pricing system, and how and by whom the hotel will be run (e.g. franchising, management contract or owner).

Once these three elements have been defined, we can prepare a business table.

A business table – a practical example

The principles of a feasibility study were applied to a family hotel at the Belgian Coast in the mid-1990s. The market possibilities were investigated and a variety of occupancy rates were applied. The practicability was analysed and translated into investment costs. The third step is the profitability. We start from the following characteristics:

1. A hotel with 40 rooms
2. An investment of 110.4 million Belgian francs (1€ = 40.34 Belgian francs), divided as follows
   - land 7 million
   - hotel 61.7 million
   - restaurant 13.5 million
   - recreation 21.5 million
   - shops 6.7 million
3. Equity 60 million and loan capital 50.4 million Belgian francs
4. Construction period one year
5. Average room rate, 3000 Belgian francs
6. Interest rate, 8 per cent
7. Depreciation:

	30 years	10 years
■ land	–	–
■ hotel	45.4	16.3
■ restaurant	8.1	5.4
■ recreation	15.5	6.0
■ shops	6.7	

8. The hotel had a tax exemption during the first 10 years of operation
9. The residual value after 10 years of operation is expected to be 57.5 billion Belgian francs.

Based on these assumptions, it is possible to forecast the annual results and the NPV and IRR of the project (see Table 8.2). The calculation is restricted to 10 years with a residual value at the end of the tenth year of operation. To a certain extent the procedure is unusual; a 30-year period of operation is more common.

Table 8.2 provides a lot of useful information with respect to the profitability of the hotel and the financial side of the project. First, the NPV equals 18.3 million Belgian francs and the IRR amounts to 11.0 per cent. Compared to the prevailing interest rate for investments and the inherent risks of any investment project, this result is not very profitable. A 50 per cent occupancy rate reduces the IRR to 8.4 per cent.

Secondly, the project shows a net profit throughout the whole lifecycle considered. As a consequence, the cash flow or the sum of net profit (losses) and depreciation is positive for every year of operation.

Thirdly, the cash flow sufficient each year to finance the annual debt payments.

Finally, notice that the calculation of the NPV or IRR is not based on the cash flow but on the row cash in/out of Table 8.2. (see definition of positive and negative cash flows in the application of dcf methods). The amount of 15.0 million Belgian francs for the first operational year is the sum of the G.O.P. (gross operational profit) of 9.9 million and the grants (5.1 million) to support the hotel modernization.

Table 8.2 Business table for a family hotel – 1995

Year	1	2	3	4	5	6	7	8	9	10	11
Investment											
Land*	70										
Hotel	617										
Horeca	135										
Recreation	215										
Shops	67										
Receipts											
Hotel		158	210	263	263	263	263	263	263	263	263
Horeca		12	12	12	12	12	12	12	12	12	12
Recreation		30	30	30	30	30	30	30	30	30	30
Shops		3	4	5	5	5	5	5	5	5	5
Total		203	256	310	310	310	310	310	310	310	310
Running costs											
Hotel		95	126	158	158	158	158	158	158	158	158
Recreation		9	9	9	9	9	9	9	9	9	9
Total		104	135	167	167	167	167	167	167	167	167
G.O.P./Ebitda**		99	121	143	143	143	143	143	143	143	143
Financial costs											
Depreciation		53	53	53	53	53	53	53	53	53	53
Interest		40	37	33	30	27	23	20	16	13	9
Grants		51	51	31	31						
Total		42	59	55	52	80	76	73	69	66	62
Ebta***		57	62	88	91	63	67	70	74	77	81
Taxes		–	–	–	–	–	–	–	–	–	–
Net profit		57	62	88	91	63	67	70	74	77	81
Amortization		43	43	43	43	43	43	43	43	43	43
Residual value											575
Cash flow		110	115	141	144	116	120	123	127	130	134
Cash in/out	(1104)	150	152	174	174	143	143	143	143	143	143
IRR	11.0%										

* in 10 000 Bfr
** Ebitda: Earnings before interest, taxes, depreciation and amortization
*** Ebta: Earnings before taxes and amortization (debt payments).

Cost–benefit analysis

Foundations of CBA

In a preceding section we defined CBA as a practical way of assessing the desirability of projects, where it is important to take a long view and a wide view – i.e. it implies the enumeration and evaluation of all relevant costs and benefits. In CBA, we try to consider all of the costs and benefits to society as a whole. That is the reason why some people refer to CBA as social cost–benefit analysis.

For Boardman *et al.* (2001), cost–benefit analysis 'is a policy assessment method that quantifies in monetary terms the value of all policy consequences to all members of society. The net social benefits measure the value of the policy. Social benefits minus social costs equals net social benefits'. The broad purpose of CBA is to help in social decision-making.

The foundations of CBA are the Pareto efficiency, willingness to pay (see consumer surplus) and producer surplus. An allocation is Pareto-efficient if no alternative allocation can make at least one person better off without making anyone else worse off. An allocation is inefficient, therefore, if an alternative allocation can be found that would make at least one person better off without making anyone else worse off. Boardman *et al.* state that 'one would have to be malevolent not to want to achieve Pareto efficiency – why forgo gains to persons that would not inflict losses on others?'. These writers make the link between positive net benefits and Pareto efficiency. If a policy has positive net benefits, then it is possible to find a set of transfers, or side payments, that makes at least one person better off without making anyone else worse off. A full understanding of this link requires some knowledge of how to measure costs and benefits in CBA. It is necessary to consider willingness to pay as the method for valuing the outputs of the policy, and opportunity costs as the method for valuing the resources required to implement the policy.

The costs are measured in terms of its opportunity costs, or what level of output would be reached if the factors of production were utilized in the rest of the economy. Benefits are the additional benefits to the community that would result from the realization of the project. Costs and benefits of a project are the time streams of consumption foregone and provided.

In a CBA, there are four important steps:

1. Identification of the cost and benefit items
2. Quantification of the cost and benefit items
3. Valuation of the cost and benefit items
4. Calculation of net present value (NPV) and/or internal rate of return (IRR).

Identification of cost and benefit items

The identification of cost and benefit items is directly related to the externalities dealt with earlier in this chapter. Table 8.3 might be helpful in identifying the cost

Table 8.3 Cost–benefit scheme

Level	Costs	Benefits
Project or paymaster's	Ca: investment Cb: running costs	Ba: direct receipts
'Unpaid' level	Cc: unpaid use of factors of production	Bb: unpaid satisfaction of needs
'Underpayment' level	Cd: underpayment of factors of production	Bc: underpayment of products and services
Side effects	Ce: side effects on competitors	Bd: side effects on complementary sectors, firms or projects

and benefit items from the viewpoint of society as a whole. We distinguish four levels of costs and benefits. The first level is the micro-level, also called the project or paymaster's level – in other words, who pays for the project. The other three levels are related to the externalities dealt with earlier in this chapter.

Table 8.3 can be applied to the identification of possible cost and benefit items of a big event (see Table 8.4).

This is not the only possible cost–benefit scheme. Another possible scheme is described by Scherly and Breiter (2002). Their approach is thematic and applied to a sports event. They make a distinction between:

1. Economic impact (based on national accounts)
    - direct economic impact
    - indirect economic impact
2. Ecological aspects
    - transport
    - energy, air and climate
    - waste
    - landscape

Table 8.4 Cost–benefit scheme for an event

Level	Costs	Benefits
Micro-level	- infrastructure costs - running costs of the event	- receipts from consumers - support from sponsors
'Unpaid' level	- public security costs - increased garbage collection - deterioration of site - social effects on local population or inconvenience costs to local people (circulation, noise, lost time, property damage, etc.)	- image-building - improvement of international liquidity position - improvement of infrastructure of the region
'Underpaid' level	- opportunity costs employment of unemployed labour (negative cost)	- consumer surplus - improvement of infrastructure of the region in case of local financial contribution

Side effects on competitive and complementary activities	- possible effect on a competitive event	- additional value added creation in:
		  – hotels and other lodgings
		  – restaurants, pubs, etc.
		  – shops
		  – other tourism activities
		- indirect effects and/or multiplier effects
		- induced effects
		- creation of new economic activities

3. Social aspects
4. Image (perception of the organization, visitors and local population).

In reality, this approach is closer to a general impact analysis than a genuine CBA. The sub-title of the study, 'Economic impact of major sports events in Switzerland', indicates in this direction.

Quantification of cost and benefit items

The next step is to express the items of Table 8.3 in quantitative terms – arrivals, nights, meters, cubic meters, volumes, etc. We can be confronted with two possibilities; either the cost and benefit items are measurable, which is the normal situation, or the items cannot be expressed in a quantitative unit; in that case they are called intangible items. A typical intangible cost item is a destruction of natural beauty of a landscape.

With respect to the quantification of cost and benefit items, a number of principles should be respected. The first quite evident – it is important to avoid double counting. The cost–benefit scheme can be very helpful in avoiding one or more cost or benefit items being counted twice, but even so double counting is not impossible. The development of a camping area cannot lead to higher land value of the area and to additional value added created in the accommodation firms on the site; it should be either higher land value or additional value added.

More important is the application of the 'with and without' principle rather than the 'before and after' principle. The first principle compares the tourism development of the project with the situation that would occur without the project – in other words, it is an evaluation in terms of the difference it makes. The 'before and after' principle attributes to a project effects that are not caused by it, but which occur because of the passage of time or for other irrelevant reasons (e.g. what were the costs before the new facility was implemented, and what will they be afterwards?).

An example makes it clear. The construction of a congress centre in a city will boost the number of nights stayed. It would be incorrect to attribute all additional nights to the congress centre; the number of nights would still probably have increased without the congress centre. The 'with and without' leads in this case to a lower benefit than the 'before and after'. However, there are cases where we have the opposite situation (e.g. a declining trend of nights in the city where the congress centre is built).

It is furthermore important to emphasize that, in Table 8.3, technological spillovers should be taken into account insofar as they alter the physical production possibilities of other producers or the satisfaction that consumers can get from given resources. On the other hand, pecuniary spillovers should not be taken into account if the sole effect is via prices of products or factors. There are cases involving transfers of resources from one group in the economy to another.

The comments made in Chapter 7 concerning crowding-out effects, expenditure switching and retained expenditure should be considered in the quantification of the different items.

Valuation of cost and benefit items

A third step in CBA is the valuation of the quantified items; the latter must be expressed in monetary units for each period of time over the economic life of the project.

In general, market prices are considered to be a proxy of the social valuations; market prices of final outputs indicate the 'proper' valuation of benefits, and market prices of resources the 'proper' valuation of costs. 'The prices placed on goods and services through the exchange process afford a means of measuring the value attached to those goods and services by those who participate in the exchange, and provide a basis for evaluating project effects in monetary terms' (US Government, Federal Inter-Agency River Basin Committee, Subcommittee on Benefits and Costs, 1950 – *The Green Book*).

In evaluating costs, attention should always be fixed on estimating the social opportunity cost of the resources used in the project; in other words, the social value of goods and services that would have been produced if the resources had been employed in the next best alternative public or private use. For most goods and services bought by public authorities from commercial firms, as well as for labour hired in competition with private sector, the market price is an adequate measure of social opportunity cost.

In practice, there is not always a market price. In these cases, a shadow price or accounting price can be used (Sassone and Schaffer, 1978; Mishan, 1994; Boardman *et al.*, 2001). This is the price an economist attributes to a good or a factor on the argument that it is more appropriate than the existing price, if any. So the price of a water purification plant down the river can be the shadow price for the waste water from a big tourism project discharged into the river, and for which the tourism project is not charged.

Many writers reserve the term 'shadow price' for outputs that are not sold in a direct market. However, shadow prices may also be used to correct the underestimation or overestimation of the value of a particular resource.

Other price standards in the absence of market prices include:

- The alternative production cost
- Individuals' willingness to pay
- Surrogate prices based on the behaviour of economic agents
- The prices of similar things elsewhere.

There are still items that are incommensurable (see Figure 8.4), such as the improvement of a landscape by a park (in the opposite case, the value of destruction of a landscape) or increase or decrease in the rate of juvenile delinquency due

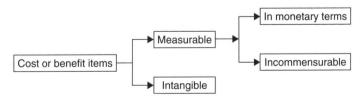

Figure 8.4 Various types of cost and benefit items

to tourism development. Another example is the saving of lives due to a better infrastructure. Although the number can be measured, for ethical reasons no value is given to saving a human being.

Sometimes there is opposition to the application of CBA because of the existence of intangible and/or incommensurable cost or benefit items. This is not a sufficient argument. We should recognize that some items cannot be expressed in monetary terms, without saying that those items should be neglected. Therefore we recommend adding (beside the table of quantifiable items) a qualitative table with costs and benefits that are intangible and/or incommensurable. We call this an itemization of the incommensurable physical benefits and costs associated with the project; it is suggested that a short description of the expected intangible effects should be added. This itemization can be helpful for the decision-makers of the project.

Very often the question is raised as to what should be done in case of price inflation and relative price changes. As a rule, we recommend the application of constant prices. For convenience, this will usually be the price level in the first year. Adjustments need not be made for inflation or general price increases. Uniform change in all prices can be ignored, and have no influence on the value of NPV or IRR. Adjustments need to be made for relative price changes. If some prices are likely to change relative to others, this should be reflected in CBA.

A special case is when there are adjustments to the market prices relative to taxes and subsidies. Indirect taxes are a cost to those who pay them, but it does not necessarily reflect economic costs to the country or the region as a whole in the sense that an increase of tax does not mean that more economic resources are required. From the viewpoint of the economy, taxes and subsidies must be viewed as transfer payments which normally should be excluded in valuating the costs of a project. Thus an import tax on beef consumed in the tourism sector should not be regarded as a cost to the economy, since it merely represents a transfer from the hotelkeeper to the government. Conversely, a grant on vegetable growing is clearly a benefit to the farmer but is not a benefit to the economy.

On the benefit side, an indirect tax on final output should be deducted as a cost by the producer paying it, but it should not be deducted from the valuation of the benefits for social cost–benefit analysis. In practice, market prices (including VAT) are the rule to valuate benefits based on the principle of 'willingness to pay'. Indirect taxes are part of the price people are willing to pay. In any case, indirect taxes paid by foreigners are a net benefit for the country; in tourism, the share of inbound tourism can be very important. All purchases must be cleared of VAT and other sales taxes. A tax paid to the government is a tax paid to society. This can lead to a real difference in profitability between a social cost–benefit application and a pure financial assessment.

This rule cannot be applied in all circumstances. A higher tax for pure budgetary reasons has nothing to do with willingness to pay. Thus a higher tax on fuel leads to higher transport cost savings in a CBA of a new highway project, but in this case the tax has a pure transfer effect and does not contribute to any increase of welfare.

Calculation of NPV and/or IRR

Now we have all the elements to calculate the NPV or IRR. Table 8.3 can be transformed into the form of Table 8.5. For each cost and benefit item, a column

Table 8.5 Calculation table in CBA

Year	Ca	Cb	Cc	Cd	Ce	ΣC	Ba	Bb	Bc	Bd	ΣB	Σ(B − C)
1												
2												
3												
4												
5												
6												
7												
8												
9												
10												
30												
NPV												

is provided (there can be more than one column for each generic cost and bene-fit item). Table 8.5 also contains special columns for the sum of the costs, the sum of the benefits and finally for the sum of (B − C). This allows us to calculate the NPV and the IRR.

A crucial point in the NPV calculation is the choice of the discount rate. The role of the discount rate is two-fold. First, it makes costs and benefits accruing at different points of time commensurable. Secondly, in considering the net benefits achieved by an investment project attention has to be paid to its costs, which means the opportunity foregone. The role of the discount rate is to help to ensure that these opportunities foregone, which are themselves time streams of costs and benefits, are properly taken into account. The opportunities foregone can be in:

1. The public sector
   - consumption
   - investment
2. The private sector
   - consumption
   - investment.

In other words, the discounting is necessary to allow for the time factor and the cost of capital.

In theory, the social time preference or the social opportunity cost as social rate of discount can have several foundations. It is not our intention to explore this aspect in this publication – the literature on that topic is immense, sufficient to fill up many shelves of a library. In reality, four different schools of thought can be distin-guished (Dasgupta and Pearce, 1972; Mishan, 1994). The first is the 'social time pref-erence' (STP) school of thought. This means that consumption in the near future is preferable to consuming something of the same market value in the more distant future. This school argues that the social discount rate should reflect society's pref-erence for present benefits over future benefits. STP expresses the social substitu-tion ratio of actual and future consumption. STP can be expressed in real terms and in nominal terms; the difference between them is the depreciation of the money.

The second is the 'social opportunity cost' (SOC) school of thought. The SOC of a project (of the public sector) is the present value for society of the best alternative project that at the same time is excluded by the project. SOC is the present value of the consumption flows that would arise without the project. The second school of thought suggests that the social discount rate for use should reflect the rate of return foregone on the displaced project.

Others prefer to apply the government's borrowing rate or the average rate of return of long-term treasury bonds. Although this third alternative is quite often used, this approach is sometimes considered as a second-best solution. Indeed, people neglect more productive investment for bonds without risk (underestimation of SOC), and interest rates are influenced by market imperfections (influence of monetary and fiscal policy).

The fourth school of thought advocates the rate of return on private investments. Public projects should earn a rate of return equal to good private projects, and hence the interest rate equal to private rates of return can be used in the CBA.

If benefits and costs are expressed in constant prices, it is recommended that the real interest rate should be used. The market interest rate is in theory the sum of the real interest rate and inflation; however, the reality is quite often different. The real interest rate R can be deduced from the following formula:

$$(1 + r) = (1 + R)(1 + i) \tag{8.15}$$

$$R = [(1 + r)/(1 + i)] - 1 \tag{8.16}$$

where

R = real interest rate
r = market interest rate
i = inflation rate.

Risk and uncertainty

In the application of CBA, we can be faced with a number of special problems. The first is risk and uncertainty. Here we take the two terms as synonyms, although this is not completely correct. Risk is inherent in all investment projects, but for some projects the uncertainty might be bigger. In the tourism sector there are many projects with uncertain factors. How do we tackle risk and uncertainty? In the literature, several procedures are proposed (see US Government, Federal Inter-Agency River Basin Committee, Subcommittee on Benefits and Costs, 1950 – *The Green Book*). Two have little value:

1. Risk premium to the discount rate
2. Shortening of project life.

These procedures have little value because nobody can tell us what risk premium should be taken, or by how many years a project should be shortened.

We prefer to recognize that there are risks, and thus recommend that two or three variants be taken for one or more cost or benefit items. The consequence of this approach is a multitude of NPVs or IRRs. However, it cannot be the intention to present 50, 100 or 200 results. Therefore, we propose to stick to three combinations:

1. The most pessimistic approach. In this case, the highest value is taken for each cost item and the lowest for each benefit item. If the NPV > 0, we get a positive sign, in favour of the project.
2. The most-optimistic approach. This uses a combination of all the lowest cost and all the highest benefit alternatives. An NPV < 0 is a negative indication, against the project.
3. The most likely result. Here, NPV or IRR is based on a combination of all the most likely estimations of cost and benefit items.

This brings us to the sensitivity analysis (Boardman *et al.*, 2001), with worst-and-best case analysis, the most plausible estimates and partial sensitivity. The latter is most appropriately applied to what the analyst believes to be the most important and uncertain assumptions. It can be used to find the values of numerical assumptions at which net benefits equal zero. The partial sensitivity analysis can also be applied with respect to the right choice of the discount rate.

Another approach of risk analysis is 'component analysis', based on the composition of the cost components as well as the composition of the benefit components of the NPV. Here, we refer to the composition of the last row of Table 8.5. It must be reassuring for an investor if one cost component represents 60 per cent of the NPV of the costs and there is not much uncertainty about the estimation of that item; similarly if a benefit component has a high share in the NPV of benefits and shows little risks.

Limitations in space and time

Any project is influenced by the definition of space and time. The NPV or IRR of a project can be calculated for a resort, destination, region, county or country. The result will most probably be different with respect to the space (or area) level. Two examples make this clear. A major event, financed by the destination, can lead to important side effects (see Bd items in Table 8.3) which do not accrue to the inhabitants of the destination and as such cannot be considered as a benefit for the destination. However, from the national point of view these benefits should be taken into account. Another relevant example is the building of a congress centre in a city subsidized by the national government. For the city the grant means a reduction of the investment and/or operation costs, but from the national point of view the subsidy should be disregarded.

Limitations in time are of a different nature. The question arises as to how long a period we should take into account in order to get a reasonable estimate of the total effect of the investment. The answer depends on many elements. The first factor is the height of the social discount rate. A high discount rate leads to a negligible NPV of a benefit accruing in 30 years or more. Other important elements include physical length of life, technological changes, emergence of competing products or projects, and shifts in demand.

Final remarks

In many applications of CBA there is confusion between the costs and receipts of the project on the one hand, and the public expenditure and tax receipts on the other. A clear distinction must be made between the macro-evaluation of a project and the financial account of the public sector. The financial account of the public sector relates to the expenses and taxes, both reduced to a present value. Taxes are a transfer, and can never be considered in a CBA.

A special problem is the comparability of the profitability of a project with other projects. In most cases this is a theoretical problem; in practice, there is not a similar project. A comparison of a project in one field with a one in another field does not make much sense. A choice between a tourism project and an education project cannot be based on the difference in IRR; the choice is purely a political decision.

Case study: Congress Centre in Bruges

At the beginning of the 1970s, a feasibility study was commissioned for a new congress centre in Bruges. The study started from the important assumption that 50 per cent of the cost could be transferred to a cultural function. In the town there was at that time a need for a cultural centre and a congress centre, and it was assumed that the new project could fulfil both functions. As a consequence, part of the project was eligible for grants from the national government.

The first part of the study dealt with the market possibilities for attracting conferences to Bruges. In a second part, investment costs and running costs were estimated.

The two main parts analysed the micro- and macro-profitability. This case is a good example for showing the difference in profitability between a micro- and a macro-approach.

From the micro-profitability point of view, the congress centre showed a very negative result during each year of operation. The first, second, sixth and tenth years of operation showed the following losses:

- First year: €–130 000
- Second year: €–111 000
- Sixth year: €–57 000
- Tenth year: €–40 000

The application of Table 8.3 to the Bruges case resulted in cost and benefit items as listed in Table 8.6.

With a discount rate of 8 per cent, the project resulted in an NPV of €5 million or an IRR of 33.5 per cent. This macro-profitability is in sharp contrast to the micro-profitability.

From the composition of the macro-benefits it can be deduced that less than one-fifth of the present value of the receipts accrue to the investor of the congress centre:

- Ba: €1 247 million or 18.0 per cent
- Bb: €1 800 million or 25.6 per cent
- Bd: €3 949 million or 56.4 per cent.

Table 8.6 Cost–benefit scheme, Congress Centre, Bruges

Level	Costs	Benefits
Project	Ca: investment congress centre Cb: running costs	Ba: direct receipts congress centre
'Unpaid' level	Cc: security cost, reception costs	Bb: prestige and promotion value
'Underpayment' level	Cd: transfer of investment and running costs to the cultural function	Bc: nihil
Side effects		Bd: additional value added hotels, restaurants and shops

It is quite remarkable that more than half of the benefits of the project accrue to hotels, restaurants and shops. This case shows that a very negative micro-profitability can be paired with a more than acceptable macro-profitability. This can be a sufficient argument for a local authority to finance the losses at the micro-level in order to harvest the benefits at the macro-level for the local community.

References and further reading

Baade, R. and Matheson, A. (2004). The quest for the Cup: assessing the economic impact of the World Cup. *Regional Studies*, 4.

Beritelli, P., Bieger, T., Müller, H. *et al.* (2004). *Assessing the Economic Impacts of Hallmark Sport Events – The Case of the World Ski Championship 2003 in St Moritz-Engadine*. Paper presented at TRC Meeting in Guildford, 2004 (unpublished).

Bierman, H. and Smidt, S. (1990). *The Capital Budgeting Decision. Economic Analysis of Investment Projects*, 7th edn. New York: Macmillan Press.

Boardman, A., Greenberg, D., Vining, A. and Weimer, D. (2001). *Cost–Benefit Analysis. Concepts and Practice*, 2nd edn. New Jersey: Prentice Hall.

Bull, A. (1995). *The Economics of Travel and Tourism*. Sydney: Longman.

Burgan, B. (2001). Reconciling cost–benefit and economic impact assessment for event tourism. *Tourism Economics*, 4.

Dasgupta, A. and Pearce, D. (1972). *Cost–Benefit Analysis. Theory and Practice*. London: Macmillan.

Ganchev, O. (2000). Applying Value Drivers to Hotel Valuation. *Cornell Hotel and Restaurant Administration Quarterly*, Oct.

Hawkins, C.J. and Pearce, D.W. (1971). *Capital Investment Appraisal*. London: Macmillan.

Hefner, F. (2001). The cost–benefit model as applied to tourism development in the state of South Carolina, USA. *Tourism Economics*, 2.

Klaassen, L.H. and Botterweg, T.H. (1974). *Projectevaluatie en imponderabele effecten: een schaduwprojectenadering*. Rotterdam: NEI.

Klaassen, L. and Vanhove, N. (1971). Macro-economic evaluation of port investments. In R. Regul (ed.), *The Future of the European Ports*. Bruges: College of Europe.

Layard, R. and Glaister, S. (eds) (1994). *Cost–Benefit Analysis*, 2nd edn. Cambridge: Cambridge University Press.

Mintel (2003). Hotels in Australia. *Travel & Tourism Analyst*, Aug.

Mishan, E.J. (1994). *Cost–Benefit Analysis*. London: Routledge.

Pandit, S.N. (1986). *Hotel Project – Feasibility Evaluation*. Vienna: Schriftenreihe für empirische Tourismusforschung und hospitality management.

Pearce, D.W. (1983). *Cost–Benefit Analysis*, 2nd edn. London: Macmillan.

Prest, A. and Turvey, R. (1967). Cost–benefit analysis: a survey. *Surveys of Economic Theory*, Vol. II. London: Macmillan.

Raybould, M. and Mules, T. (1999). A cost–benefit study of protection of the northern beaches of Australia's Gold Coast. *Tourism Economics*, 5.

Rushmore, S. (1992). Seven current hotel-valuation techniques. *Cornell Hotel and Restaurant Administration Quarterly*, Aug.

Sassone, P.G. and Schaffer, W.A. (1978). *Cost–Benefit Analysis: A Handbook*. London: Academic Press.

Scherly, F. and Breiter, M. (2002). *Impact économique des grandes manifestations sportives en Suisse, Etude de cas 'Athletissima' Lausanne 2001*. Lausanne: HEC Lausanne.

Sinclair, T. and Stabler, M. (1998). *The Economics of Tourism*. London: Routledge.

Smith, S. (1997). *Tourism Analysis. A Handbook*, 2nd edn. Edinburgh: Longman.

Sugden, R. and Williams, A. (1988). *The Principles of Practical Cost–Benefit Analysis*. Oxford: Oxford University Press.

United Nations (1993). Feasibility study on the Arona Valley Tourism Development Project. *Escap Tourism Review*, 12.

United Nations (1999). *Guidelines on Integrated Planning for Sustainable Tourism Development*. New York: UN.

US Government, Federal Inter-Agency River Basin Committee, Subcommittee on Benefits and Costs (1950). *Proposed Practices for Economic Analysis of River Basin Projects* (The Green Book). Washington: US Government.

Vanhove, N. (1978). Tourism planning: economic instruments – an evaluation at the project level. *Tourism Planning for the Eighties*, 28th AIEST Congress, Cairo. Bern: AIEST.

Vanhove, N. (1997). Mass tourism: benefits and costs. In Wahab, S. and Pigram, J.J. (eds), *Tourism Development and Growth*. London: Routledge.

Vanhove, N. (2003). Externalities of sport and tourism investments, activities and events. In Keller, P. and Bieger, T. (eds), *Sport and Tourism*, 53rd AIEST Congress, Athens. St-Gall: AIEST.

Van Rompuy, V. and Vertonghen, R. (1982). *Sociaal-economische kostenbatenanalyse*. Leuven: Acco.

Ward, T.J. (1991). The hotel feasibility study – principles and practice. In Cooper, C. (ed.), *Progress in Tourism, Recreation and Hospitality Management*. London: Belhaven Press.

WES (1971). *Micro and Macro ekonomische rendabiliteit van een kongresgebouw te Brugge*. Brugge: WES.

Witt, S., Brooke, M. and Buckley, P. (1991). *The Management of International Tourism*. London: Unwin Hyman.

9

Epilogue

The preceding chapters give an optimistic view of the growth of tourism and the role of tourism as a vehicle for economic development. However, we might ask the question, 'Is this view not too optimistic and too generalized?'

'Beyond the myth of growth in tourism'

In Chapter 3 we noted the WTO figures of inbound tourism by region. For the period 1995–2020 the expected average growth rate is 4.1 per cent, and varies from 3.0 per cent for Europe to 7.1 for the Middle East. This already provides a warning that the generalization of growth rates should be avoided. Most European and North American countries will show a high but not very high growth rate. Smeral (2004) shows even lower growth rates for the tourism exports (expenditure) of Japan, the USA and the EU for the period 2010–2020 (see Chapter 6). This is not surprising. Edwards (1988) was the first to recognize the ceilings in annual leave and public holidays and in holiday participation. We find confirmation of these phenomena in Chapter 3. In many European countries, public leave has not changed very much during the last two decades. The evolution in the last decade of net holiday propensity in several developed European countries is very surprising; even the gross holiday propensity shows signs of stagnation in some European countries.

This trend is related to a shift from holidays to short holidays. Should this evolution be interpreted as a sign that tourism in developed countries will not always be such a strong vehicle of economic development as is often suggested?

This brings us to 'the seven stylized facts of global tourism growth' of Smeral (2001), developed on the occasion of the AIEST Congress in Malta, where 'Tourism Growth and Global Competition' was the central theme. In his contribution 'Beyond the myth of growth in tourism', Smeral underlined his seven stylized facts:

1. Tourism grows faster than the world economy, its income elasticity is above 1. Given that, tourism services are a luxury good.
2. Tourism services are not among the fastest growing activities; other services grow at a significantly quicker rate.
3. Employment in the hotel and restaurant industry is making up an increasing share of total employment.
4. In the long term, tourism services get more expensive than manufacturing goods or other services which have better options for rationalization.
5. Growth rates in tourism decline with increasing living and income standards; tourism in low income countries grows faster than in high income countries.
6. Country-specific growth rates in tourism show significant variations. Tourism is not a luxury for each country or region. Even highly developed countries have opportunities to realize high growth rates in tourism.
7. Conflicts have sprung up between tourism growth and the principles of sustainable development. This is true not only for quantitative development strategies, but also for qualitative approaches.

Underlying factors in the 'stylized facts'

Smeral (2001) explains the stylized facts of tourism growth by a number of factors that apply to one or several of these stylized facts:

Factors	Stylized facts of tourism growth						
	1	2	3	4	5	6	7
Structural change	+	+				+	
Productivity differentials		+	+	+	+		
International division of labour	+				+	+	
Growth and development theory					+	+	
Limits of sustainable development							+

- *Structural change in tourism demand (demand bias)*: changes in taste and lifestyle and fashion trends have an impact on the development of country- and product-specific market shares. In Chapter 3 we saw that experience-driven short trips with cultural, sporting and gourmet themes are in. The same can be said about long-haul tourism and experience-based trips. On the other hand, destinations based on mass customized tourism supply, such as beaches, are losing market share.

- *Productivity differentials (productivity bias)*: the relatively slow growth of labour productivity growth in the tourism sector is one of the main reasons why tourism scores quite well as a employment generator. However, tourism prices have grown at a faster pace than prices of manufactured goods, communications and information (Smeral, 2003). The productivity gap between manufacturing or disembodied (separation of production and consumption) services and tourism increases with the development level of the economy: In other words, in several developed countries tourism is becoming relatively expensive (Smeral, 2001). We should not underestimate the impact of this phenomenon when the sector is confronted with a price elasticity of about −1.
- *International division of labour or international specialization and globalization*: Smeral refers to the Heckscher–Ohlin theorem (a country's comparative advantage is in its endowment with factors such as nature, labour and capital) and the new theory of international trade (this theory focuses on the exchange of differentiated products and services between countries of similar development levels and similar preferences – e.g. Italian winter sports resorts vs the French Alps, or Florence vs Prague). Globalization is another factor that stimulates tourism growth and specialization. The most important impact of globalization is greater competition. An increasing number of destinations compete with each other.
- *Growth and development theory*: here, Smeral refers to (a) the diminishing marginal returns of capital (in tourism, diminishing capital returns will become effective when thresholds in the development level are exceeded); (b) the advantage of backwardness (this applies particularly to tourism – the Gershenkron hypothesis); (c) the product cycle; and (d) the new growth theory. The latter explains why highly developed countries can still achieve high tourism growth rates, by focusing on public infrastructure, quality and human resources to stimulate innovation.
- *Limits of sustainable development*: Growth in tourism is to a large extent dominated by the issue of sustainability (Krippendorf, 1991; see next section).

For the coming two decades, another factor should be considered. In all developed countries, particular attention should also be paid to the ageing of the population. This ageing will have a negative impact on holiday participation in the long run. Early retirement will come under pressure, and the active population will be confronted with the growing social costs of the ageing process.

Sustainable development

It cannot be denied that there is growing attention to sustainable development. The Brundtland Report *Our Common Future* (1987) defines sustainable development as 'development that meets the needs of the present without compromising the ability of future generations to meet their own needs'. The World Travel and Tourism Council, WTO and the Earth Council adopted what is known as 'Agenda 21 for the Travel and Tourism Industry', which adapts the concept of sustainable development to tourism. Sustainable tourism is presented as a wise business practice (Bosselman *et al.*, 1999). If the development of tourism destroys the natural and cultural resources that attract visitors to a destination, tourism cannot be sustained: 'Quantitative tourism growth appears incompatible with the sustainable use of natural and cultural assets' (Mazzanti, 2002). It is in the interests of the tourism sector to ensure a balance between growth and the capacity to sustain growth. The Agenda 21 report emphasizes appropriate planning to ensure that tourism development will avoid environmental and cultural degradation.

Sustainability has several dimensions. Ritchie and Crouch (2003) make a distinction between ecological, economic, socio-cultural and political/governance environments.

Natural environment is a major attraction for many destinations, and in many cases it is the core of a destination's tourism product. Residents and the tourism industry have a great responsibility. Ritchie and Crouch see a dual role for the tourism sector: first, to ensure that any tourism development minimizes harm to ecology; and secondly, to provide an economic incentive that encourages preservation and protection. Any harm to the ecology of an area means external diseconomies in economic terms (see Chapter 8). In fact, this is not new.

Economic sustainability must aim to meet the economic needs and aspirations of residents in the long run. According to Ritchie and Crouch, the following considerations may be influential in determining economic sustainability: (a) tourism should benefit the many, not just the few; (b) utilization of local labour should be encouraged; and (c) any efforts to enhance job security will improve economic sustainability.

Socio-cultural sustainability means, for Ritchie and Crouch, minimizing adverse social and cultural impacts such as crime, prostitution, alienation of certain segments of the population, trivialization of culture and the disintegration of a way of life, while fostering an interest and pride in those things that define a culture or society without placing it in a time warp.

If tourism destination development is sustainable from the three above-mentioned points of view, it is likely that it may be acceptable politically.

Smeral also considers four dimensions of sustainability: ecological, social, cultural and economic perspectives. The content of the different aspects is not always the same as with Ritchie and Crouch.

The ecological dimension is in line with Ritchie and Crouch (2003); it focuses on avoiding or minimizing the environmental impact of tourism activities. Knowledge of the carrying capacity can be very helpful in assessing environmental impact. It sets the limits to ecologically sustainable development and, indirectly, quantitative tourism growth.

Social sustainability refers to the ability of a destination to absorb additional demand and be able to continue functioning without social disharmony. Sources of disharmony include the increasing differences between those who benefit from tourism and those who are marginalized by it, and the creation of tourist ghettos.

Cultural sustainability refers to 'the ability of people to retain or adapt elements of their culture which distinguish them from other people' (Smeral, 2001). Customs, traditions and lifestyles are subject to change through the introduction of tourists. To a certain extent changes are unavoidable; culture itself is dynamic and tourism is not the only factor that has an impact on the local culture. Television programmes have considerably more influence on cultural changes than tourism.

Smeral has a different view of economic sustainability: 'It refers to a level of economic gain from the activity which is sufficient to cover the cost of any special measures taken to cater to the tourists and to mitigate the effects of the tourists' presence or to offer an income appropriate to the inconvenience caused to the local community visited'.

Very important is Smeral's (2001) statement that

> in most cases the ecological carrying capacity, and especially the environmental assimilation capacity, limits quantitative growth. Once quantitative growth has reached a limit at which the environment begins to be degraded by excessive burden, only sustainable policies that take into account ecological limits can stimulate tourism development.

Managing tourism growth

Managing tourism growth has become a new paradigm. Godschalk and Brower (1979) define growth management as a 'conscious governmental program intended to influence the rate, amount, type, location, and/or quality of future development within a local jurisdiction'. Bosselman *et al.* (1999) condense the five objectives to three, and apply them to tourism. The three objectives are: quality (type is subsumed in quality), quantity (rate and amount) and location. A growth strategy can work towards all three of these objectives, although in practice most strategies emphasize one of the three. Bosselman *et al.* formulate the three strategies as follows:

1. The quality of development strategy, which usually has the objective of encouraging only that development that meets certain standards. They illustrate this strategy with several case studies (e.g. New Zealand; and Lake Tahoe in Nevada and California).
2. Strategy that manages the quantity of development by regulating the rate of growth and/or the capacity of development, carrying out capacity analysis, is a key element in this approach. However, this is more than the number of tourists. Other techniques are needed to mitigate unwanted impacts, such as the 'Limits of acceptable change approach' and 'Visitor impact management approach'. The authors devote several interesting case studies to this. Three of them concern the Great Barrier Reef Marine Park in Australia; Aspen (Colorado); and Bermuda.
3. Finally, many strategies focus on the location of development by either expanding or contracting existing areas, or by diverting the growth to new locations. Typical examples of a concentration strategy are the Nusa Dua project in Bali (Indonesia), and Bruges (Belgium); The Republic of Maldives is an example of a dispersal strategy.

To manage the growth of tourism a strategic planning approach is essential, whereby the different planning and development activities related to tourism are linked to an overall strategic plan to provide an integrated framework for directing tourism (United Nations, 1999). Strategic tourism planning requires careful consideration of the goals and principles of sustainable development. These goals and principles have different aspects. The United Nations report makes a distinction between five levels – economic, social, ecological, cultural and political – of principles, and these are listed below. However, we believe that some of the formulated guidelines are too theoretical, and very difficult to achieve in practice.

Economic:

- Development that takes into account the full costs and benefits of the alternatives and decision embarked upon, from an overall economic and social perspective.
- Broad-based distribution of benefits among all stakeholders.
- Provision of a quality visitor experience that is compatible with the destination's goals and values.
- Ensuring that fiscal costs of infrastructure provision and marketing do not outweigh the benefits.

Social:

- Steady employment that avoids the underemployment and unemployment associated with seasonal hiring for peak tourism periods.
- Better employment opportunities than the inferior positions typically associated with tourism services.
- Quality jobs that encourage the use of local knowledge, skills and traditions, and offer a sense of fulfilment and satisfaction to residents.
- Improvement of the standard of living and equitable distribution of benefits within (and between) generations in the present and the future.

Ecological:

- Maintenance of essential ecological processes, biological diversity and non-renewable resources for future generations.
- Planning at a scale and pace that enables effective and ongoing monitoring and mitigation of long term impacts.
- Full-cost accounting of environmental resources in cost – benefit analysis.
- An environmental and cumulative impact that analyses important prerequisites to development and environmental management systems needs to be implemented by business and organizations.

Cultural:

- Tourist activities and behaviours should be respectful of cultural activities, sites and values.
- Designs should be compatible with national and local heritage and character and should foster the community's identity or sense of place.
- Tourist types and activities should match the needs and expectations of the local people, with protection of sensitive and indigenous cultures against any adverse impact.

Political:

- Compatibility between overall economic development goals of regional and community interests and tourism goals.
- Integration of plans and planning with other relevant community and regional plans and processes.
- Balance top-down planning with resident input and participation planning and development.

(United Nations, 1999)

Tourism and economic development strategy

Let us return to the opening words of this epilogue. Has tourism a strategic role in the development of a country, a region or a destination in general? The answer to that question is not black or white. First, there is a preliminary condition. The basic requirement is the availability of tourism attractions, the necessary infrastructure and accessibility (see Chapter 4). However, not all attractions are able to mobilize a large group of visitors – tourists do not travel several thousands of miles to see what they have next door. Many interregional flows of tourists can be interesting, but insufficient to stimulate the development of a region. The degree of attractiveness of the tourism supply and the size of demand of the appealing factors are of vital importance.

Assuming that the necessary attractions are available in a country or destination, can tourism be a vehicle for development? From what we have seen in the preceding chapters of this book, by and large the answer is positive. However, quite often a distinction is made between richer and poorer countries (De Brabander, 1992; Sharpley and Telfer, 2002). This distinction appears to be too rough – not all the countries of EU can be considered as rich, and within each EU country there are both rich and backward regions.

Although any generalization should be avoided, there are doubts about the role of tourism as a vehicle of development in rich regions. Smeral's remarks cited above are indicative in this respect. Furthermore, contributions of tourism to income generation, balance of payment effects and the international liquidity position are in most cases marginal, or in any case tourism has no dominant role (De Brabander, 1992). However, from the point of view of employment there are also several drawbacks. In Chapter 7, we saw that tourism employment has a number of negative characteristics – although again, generalization is dangerous. In cities with business and/or cultural tourism, there are many jobs in hotels, restaurants, entertainment, etc. Furthermore, in richer regions tourism is a sector that offers job opportunities for unskilled people; these types of jobs are needed in all societies. It should not be concluded that tourism does not offer qualified jobs and does not employ highly qualified people.

The situation is very different in backward regions of developed countries with genuine tourism attractions. There is in most cases less competition with other sectors on the labour market, and unemployment is very often high. The advantages of tourism development mentioned in Chapter 7 apply to this type of regions (Vanhove, 1986, 1999; Williams and Shaw, 1995; Telfer, 2002a, 2002b).

243

The European Commission recognizes the role of tourism in regional development. In the framework of the Structural Funds, the EU supports several regions in their efforts to develop tourism as a vehicle of change. In the objective 1 areas (the poorest regions of the EU), interventions of structural funds (SF) for the period 2000–2006 for tourism measures amount to 4 295 million euros, or 3.2 per cent of the total SF (retained codes or fields of intervention are: encouragement for tourist activities, tourism physical investment, non-physical investments, shared services for the tourism industry, vocational training). That share is 4.2 per cent for France and 6.2 per cent for Italy. These figures underestimate the reality; tourism is also part of several other measures of the regional strategic programmes. In objective 2 regions, tourism measures represent 2 032 million euros, or 9.0 per cent of the SF expenditures. In the objective 2 regions of France this share increases to 12.9 per cent, and in Italy to 13.3 per cent. In several European countries, tourism contributes to a redistribution of wealth between regions (see also Guicheney and Rouzade, 2003).

Tourism as a vehicle for economic development is even more realistic for destinations in developing countries with interesting tourism attractions. The key arguments were developed in Chapter 7. Sharpley (2002) also cites several of these factors:

■ Tourism is a growth sector, and especially long-haul tourism.
■ Tourism demonstrates high income-elasticity.
■ Price-elasticity can do harm to tourism regions of rich countries.
■ Tourism redistributes wealth.
■ Tourism utilizes 'free' attractions such as climate, sea, beaches, mountains, monuments, way of life, architecture, etc. – in other words, resources are available and can in many cases be used in the tourism industry with marginal additional investments.
■ There are no trade barriers to tourism.
■ Tourism has backward linkages and stimulates entrepreneurial activity.
■ Tourism is a guarantee for income stability.
■ Tourism is a labour-intensive sector.

Four (critical) remarks should be made. First, many developing countries have little choice in sector development, and frequently tourism is one of the few opportunities. There are many remote regions that have few alternatives for economic growth, due to the lack of a resource base or their distance from markets, their inimical climate or lack of water. Many of these countries or regions are suitable for tourism (Christie, 2002).

Secondly, many developing countries have a shortage of capital. To develop tourism, they need capital import. As such, this should not be considered to be a disadvantage. Tourism capital import increases the capital stock and strengthens the domestic economy (De Brabander, 1992). We agree that the decision-makers are foreigners, with higher dependence from abroad. There is also the danger of repatriation of profits, and this phenomenon cannot be exaggerated. Cash flows are in many cases used for extensions and modernization. If the returns on investment are sufficient, why should a group invest the profits abroad?

The third comment is more significant. In many developing countries import leakages are very high, but they are not higher, on average, than for most other sectors – on the contrary. There is a lot that can be done to reduce the import leakages with respect to food supply, construction, souvenirs, etc. We refer to what was said in Chapter 5: 'make tourism a lead sector'. Of course, the degree of development and the availability of natural resources will influence the success of reducing import leakages.

Fourthly, and complementary to the preceding remark, there are strong linkages between tourism and other sectors. The case of handicraft is very instructive. In several countries there are real opportunities to develop their own handicraft industries out of local materials. Kenya and Bali are very successful in that respect. In Mozambique there are interesting efforts in creating and enhancing handicrafts as well as marketing them. The programme is called 'Aid to Artisans', and has the motto 'from maker to market'.

We would like to finish this epilogue with an interesting statement by Ian Christie (2002), expert at the World Bank, on the occasion of 'Sommets du Tourisme' at Chamonix. To a certain extent this quotation is a synthesis of the epilogue:

> Not all countries can benefit from tourism but those with the potential must be concerned with the quality of growth and its sustainability. In other words, growth alone is not enough – distribution and quality can enhance or stifle its impact. Investments can be single sector, cross-sectoral and have backward linkages which can create greater or lesser value added. The profile of the investor – public, private or mixed – will determine management of the investment and the mechanisms for financing will also produce varied results. In short, the composition of growth and its quality are important determinants of sustainability. Complementary investments and corollary measures may be needed to ensure the sustainability of growth – enhancing local participation; regulations on land use and zoning, environmental protection and building codes. On most of these scores, tourism can be a sound source of growth with high impact on the economy. A critical element is that, although lodging and meals are a large part of any tourist expenditure, tourists also spend money outside their hotel. Thus, linkages with other industries can yield enhanced returns – agricultural production to serve foreign tourists might be a novel (and efficient) way of developing export agriculture. Too often, however, hotels and restaurants cannot rely on local supplies in terms of on-time availability, price and quality. This suggests that tourism investments must go beyond the limits of the investment itself to bring in other linked sectors, if value added is to be maximized.

References and further reading

Bosselman, F., Peterson, C. and McCarthy, Cl. (1999). *Managing Tourism Growth. Issues and Applications.* Washington: Island Press.

Christie, I. (2002). Tourism, growth and poverty: framework conditions for tourism in developing countries. *Tourism Review*, 1–2.

De Brabander, G. (1992). *Toerisme en Economie.* Leuven: Garant.

Edwards, A. (1988). *International Tourism Forecasts to 1999*. London: EIU Special Report.

Godschalk, D. and Brower, D. (1979). *Constitutional Issues in Growth Management*. Washington: Planners Press.

Guicheney, J. and Rouzade, G. (2003). *Le tourisme dans les programmes européens*. Paris: La Documentation Française.

Keller, P. and Bieger, T (eds) (2001). *Tourism Growth and Global Competition*. St Gallen: AIEST.

Krippendorf, J. (1975). *Die Landschaftsfresser, Tourismus und Erholungslandschaft – Verderben oder Segen*. Bern: Hallwag Verlag.

Krippendorf, J. (1991). Towards new tourism policies. In R. Medlik (ed.), *Managing Tourism*. Oxford: Butterworth-Heinemann.

Mazzanti, M. (2002). Tourism growth and sustainable development. *Tourism Economics*, 4.

Ritchie, J.R.B. and Crouch, G. (2003). *The Competitive Destination. A Sustainable Tourism Perspective*. Wallingford: C.A.B. International.

Sharpley, R. (2002). Tourism: a vehicle for development. In R. Sharpley and D. Telfer (eds), *Tourism and Development. Concepts and Issues*. Clevedon: Channel View Publications.

Sharpley, R. and Telfer, D. (eds) (2002). *Tourism and Development. Concepts and Issues*. Clevedon: Channel View Publications.

Smeral, E. (2001). Beyond the myth of growth in tourism. In P. Keller and T. Bieger (eds), *Tourism Growth and Global Competition*. St Gallen: AIEST.

Smeral, E. (2003). A structural view of tourism growth. *Tourism Economics*, 1.

Smeral, E. (2004). Long-term forecasts for international tourism. *Tourism Economics*, 2.

Telfer, D. (2002a). The evolution of tourism and development theory. In R. Sharpley and D. Telfer (eds). *Tourism and Development. Concepts and Issues*. Clevedon: Channel View Publications.

Telfer, D. (2002b). Tourism and regional development issues. In R. Sharpley and D. Telfer (eds), *Tourism and Development. Concepts and Issues*. Clevedon: Channel View Publications.

United Nations (1999). *Guidelines on Integrated Planning for Sustainable Tourism Development*. New York: UN.

Vanhove, N. (1986). Tourism and regional economic development. In J. Paelinck (ed.), *Human Behaviour in Geographical Space, Essays in Honour of L.H. Klaassen*. Cheltenham: Ashgate.

Vanhove, N. (1999). *Regional Policy: A European Approach*. Cheltenham: Ashgate.

Williams, A. and Shaw, G. (1995). Tourism and regional development: polarisation and new forms of production in the United Kingdom. *Tijdschrift voor Economische en Sociale Geofrafie*, 1.

Williams, A. and Shaw, G. (1998). Tourism and uneven economic development. In A. Williams and G. Shaw (eds), *Tourism and Economic Development: European Experiences*. Chichester: John Wiley & Sons.

World Commission on Environment and Development (1987). *Our Common Future*. Brundtland Report, Oxford: Oxford University Press.

Index